THE SHORES OF BOHEMIA

Wellfleet Fall 92'   Caleb William

THE SHORES OF BOHEMIA

A Cape Cod Story,

1910–1960

JOHN TAYLOR WILLIAMS

FARRAR, STRAUS AND GIROUX

NEW YORK

Farrar, Straus and Giroux
120 Broadway, New York 10271

Permission to reprint the following previously published material is gratefully acknowledged:
Excerpt from Ati Gropius Johansen interview by Christine Cipriani, 2009, quoted in
Peter McMahon and Christine Cipriani, *Cape Cod Modern: Midcentury Architecture and
Community on the Outer Cape* (New York: Metropolis, 2014), 117.
Excerpt from *The Twenties: From Notebooks and Diaries of the Period* by Edmund Wilson, edited
and with an introduction by Leon Edel. Copyright © 1975 by Elena Wilson,
Executrix of the Estate of Edmund Wilson.
Excerpt from *The Thirties: From Notebooks and Diaries of the Period* by Edmund Wilson, edited
and with an introduction by Leon Edel. Copyright © 1980 by Helen Miranda Wilson.
Excerpt from *The Forties: From Notebooks and Diaries of the Period* by Edmund Wilson, edited
and with an introduction by Leon Edel. Copyright © 1983 by Helen Miranda Wilson.
Excerpt from *The Fifties: From Notebooks and Diaries of the Period* by Edmund Wilson, edited
and with an introduction by Leon Edel. Copyright © 1986 by Helen Miranda Wilson.

Illustration credits can be found on pages 341–343.

Library of Congress Cataloging-in-Publication Data
Names: Williams, John Taylor, author.
Title: The shores of Bohemia : a Cape Cod story, 1910–1960 / John Taylor Williams.
Description: First edition. | New York : Farrar, Straus and Giroux, 2022. | Includes
  bibliographical references and index. | Summary: "The history of a generation of artists,
  writers, activists, and dreamers who created a Bohemian utopia on the windblown
  shores of Cape Cod" —Provided by publisher.
Identifiers: LCCN 2021059691 | ISBN 9780374262754 (hardcover)
Subjects: LCSH: Bohemianism—Massachusetts—Cape Cod—History—20th century. |
  Cape Cod (Mass.)—Biography—Anecdotes. | Cape Cod (Mass.)—Intellectual life—
  20th century. | Cape Cod (Mass.)—Social life and customs—20th century. | Arts—
  Massachusetts—Cape Cod (Mass.)—History—20th century—Anecdotes.
Classification: LCC F72.C3 W487 2022 | DDC 974.4/92—dc23/eng/20211214
LC record available at https://lccn.loc.gov/2021059691

Designed by Gretchen Achilles

Our books may be purchased in bulk for promotional,
educational, or business use. Please contact your local bookseller or the Macmillan
Corporate and Premium Sales Department at 1-800-221-7945, extension 5442,
or by email at MacmillanSpecialMarkets@macmillan.com.

www.fsgbooks.com
www.twitter.com/fsgbooks • www.facebook.com/fsgbooks

1   3   5   7   9   10   8   6   4   2

Frontispiece: *Wellfleet, fall 1992*

For Noa Hall
and
Charles Jencks,
my guides to bohemia

My candle burns at both ends;
It will not last the night;
But ah, my foes, and oh, my friends—
It gives a lovely light!

—EDNA ST. VINCENT MILLAY

CONTENTS

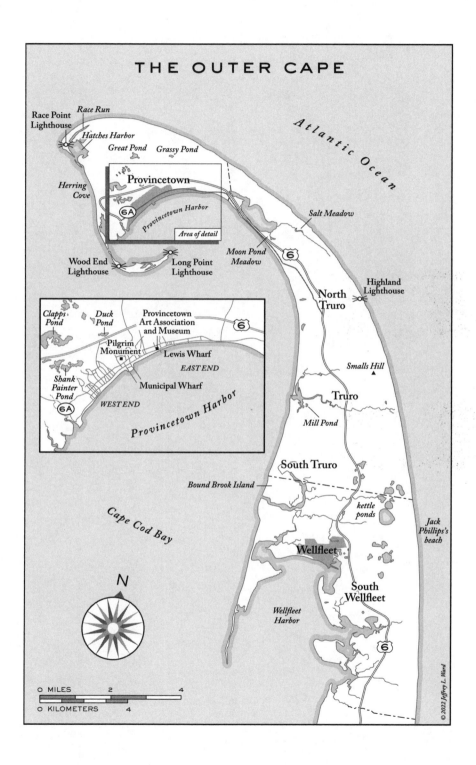

THE OUTER CAPE

Race Point
Lighthouse
Race Run
Hatches Harbor
Great Pond
Grassy Pond

Herring
Cove

Provincetown

6A
Provincetown Harbor

Area of detail

Wood End
Lighthouse
Long Point
Lighthouse

Moon Pond
Meadow

Salt Meadow

Atlantic Ocean

6

Highland
Lighthouse

North
Truro

Smalls Hill ▲

Clapps
Pond
Duck
Pond
Provincetown
Art Association
and Museum

Pilgrim
Monument

Lewis Wharf

EAST END

Shank
Painter
Pond
Municipal Wharf

6A
WEST END

Provincetown Harbor

6

Truro

Mill Pond

South Truro

Bound Brook Island —

*kettle
ponds*

Wellfleet

Jack
Phillips's
beach

Cape Cod Bay

South
Wellfleet

*Wellfleet
Harbor*

6

N

MILES   2   4

KILOMETERS   4

© 2022 Jeffrey L. Ward

PREFACE

Certain historians of the obscure claim that at some point during the Holy Roman Empire, Bohemia, which today constitutes the landlocked western part of the Czech Republic, actually possessed a small section of the Adriatic coast. Like Shakespeare's Arden or Malory's Camelot, the shores of Bohemia continue to exist in our collective unconscious geography, troubling and alluring. A less romantic origin for the word "bohemians" might have been its use by the French as a pejorative for the Gypsy or Roma who had entered France from the east.

For a brief time in America, beginning about 1910, those dedicated to radical political reform, a new exploration of personal relationships free from Victorian strictures, and the search for a new "American" voice in writing, painting, architecture, and theater congregated in two locales: New York's Greenwich Village below Fourteenth Street, in the maze of narrow streets that radiated from Washington Square at the base of Fifth Avenue; and three fishing villages—Provincetown, Truro, and Wellfleet—that cling to the end of the massive flexed arm of sand that thrusts into the Atlantic toward Europe, named Cape Cod in 1602 by the English explorer Bartholomew Gosnold.

These idealists, like the shapers of most revolutionary movements, especially in the arts, were primarily drawn from the middle and upper classes, young men and women searching to build a life free from Victorian restraints amid the sprawling post–Civil War industrialization of the country and the shifting of political control to a small group of increasingly wealthy robber barons. The early bohemians' anticapitalism wasn't based on Marxist principles as much as it was on their own perception that the now wealthy owners were paying their workers the lowest wages possible and punishing them (with judicial and police support) if they organized in protest over their wages or working conditions. Until the Sixteenth Amendment in 1913, there was no federal income tax and only a small inheritance tax. The 1913 tax rate for the highest bracket was 7 percent on income over five hundred thousand dollars (approximately eleven million dollars in today's money), and the average worker in 1913 was lucky to earn more than a thousand dollars a year working a six-day, sixty-hour week.

Whether they were American-born or European immigrants, the bohemians of the early twentieth century saw an America in which work, for most, had become a Chaplinesque automaton's labor in vast coal and copper mines, textile mills, factories, and cotton fields in a debased landscape of clear-cut forest, hills imploded by dynamite, factories spewing smoke night and day, and rivers fouled with industrial waste. These radicals turned from this world in disgust, bent on creating a new world of their own.

For many, it was the golden arm of Cape Cod that lured them from overcrowded Greenwich Village to a new arcadia for their comrades. Provincetown's calm harbor on one side and the treacherous Atlantic surge on the other bound its neighboring towns with a tolerance characteristic of maritime cultures. In the years between 1910 and 1960, you could still rent a house or studio for the summer or all year on Provincetown's harborside Commercial Street for less than anything in Greenwich Village. If you could scrape together just a few thousand dollars, you could even purchase an abandoned farmhouse or woodlot in the adjacent towns of Truro and Wellfleet, where many of the old Pilgrim families had abandoned their homes as the forests were timbered off and the topsoil blew away, exposing the Cape's glacial sand foundation. Until the 1950s, there were really only two ways to reach the far end of the Cape:

either on the *Dorothy Bradford*, the day boat from Boston (named after the wife of the first Pilgrim governor), which ran in good weather only, or on the trains to Provincetown from Boston or Fall River if you were coming from New York. The ferry was best, because the trains were really mainly for freight and fish, and taking an automobile—still a novelty then—meant a long day's journey from the Cape Cod Canal, where the traveler left the mainland, through a spiderweb of one-lane roads, often just sand, to Provincetown.

Cape Cod was almost preindustrial in 1910. Although the great whaling and cod-fishing days were over in Provincetown, for generations of predominantly Portuguese Azorean and old Yankee families, fishing from wooden-hulled boats in the Grand Banks remained a way of life akin to what Kipling described in *Captains Courageous*.

It was this glimpse of an almost pre–Civil War America—free from mines, factories, or any evidence of national corporations, governed by Athenian-style town meetings, where each family worked not to amass wealth, or even much in savings, but only to support themselves amid an ever-changing world of sea and light—that captured the bohemians' longing for a return to an America where individuals found meaning and dignity in their work.

They had enlisted in a sacred campaign against capitalism and for restoring individual Americans' control over a government seemingly intent upon the limitation of political freedom, the suppression of organized labor, and the denial of basic rights to women and Black people. These reformers, both men and women, spent significant time in New York, either to organize or to join the great labor strikes by the silk workers of Paterson, New Jersey; or the mill girls' Bread and Roses strike in Lawrence, Massachusetts; or strikes by the Industrial Workers of the World's mine workers from the coalfields of Pennsylvania to the Rockefeller copper mines in Colorado. Other bohemians returned to run the magazines and newspapers that represented their movement from its socialist progressive beginning.

The bohemians brought to their new arcadia easels and typewriters and a distaste for money not earned by creativity; their obsession with alcohol as a muse; their commitment to sexual freedom for both men and women, married or unmarried; and very little interest in their own children, if child-rearing in any way interfered with these pursuits.

Their brief reign was an intellectually anarchist period, but during that fifty-year occupation of the Cape, they left us with new American voices. In the theater they produced new plays based on working people's lives, first those of Eugene O'Neill and Susan Glaspell and the Provincetown Players and later Tennessee Williams's *A Streetcar Named Desire*. In publishing their political thinking, they created a radical truth-seeking press first in *The Masses* and then in *The Dial*, *The New Republic*, and the *Partisan Review*. The American novel and books of nonfiction found a new, politically aware voice in the writings of John Reed, John Dos Passos, Edmund Wilson, Mary McCarthy, Alfred Kazin, and Norman Mailer. In painting, the school Charles Hawthorne founded in 1899 attracted painters like Edward Hopper, Edwin Dickinson, Charles Demuth, Marsden Hartley, and William Zorach. Hawthorne's 1934 successor was the German émigré Hans Hofmann, who lured Josef Albers, Robert Motherwell, Jackson Pollock, Lee Krasner, Mark Rothko, and Helen Frankenthaler to explore the Cape light. Last, America's architecture and design was transformed by the refugees from the Bauhaus led by Walter Gropius and its adherents Marcel Breuer, György Kepes, and Serge Chermayeff, who sited their modern, low-slung houses on the ponds and hills of Truro and Wellfleet and, in turn, brought Eero Saarinen, Hans and Florence Knoll, and Charles and Ray Eames to refashion American furnishings.

But it is not a mere cataloging of those who have lived, created, or loved at the far end of the Cape that is my purpose. Like Anthony Powell's narrator, Nicholas Jenkins, in *A Dance to the Music of Time*, who gave readers an intimate view of the lives of those who shared the interwar bohemian England he knew and admired, for me the American bohemia was informed by the lives of my father-in-law, Jack Hall, and his four wives.

The bohemians' half century from 1910 to 1960 encompassed their attempt to found a society in which members could free themselves from their past, whether they were upper-class Victorian children; immigrants in search of the possibility of building a new, just society; Jewish, Catholic, and Protestant intellectuals yearning to abandon religion and its pre-

judices; or the restless young women who longed to have the same freedom men did to explore their sexuality. And, of course, finally, they had
a common goal to write, paint, or build something based on American
themes. Indeed, the impulse was to escape the rigid, class-bound world
of their parents and to embrace the new revelations of Freudian and
Jungian psychiatry, which seemed to legitimize their revolt. The Edenic
world they created was evanescent, but few movements have done more
to transform American culture.

This is not a scholarly history of American bohemianism. I make no
attempt to analyze its predecessors, the Victorian socialist movement
in England and the earlier anarchist movements against any authority in
France and czarist Russia; nor does this account encompass many who
made the movement politically and socially effective on a national level
but never spent time in Provincetown and its environs. This is a Cape story,
pure and simple, an account of how a movement that shaped American
art, literature, design, and theater rose and fell like the tides on its shores.

I have tried to create a picture of Cape Cod's bohemia through people
who lived much of their time on the Outer Cape and do it through their
own words, or through the words of those who knew them best, over
five decades, bounded by the four seasons that shape the unique life and
landscape of Cape Cod and the radical political movements to which
they clung.

PART I

SPRING

I.

ARCADIA

At the close of the Ice Age, the first nomadic hunters met the ocean and realized their journey had ended. From atop the carved, forested mound of glacial till, which geologists call a tombolo, they could see nothing but endless water. The great Wisconsin glacier had pushed its frozen treasure of boulders and gravel across North America until it encountered the even mightier Atlantic, which melted its ice and pulverized its stone cargo into a long, curved sand spit, embracing at its far end a calm harbor shielded from the dangerous Atlantic surge. That sand had slowly spawned a woodland of primeval oaks, cedars, and red pines, dotted with freshwater kettle ponds formed by the melting of isolated masses of ice and fringed by small islands and marsh, which provided abundant game: deer, rabbit, grouse, turkey, fish, and shellfish.

The hunters' descendants, the Nauset, Pamet, and other related tribes, had a familiarity with Europeans stretching back to the fifteenth-century fishing ships manned by Basque, Catalan, Breton, and Spanish crews, who had come ashore to trade and split, smoke, salt, and barrel their cod for their return trip. None of these visitors had any intention of staying, until the *Mayflower*, far off course from its planned landing in Virginia, struggled into Provincetown Harbor on November 11, 1620. In a few lifetimes, the great Cape forests were cleared for British naval spars and plank. The land, once subject only to yearly slash-and-burn farming so the first people could plant their Three Sisters mounds atop a fertilizer of netted shad to produce an abundance of corn, squash, and beans for the long winters, was now plowed year-round.

With no tradition of legal ownership of land, the first people soon found themselves fenced out of their traditional hunting grounds and decimated by a plague of new European diseases, including smallpox and cholera. By 1800 they were nothing but a memory evoked by an occasional arrowhead or shell midden and the names they had given to the Cape's ponds, rivers, and marshes. From their Algonquin language came the names of places, people, and things: Massachusetts (the Massachusetts were a subtribe whose Algonquin name meant Great Hill, probably referring to the sacred Blue Hills adjacent to what is now Boston), sachem (leader), sagamore (tribal head), succotash (a mix of corn and beans), quahog (clam), wampum (beads made of shells, strung together on a belt and used as money), hubbub (their favorite board game of chance), and the animals they named, such as raccoon and moose.

By the early twentieth century, the Outer Cape from Provincetown to Wellfleet had reverted to its original postglacial landscape, cleared of forests except for small clusters of locust trees around abandoned farmhouses whose fields were now moors, their topsoil gone. The cod and whales had been fished out or had migrated north to the Grand Banks, where the waters were still cold. For the old Yankee settlers it was a dark period, but to the bohemians, who first encountered the Cape in 1910, it was the most magical of landscapes. Golden beaches beneath towering dunes ran unbroken south from Provincetown on both the bay and the ocean sides, for miles and miles, down to the elbow of the Cape at Chatham. The land, now covered by hog cranberry and beach grass, flowed gently over low hills, from the tops of which one could see the ocean on both sides, as well as small clusters of eighteenth-century shingled houses, barns, and the occasional white church spire that marked a town.

The sea surged around them, providing not only an ever-changing palette but a concert shifting from lulling rhythmic waves to surging Wagnerian storms. The light was clear, dazzling at high noon and more dappled and complex at dawn and dusk. Later, the abstract expressionist Robert Motherwell would report how deeply he was impressed by the Outer Cape's golden Mediterranean glimmer, so different from the blazing clarity of Mexico, where he had been working. In his memoir, he wrote:

> the radiant summer light of Provincetown that rivals the Greek islands, because, I have always supposed, like them, Provincetown is on a narrow spit of land surrounded by the sea, which reflects the light with a diffused brilliance that is subtly but crucially different from the dry, inland light of Tuscany, the Madrid plateau, of Arizona or the Sierra Madres in Mexico, where the glittering light is not suffused, but crystal clear, so that each color is wholly local in hue, as in the landscape backgrounds of Quattrocento Italian painting or in the late collages of Henri Matisse.[1]

The bohemians' diaspora from Greenwich Village began to arrive in Provincetown by the day boat from Boston or the night boat to Fall River from New York, which connected to the freight and passenger train that stopped on the hill above Provincetown Harbor. The roads were still mainly sand, and cars were rare. Apartments and old farmhouses at the Cape's end were cheap to rent, and on a beautiful summer day it didn't really matter that most had no electricity, indoor plumbing, or heat, other than a stove or fireplace.

2.

GREENWICH VILLAGE AND PROVINCETOWN

By 1910, Greenwich Village was the acknowledged center of those who claimed to be bohemians and whose lifestyle caused others to label them as such. America's bohemian movement had deep artistic and political roots in nineteenth-century England and France. The English suffragist movement and the international progressive, socialist, Marxist, and French syndicalist labor movements had found many American adherents. These social and political passions were further fueled by the influx of German and Russian Jews into New York during the period, many fiercely committed to labor reform, anarchism, or socialism and early converts to the new psychology movement inspired by Freud and Jung. The arts were now influenced by the work of the French avant-garde led by Alfred Jarry, Henri Rousseau, and Guillaume Apollinaire, so beautifully depicted in Roger Shattuck's *Banquet Years*.

However, America's bohemian movement was both more inclusive as to one's class, religious adherence, or ethnicity and more directed to establishing a new "American" definition of democratic socialism and an "American" voice and style in literature, theater, and painting. These would be unique because by 1900 America was the only great nation without a state religion and already had the most polyglot population.

America was a new nation in search of an identity separate from its

European origin. As Henry Adams observed in his *Education*, many Americans were becoming appalled by the gigantic and brutal forces that post–Civil War capitalists like Rockefeller, Frick, and Morgan had loosed on both the landscape and its formerly independent agricultural and skilled workforce. The mines, the blast furnaces, the textile mills, and the factory production lines, lampooned in Chaplin's *Modern Times*, had already stripped much of the country of its forests, polluted its rivers, and resettled its laborers in squalid tenements and tent camps. These "captains of industry" had seized control of state legislatures, and finally Congress, by such unabashed bribery that two of the most powerful states, New York and Pennsylvania, moved their capitals in a futile attempt to escape the stranglehold of corrupt political machines like New York City's Tammany Hall. "Fighting Bob" La Follette, who was first Wisconsin's congressman, then governor, and finally senator from 1906 to 1925, joined Teddy Roosevelt's progressive wing of the Republican Party in opposition to these "bosses" and "vast corporate combinations." TR had helped lead the progressive Republicans to victory in 1900 under his Square Deal for labor policy (later to be transformed by his cousin FDR into the New Deal).

Social reform was a major goal for many bohemians deeply influenced by Jane Addams's Hull House home for desperate women and Jacob Riis's daring exposé of the plight of the poor, *How the Other Half Lives*, particularly for the many young women who had come to the Village to work in its poorer tenements and schools, which housed Irish, Italian, and Jewish immigrants. Many marched with their hero Eugene V. Debs, the leader of the Socialist Party, whose motto was "The class which has the power to rob upon a large scale has also the power to control the government and legalize their robbery."

The original Greenwich Village community of artists, writers, and activists centered on Washington Square, where Fifth Avenue ended at Stanford White's new towering arch. Some resided in well-maintained brick houses like 61 Washington Square, nicknamed the House of Genius due to the brilliance of its inhabitants, including Willa Cather, Stephen Crane, and Theodore Dreiser. While a group referred to by the conservative press as "the muckrakers," the new socialist writers and organizers

Emma Goldman, Frank Norris, Upton Sinclair, Jack London, John Reed, and Lincoln Steffens, packed into cheap boardinghouses. A few, like Mabel Dodge, lived in rather grand town houses, but none dared live above Fourteenth Street and claim to be a bohemian.

Dodge, an heiress from Buffalo, was in her early thirties when she arrived in New York in 1912 and established herself as a patron of the arts. After a decade in France and Italy, now divorced with a young son, she had through pure force of personality attracted bohemia's leaders to her new Village salon. Her young friend Max Eastman wrote of her, "She has neither wit nor beauty, nor is she vivacious or lively-minded or entertaining. She is comely and good-natured, and when she says something, it is sincere and sagacious, but for the most part she sits like a lump, and says nothing."[1]

In her fabulous house at 23 Fifth Avenue, complete with polar bear rugs, Venetian chandeliers, and an English butler, she entertained lavishly, not just for her social peers but for almost any person of intellect or talent.

Emma Goldman (1869–1940)

With the encouragement of dedicated radicals Lincoln Steffens and Hutchins "Hutch" Hapgood, Mabel began to host Wednesday evening discussions based on themes she proposed. Many of these "Radical Evenings" included provocative featured guests. The Jewish radical immigrants Emma Goldman, Alexander Berkman, and Ben Reitman (both lovers of Goldman's) came to discuss anarchism and violent revolution; the radical leaders of labor strikes "Big Bill" Haywood, Carlo Tresca, and his lover Elizabeth Gurley Flynn spoke on their new union, the Industrial Workers of the World (IWW), and a worker's right to sabotage or strike; and the radical writers William English Walling, Walter Lippmann, and Hutch Hapgood talked of the Socialist Party leader Eugene Debs and socialism. When these often-violent discussions reached midnight, Dodge's butler threw open the dining room doors to a vast Victorian repast (which was often the sole good meal of the poorer attendees).

John Reed, who was to become the hero of both Villages, was born to a well-off lumber family in Portland, Oregon, on October 22, 1887. In 1906, at his father's insistence, he gained admission to Harvard, where he was a football cheerleader, swimmer, member of *The Harvard Lampoon*, and president of the Glee Club. Among his classmates were T. S. Eliot and others who became lifelong friends, including Walter Lippmann, Van Wyck Brooks, the stage designer and producer Robert Edmond "Bobby" Jones, and the poet Alan Seeger. Charles Townsend Copeland, or "Copey," became his English professor and mentor and, sensing Reed's poetical romanticism, urged Reed to go to Europe upon graduation to capture the spirit of Villon and Byron. Reed was a force of nature: tireless, broad shouldered, tall, with a head of tousled brown hair that fell over his high forehead. Although his face was somewhat oddly proportioned, women found him fascinating, as did men. With his enormous energy,

John Reed (ca. 1912)   *Lincoln Steffens (1866–1936)*

curiosity, and growing writing skills, he was becoming a leading figure in both Villages from 1911 to 1919.

Reed began sharing rooms on Washington Square with his mentor and muckraking hero, the forty-four-year-old Lincoln Steffens, whose wife had recently died. Their rooms cost thirty dollars a month with a bathtub on a platform in the kitchen and a "juke," or outside toilet. Of their tenement Reed wrote,

Inglorious Miltons by the score,—
Mute Wagners,—Rembrandts, ten or more,—
And Rodins, one to every floor.
In short, those unknown men of genius
Who dwell in third-floor-rears, gangreneous,
Reft of their rightful heritage
By a commercial, soulless age.
Unwept, I might add,—and unsung,
Insolvent, but entirely young.[2]

A Harvard classmate described him thus: "Even as an undergraduate, he betrayed what many people believed to be the central passion of his life, an inordinate desire to be arrested."

Bill and Lucy L'Engle knew just about everybody in Greenwich Village and in Provincetown. William J. L'Engle Jr. came from a wealthy and distinguished Florida family. He graduated from Yale in 1906, having studied architecture, but more important having become a skilled draftsman. Leaving the Art Students League for France, he studied at the Académie Julian and traveled to Spain in 1910 with the lawyer turned painter George Biddle and Waldo Peirce, the towering former Harvard football captain and painter who later became a lifelong friend and role model for Hemingway.

L'Engle had met Lucy Brown, or "Brownie" as she was known to friends, at the Académie Julian and married her in 1914. Lucy had already visited Provincetown in 1909 to study with Charles Hawthorne at his new painting school. The couple lived mainly in Paris until 1915, when the war threatened the city. They had two girls, Madeleine and Ca-

Lucy Brown L'Engle, 1919, by William L'Engle

mille, or "Cammie." Upon their return in 1917 they began to spend every summer in Provincetown.

Many of their New York friends also spent the winters in New York and summers in Provincetown, but Greenwich Village was the hub on that wheel, and by 1910 its character was almost set. Large groups of restless, young, well-educated men and women from the East Coast and the Midwest and others from more distant parts had assembled in Greenwich Village to explore building a free, progressive socialist society dedicated to equality and "comradeship" and the uninhibited search for a fresh creative standard in the arts. One was most likely to encounter these early bohemians at the Liberal Club, in the heart of the Village. The club had been founded in 1912 by Percy Grand and Lincoln Steffens to advance women's rights, but its women members were not convinced these founding males really grasped what women wanted. Henrietta Rodman, a radical feminist member and high school teacher, believed in "free love" for all women, married or unmarried, and had become a magnet for young women who modeled themselves on her, both in her dress (loose hair and bright-colored clothes, long earrings, sandals, and cigarettes!) and in her causes: Margaret Sanger's birth control movement and women's suffrage.

In 1913, Rodman tore the club apart after she encouraged an affair between a young unmarried girl and a married club member and then led a protest when the club refused to elect Emma Goldman and W. E. B. Du Bois as members. Du Bois, one of Harvard's first Black graduates, and the first Black man to earn a PhD at the school, had come from Atlanta to help edit William English Walling's NAACP magazine *The Crisis*. Goldman—plain, short, and fierce with her white shirtwaists and steel-rimmed glasses (John Dos Passos later described her at their first meeting in 1917 at the Hotel Brevoort as "a Bronxy fattish little old woman who looks like a rather good cook"[3]—had become an early feminist and labor organizer, influenced by the powerful International Ladies' Garment Workers' Union (ILGWU), in which, as a poor immigrant, she had first found work.

Margaret Sanger

Nineteen thirteen was a tumultuous year for Goldman, Rodman, the birth control advocate Margaret Sanger, the Provincetown-based fiction writer Mary Heaton Vorse, and their women "comrades" who participated in the largest women's suffrage march Washington had yet seen on March 3, the day before President Wilson's inauguration (he hid in the White House). More than a hundred of the five thousand marchers were injured by hostile crowd members and police. The artists wore pink; the writers wore white. They were led by the beautiful feminist Inez Milholland, wearing a crown and long white robe and riding on a white horse.

Milholland was a Vassar graduate as well as a practicing labor lawyer who married Eugen Boissevain, who was later to marry her fellow Vassar graduate Edna St. Vincent Millay.

Inez Milholland, women's suffrage procession, 1913

Rodman's adherents, both male and female, moved the club into rooms at 137 MacDougal Street above Polly's Restaurant, with its plain entryway and paintings by club members hung on the bright orange and yellow walls.

Polly's Restaurant, 137 MacDougal Street, Greenwich Village, ca. 1915

Polly's had been started by Paula Holladay, a tall redhead from Evanston, Illinois, with her older lover and fellow anarchist, Hippolyte Havel, who came complete with spectacles, goatee, and Nietzsche mustache. Polly was a gifted cook, and her food, prices, and affinity for radicals gradually made Polly's the bohemians' restaurant of choice. Havel had been arrested for anarchist activity in both Europe and the United States and ridiculed diners he viewed as bourgeois. He always reserved a table and bench, meals always free, for his fellow anarchist heroes Emma Goldman and her lover Alexander Berkman. It was Havel who declared, "Greenwich Village is a state of mind; it has no boundaries."[4] Polly and Hippolyte often kept the restaurant open all night for dancing and exhibits of new works by modernist and cubist painters. They moved the restaurant to Provincetown in the summers.

The upstairs space, now occupied by the "new" Liberal Club, consisted of two large parlors, a sunroom with a large fireplace, and stairs that led to a garden and the privy behind the building. The front room became the choice for meetings and in the evenings for dancing. Friday night was the major night for dancing the turkey trot, grizzly bear, tango, and shimmy to the club's Victrola. The club also became notorious for its annual costume ball: the Blaze and the Pagan Rout, held at nearby Webster Hall. "Notorious" was exactly how these artists wanted to be seen.

The club's members embodied its motto: "A Meeting Place for Those Interested in New Ideas." Many divided their time between New York and Provincetown, such as the handsome Village "tramp" (so named for his vagabond years trekking by boxcar across the country), poet, boxer, and ladies' man Harry Kemp; the socialist labor writer Mary Heaton Vorse; William English Walling and his wife, the Russian-born socialist Anna Strunsky; Hutch Hapgood and his wife, Neith Boyce; John Reed; Max Eastman (a recent Williams College graduate and now editor in chief of *The Masses*), nicknamed the Sleepy Adonis, and his new wife, Ida Rauh (a rising actress and labor lawyer); Eugene O'Neill (already an alcoholic, having been thrown out of Princeton and become a tramp steamer deckhand); the Harvard graduate and rising critic Gilbert Seldes; the Village bookstore owner Frank Shay; and the editors of *The Masses* Art Young and Floyd Dell.

The club became even more popular when it arranged to create a passage into the neighboring building where the brothers Albert and Charles Boni's Washington Square Bookshop was located. The Bonis had established the store with money their father unwisely gave them to attend Harvard Law School. Unfortunately, members with no money "borrowed" the books and took them back into the club to read. Their store never made a profit until it moved to Eighth Street with the assistance of the curly-red-haired Frank Shay (with temper to match), who was soon to open a bookstore of his own on Christopher Street and start a small publishing imprint, the first to publish another certain redhead, the beguiling Edna St. Vincent Millay, whom her first lover, Floyd Dell, described as "a New England nun; a chorus girl on a holiday; the Botticelli Venus."

Within the Liberal Club existed a much more exclusive group, the Heterodoxy Club, founded in 1912 and limited to twenty-five women. It met every other Saturday until 1940. They adopted the Greek word for equality, "heterodoxy," and its members included straights and lesbians, whites and Blacks, Protestants, Catholics, and Jews. Many of its leading members were "Two Villagers," Mary Heaton Vorse, the playwright Susan Glaspell, the labor lawyers Ida Rauh and Crystal Eastman, and Mabel Dodge. They adopted the feminist/suffrage goals of Inez Milholland and Henrietta Rodman but also those of radical labor leaders like their fellow member Helen Gurley Flynn, later a founder of the Communist Party of the United States of America (CPUSA).

The Heterodoxy Club was an extremely strong bond for its members and is often mentioned in its members' diaries and letters.

MacDougal Street's bohemian "pleasure dome" became an even greater attraction when the Provincetown Players moved in 1916 from Mary Heaton Vorse's Lewis Wharf in Provincetown to 139 MacDougal Street, next to Polly's Restaurant and the Liberal Club. The transition between the Liberal Club's amateur plays and the Provincetown Players' sophistication attracted new gifted bohemians. When any of the bohemians had money, they would follow an admonition of the modernist painter and heavy drinker Niles Spencer, "Let's resort to the Brevoort," their favorite hotel and restaurant, located at Ninth Street and Fifth Avenue, or its equally popular rival the Hotel Lafayette at University Place and Ninth Street, with its faux French bar and outdoor tables.

The young Floyd Dell had moved to the Village from Chicago to join his two oldest friends, the writers George Cram "Jig" Cook and his new wife, Susan Glaspell. The pair had met in Davenport, Iowa, where Cook's family was prominent and where he retreated after Harvard and a teaching stint at Stanford. The Cook estate, called the Cabin, was actually large, complete with butler and liveried footmen. Dell was smitten at first exposure to the Village and traded in his detachable collar and tie for a flannel shirt. Of the Village he wrote,

> *Where now the tide of traffic beats,*
> *There was a maze of crooked streets;*
> *The noisy waves of enterprise,*
> *Swift-hurrying to their destinies,*
> *Swept past this island paradise:*
> *Here life went to a gentler pace,*
> *And dreams and dreamers found a place.*

The tall, burly Cook was separated from his first wife and engaged to a fellow writer whom he was to marry next and who became the mother of his only children, Harl and Nilla. Despite these commitments, he had fallen deeply in love with Susan Glaspell, a young novelist and journalist. To avoid Jig's entanglements, Susan retreated to Greenwich Village, but Jig pursued her, and they were married in 1913, the year of the famed Armory Show of European modern paintings and the violent Paterson silk strike.

The two individuals who first lured the Greenwich Villagers to Provincetown were Mary Heaton Vorse, one of the most popular members of both the Liberal and the Heterodoxy Clubs, and Charles Hawthorne, whose painting school had already attracted Village painters like the L'Engles and their friends.

The bohemians' companion village (or as Floyd Dell called it, "Greenwich Village sunburnt") was as remote as Greenwich Village was accessible. As difficult as it was to get to Provincetown in 1910, the Cape was part of one modern venture, as the first Marconi telegraph cable connecting America directly to Europe was completed in the town of Orleans in 1879; as Cole Porter was later to sing, "They all said Marconi was a phony," to buffoon those who had claimed it would never work.

Provincetown had been a leading Yankee fishing port since the Puritans resettled it after the Pilgrims' ignominious flight on the *Mayflower* to Plymouth under a hail of arrows launched by the initially welcoming Indigenous people, whom the Pilgrims had immediately abused by stealing their winter corn supply. "This outside shore, this long hook of the Cape, is the remaining rampart of an old continent," Mary Vorse wrote. "The never-ending battle of land and sea has been going on for untold centuries. . . . [W]hen the town is bathed in the winter quiet and the night is ghostly still, five miles away the crashing roar of the surf can still be heard." Provincetown Harbor provided a deep anchorage for early European cod boats, for the Pilgrims and privateers both before and after the Revolution, and, finally, for the U.S. Navy as a base to hunt for German submarines in both world wars. During Prohibition, it was one of the great rum-running destinations.

Between 1700 and 1800, Provincetown and Wellfleet (named after famous English oyster beds) had a whaling fleet that rivaled Nantucket's or New Bedford's, with ships that plied the waters as far away as China and Hawaii. But when the whales were gone (although many front yards still featured whale jawbone gates in 1910) and the local cod fished out, its fishermen resorted to Newfoundland's dangerous and fogbound Grand Banks, painted by Winslow Homer, where cod were still plentiful. The Yankee crews were no longer ascendant. The mainland residents, and the Azorean Portuguese they had recruited beginning in the eighteenth century to man their whaling vessels, had thrived and now owned boats of their own. Perhaps this new mix of Portuguese and Yankees was best exemplified in the erection of the Provincetown Pilgrim Monument in 1910. Designed by Willard Sears, who based it on the Torre del Mangia in Siena in the absence of any grand Pilgrim architectural model, it loomed over the Portuguese East End, in 1910 the biggest Portuguese-speaking community other than Brazil in the New World.

Like all ports, Provincetown had a certain swagger and plenty of tolerance for sex and alcohol. Its houses are arranged upon a ladder of streets, the two frames being Commercial, or "Front," Street, paralleling the harbor, and the other Bradford, or "Back," Street, closest to the dunes stretching to the wild Atlantic Back Shore. The rungs of the ladder are the narrow streets running between them beginning in the East End nearest Truro and ending in the West End at the ocean. Until the late 1930s, Provincetown still had double-tiered buses with oilskin weather curtains carrying locals and tourists from the West End to the East End for five cents. Until the late 1920s there were no home phones; one went to Adams Pharmacy on Commercial Street to place a call. It did have a rather good newspaper, the *Provincetown Advocate*, founded in 1869 with a Yankee motto: "It belongs to no party or clique."

When the returning cod- or mackerel-fishing fleet was spotted along Provincetown's dangerous Back Shore headed for Wood End at the harbor's entrance, the Portuguese wives and children would hurry to the harbor beach to see if the ships' flags were at half-mast; if so, the weeping began for lost husbands and sons, but if not, they returned to their kitchens to prepare the welcoming dinner.

Outdoor painting class, Provincetown, 1928

A nineteenth-century critic wrote that "the summer belongs to the artist by an inalienable right," and that became true in Provincetown as Charles Hawthorne departed William Merritt Chase's Long Island painting school in 1899 to open his own in Provincetown. Many who had been Chase's students followed him to Provincetown, including Marsden Hartley, Charles Demuth, and Edward Hopper. Hawthorne had little money, a wife who was a fellow painter, and two small sons.

The tall, magnetic Hawthorne had grown up in Maine, where his father captained coastal sailing ships, and he had never lived far from the sea. At eighteen he came to New York to study at the Art Students League and then with William Merritt Chase at his famous Shinnecock Hills Summer School of Art. Both Chase's impressionistic teaching methods and the plein air classroom dedicated to the natural world were ideal for Hawthorne. He named his new school the Cape Cod School of Art. Usually dressed in white, he taught his students in good weather on the harbor docks and in bad weather at a studio he had built on Miller Hill Road off Bradford Street, where they worked from the figure or did still lifes.

Among them was the young Norman Rockwell, then living in Provincetown with his wife and son, and William Henry Johnson, the African American painter. When Johnson was denied a scholarship because of his race, Hawthorne raised the money for him to study in Europe. Like Chase, he encouraged his women students and surrounded himself with assistants who went on to major careers of their own, including Henry Hensche, Richard Miller, and Max Bohm. He formed a direct relationship with his students, candid and supportive, which usually led to lifelong friendships.

Hawthorne was famous for his aphorisms about painting: "Painting is just getting one spot of color in relationship to another spot. . . . Let color make form, do not make form and color it!"

"Swing a bigger brush. Have enthusiasm."

He resisted middle-class sensibilities in art and embraced gestural painting, approaching the canvas with a "premier coup," or first attack on the color before you. His successor, Hans Hofmann, while an abstract painter, admired Hawthorne and shared his belief that color was the key to great painting. Hofmann remarked, "As a painter Hawthorne cast aside every doctrine so that he might surpass the limitations of calculation and construction."

Hawthorne did have a temper, as one young student discovered when she showed him her sentimental painting of two children on a beach. At first he responded, "I'm not going to say a thing about this picture," but then, thought again, and roared, "This is a damnable thing!" The woman fainted and had to be assisted by Hawthorne. He might have treated his students roughly at times, but the women painters he mentored remained lifelong friends. Brownie L'Engle returned again after the war, bringing her new husband, Bill, back from Paris. Edwin Dickinson, like so many students of Hawthorne's, met his wife, Pat Foley, while they both were Hawthorne's students. They married at the Hotel Brevoort in 1928 and returned to the Smooley, the cottage Pat, her sister Edy, and Katy Smith rented from Mary Heaton Vorse. The czarist immigrants Biala Tworkov and her brother Jack came to study with Hawthorne in 1923, having left their village in the Pale to come to America. Biala appreciated Hawthorne's support but found Edwin Dickinson's less representational style more sympathetic, as did her friend Shelby Shackelford, a young Virginia girl who had also made the transition from Hawthorne to Dickinson. Biala's brother, Jack, had moved from Hawthorne to Karl Knaths, who was beginning to teach in a totally abstract vein.

In 1910, Hawthorne's students discovered incredibly cheap rooms in houses or abandoned warehouses along Commercial Street. A favorite of the early artists were the unheated storerooms above Frank Days's Pearl Street lumberyard's second floor, with no bathrooms on the entire floor. By 1914, Ross Moffett, Charles Hawthorne, Edwin Dickinson, and Charles Kaeselau were renting their studios at fifty dollars for the season (from May until as long as they could stand the cold). Dickinson would buy a cheap bottle of liquor and then invite all his friends to tack brown paper over the windows and nail canvas to the floor to see how long he could withstand the winter. The brown paper came down in the spring to welcome the Cape light. The Days family (originally from Portugal, where their name was Diaz) were well-known friends to artists and rented out other buildings they owned, including 4 Brewster Street (where the soon-to-be-famous Myron Stout and later Robert Motherwell and Jim Forsberg rented). The Days family were tolerant of late rent, and as a result their tenants never stole coal from the open bins at the lumberyard.

Moffett had come to study with Hawthorne in 1913 and married a fellow painter and Hawthorne student, Dorothy Lake Gregory (who became the illustrator of Andrew Lang's enormously popular *Fairy Books*). Tall, thin, and serious, Moffett moved slowly from Hawthorne's portraiture to more abstract work and became, with Dickinson and Karl Knaths, the leading advocate in demanding that the Art Association include more modern nonrepresentational work in its two juried shows.

Writers, too, found dozens of cheap houses and rooms for rent or sale along elm-lined Commercial Street or on the side streets of the East End, each with its small garden full of hollyhocks and lilacs. Many early bohemians like the L'Engles, Mary Vorse, Hutch Hapgood, and Neith Boyce had settled in the East End, leaving the West End to the Portuguese and Yankee fishermen. Few houses had any heat other than via fireplace or water other than from the sink hand pump, and there were no toilets or refrigerators. Ice for iceboxes was bought in advance for the season from the De Riggs icehouse on Pilgrim Lake and delivered weekly by horse cart as the summer began.

In many ways, Mary Heaton Vorse, neatly put together and quiet at first meeting, was the glue that held Provincetown's bohemian population together. She was comfortable with the upper-class bohemians like the L'Engles, Mabel Dodge, and Hutch Hapgood, having been born into a wealthy family who had owned the Red Lion Inn in Stockbridge, Massachusetts. She traveled widely in Europe as a young woman, spoke French, Italian, and German, and had first married a yachtsman and playboy named Albert White Vorse in 1898. They moved to Provincetown in 1907, and he died three years later, leaving her in her twenties with two small children, Heaton and Mary Ellen.

Mary was an early feminist and developed an international reputation before World War I as an expert reporter on the socialist labor movement. She worked with Emma Goldman, John Reed, Dorothy Day, and the towering, one-eyed hero of WWI "Big Bill" Haywood on the major prewar union strikes. So respected was she by radical labor organizers for her support that the honorific "Mother" Vorse was given to her. Only "Mother" Jones and "Mother" Bloor, the legendary mine worker organizers, were similarly honored.

Her second husband, Joe O'Brien, with whom she had a son, died young and was perhaps more radical. Her last husband, Robert "Bob" Minor, the famed cartoonist for *The Masses*, rose to be one of the leaders of the American Communist Party. Yet somehow, she retained a reputation in both Villages as a pretty, calm, sweet, supportive friend to both women and men. Mary was always recruited to join every cultural, political, or social event that seemed to have any serious purpose from 1910 to 1960. She ended her life as the beloved chronicler of Provincetown's history in her classic book, *Time and the Town*, and because it was on her wharf that the first Provincetown Players' performances took place, she can claim to be the true muse of the American theater movement.

3.

THE 1913 ARMORY SHOW

Only a year before World War I isolated America from Europe, a group of American artists assembled one of the most transformative international exhibitions in American history, consisting of more than 1,350 works of painting and sculpture by European and American artists.

Its organizers had managed to obtain a month's lease on the cavernous Sixty-Ninth Regiment's armory at Twenty-Sixth Street and Lexington Avenue in New York City. The exhibition opened to the public on February 17, 1913, and the press vigorously responded to America's first exposure to fauvism, cubism (Picasso and Braque), and futurism (czarist Russian modernists) in highly emotional editorials. Regardless of the largely negative reaction of the critics, the crowds were immense, and it was just as popular in its subsequent exhibition in Chicago and Boston. E. E. Cummings attended the Boston exhibition while a Harvard undergraduate.

The original show was almost evenly divided into two sections, one American and the other European. But the division was really between the avant-garde in painting—including Picasso, Munch, Van Gogh, Duchamp, Matisse, and Cézanne—on one side of the armory and American Gilded Age Victorian artists and a few American realists. The realists consisted of many who illustrated for the radical socialist magazine *The*

Masses. These artists included John Sloan, George Bellows, and Robert Henri, comically referred to as the Ashcan school. The name had originated from a comment made by their fellow *Masses* artist the good-natured, rotund, ardent socialist Art Young, who, when reviewing submissions to the magazine, noted that every artist now seemed to feel they were eligible for consideration if they included an ash can in their drawing to confirm their allegiance to the poor! Art Young's work was also in the Armory Show.

The show marked the introduction of modernism to America. As the critic Patricia Cohen wrote a century later, "It required a new way of seeing. Imagine Mozart hearing Metallica." And, of course, this was the beginning of a new era of radicals: outside the armory women were marching for suffrage, workers were striking for an eight-hour day, and Margaret Sanger was promoting birth control devices in *The Masses.*

Nude Descending a Staircase (No. 2), *1912, by Marcel Duchamp*

Provincetown artists flocked to the show not only because it embraced their thirst for change but because many of them, like Marsden Hartley, John Sloan, Sonia Brown, Marguerite and William Zorach, Stuart Davis,

Oliver Chaffee, Edwin Clymer, and Ambrose Webster, had work in the show. That is not to say they were all in agreement about some of the most nonrepresentational work, such as Marcel Duchamp's *Nude Descending a Staircase (No. 2)*, which depicted a series of angular forms descending the surface of his work. The less serious reviewers seized upon this work in particular to express their dismay and horror at the show. One described Duchamp's painting as an "explosion in a shingle factory"; another renamed it *The Rude Descending a Staircase (Rush Hour at the Subway)*. President Teddy Roosevelt, not known as an aesthete, angrily shouted, "This is not art!" Perhaps the best defense of Duchamp was raised by one of the exhibition's planners, the seemingly Victorian American painter Walter Pach, who responded to a critic asking where the nude was in the Duchamp painting, "Where is the moon in the Moonlight Sonata?"

Despite these attacks, almost all who attended realized the definition of art had been forever altered as promised in the exhibition's subtitle, "The Spirit of Change." Stuart Davis described it after attending as "a masochistic reception whereat the naïve hosts are trampled and stomped by the European guests at the buffet."[1] The American painter Kenneth Hayes Miller went deeper: "It set off a blast of dynamite in a cramped space—it blew everything wide open. I feel that art can really be free here now."[2]

Sunday, Women Drying Their Hair, *Greenwich Village, 1912,*
by John Sloan

Others from Provincetown and the Village were more interested in the Ashcan school artists' biting commentary on capitalism's effect on the poor. "Big Bill" Haywood found new inspiration in them for his organizing work for the new Industrial Workers of the World, as did Mabel Dodge and John Reed, now involved in a passionate love affair.

Artists like Bill and Lucy L'Engle discovered a new way of painting figures, and their friends Bill and Marguerite Zorach became cubists, returning to their Tenth Street Village apartment and taking up their paintbrushes to create a Rousseau-style Adam and Eve in a jungle on their walls, complete with tropical plants, birds, and leopards. All their furniture was painted yellow, orange, or purple, and the stove white.

In many ways the future of what American art might become was first revealed to Peggy Guggenheim, who attended the Armory Show at age fifteen. Peggy was already referred to as the "copper mine heiress" after her father was lost aboard the *Titanic* and left her at twelve what would be about thirty-six million dollars in today's money. Thereafter she devoted her life to art and artists. She once claimed she had slept with a thousand of them. Her groundbreaking Art of This Century gallery opened in 1942 on West Fifty-Seventh Street and became the new home for American and European surrealists, cubists, and abstract painters.

Also in attendance was Betty Parsons, the thirteen-year-old child of sophisticated New York parents who later recorded her experience: "It was exciting, full of color and life. I felt like those paintings; I couldn't explain it, but I decided then that this was the world I wanted . . . art."[3] The Betty Parsons Gallery opened in 1946 and, along with Guggenheim's, was the first to show many of the early abstract painters.

After the Armory Show things began to change in every artists' community in the country. The Armory Show also turned out to have something like the effect that Martin Luther's Ninety-Five Theses had on Catholicism; suddenly artistic communities saw schisms grow between those who clung to Victorian realism and those who now embraced modernism in all its many facets: impressionism, surrealism, and cubism. With the war now engulfing Europe, many artists, including Hawthorne's former students the L'Engles and the Zorachs, returned from Paris to

Provincetown, with its cheap housing and gorgeous light. *The Boston Globe* of August 8, 1916, proudly dubbed Provincetown "The Biggest Art Colony in the World." The Zorachs had met in Paris in 1910, where both were studying and became friends of Picasso's. She was Marguerite Thompson, a sheltered girl from a wealthy California family born in 1887; he was a Lithuanian-born Jewish immigrant with the birth name of Zorach Gorfinkel. They fell in love to the horror of both their families. Zorach felt it might increase his favor with Marguerite's father if he changed his name to William Zorach. It did not, but they married anyway and moved east to begin a lifelong passionate partnership as working artists. They brought with them firsthand experience of the new European approaches to painting that had inspired the Armory Show.

The Provincetown Art Association was formed in 1914 by Charles Hawthorne and followers of his popular approach to representational work, albeit with strong hints of impressionism. The next year the association presented its first two juried shows.

Year after year more painters came from across the country to study and to rent or buy houses, and the fishermen found that their decaying oyster sheds, fish-flaking shacks, and semi-abandoned houses—most with neither electricity nor plumbing—were suddenly prized "studios,"

Charles Hawthorne, Provincetown, late 1920s

and the harbor's waterfront slowly became a montage of artists' studios and fishermen's boats and docks.

Although artists prefer solitude while working, once done, they seek company, and Provincetown could now provide it in spades as clubs, bars, and "cocktail" parties abounded, particularly with the war's end.

Even before Hawthorne's arrival, Provincetown had been a sought-after residence for marine painters, uninterested in the Armory Show's modernism and dedicated to the portrayal of the sea, the fishermen, and their boats. Provincetown's leading marine painter was Frederick Judd Waugh, better known as "Wizard" Waugh for his flamboyant enjoyment of life, similar to Augustus John, his Welsh bohemian counterpart. He made friends widely, including among the Portuguese fishermen and their large families who welcomed him to their West End community on Commercial Street. His sprawling house, studio, and sculpture-filled terrace soon won the name of Waughville. There he held court with his family, hosting large parties mixing locals and artists. In 1945, in old age, he sold it to another bigger-than-life figure, Hans Hofmann, who, while totally unlike him in painting style, reflected the same warm aura and gregarious spirit.

Beachcombers' Club, early 1920s: William L'Engle (top row, seventh from left); Charles W. Hawthorn (top row, sixth from left); Eugene O'Neill (bottom row, fourth from right)

The Hawthorne camp found refuge in the Beachcombers' Club, which had been started in 1916, meeting for drinks and dinner in the converted hulk of a beached ship at 465A Commercial Street. There the neo-impressionists like Bill L'Engle, John Whorf, and Hawthorne could share their outrage at the fauvist mob of newcomers. The club was not totally intolerant; it did admit nonconformist painters like Edwin Dickinson, "Wizard" Waugh, and the cubist Bill Zorach and even a few poets and writers like Eugene O'Neill and Harry Kemp (until he was too drunk to pay his bills). And its annual summer costume ball soon became the equal of the Liberal Club's Pagan Rout.

Days Lumberyard Studios, ca. 1940. (from left) Elaine de Kooning,
Charles Egan, Sam Kootz, Fritz Bultman, Hans Hofmann, Perle Fine
(Maurice Berezov Photograph, © A.E. Artworks, LLC)

The tension between the realists, including impressionists, and the modernists reached its apogee in 1927 when a large group of modernists led by Ross Moffett successfully petitioned the Art Association to allow its first modernist exhibition, and shortly throughout the country museums and galleries began to follow suit.

This schism often left the modernists to find their own champions to show and purchase their work. A surprising one was John D. Rockefeller Jr.'s wife, Abby, who, much to his displeasure, raised funds for the founding of the Museum of Modern Art (MoMA). It opened in November 1929 in rented space, scant days after the collapse of Wall Street.

4.

THE PROVINCETOWN PLAYERS

Mary Heaton Vorse

t was the summer of 1915, and Mary Heaton Vorse, now remarried to the radical labor writer Joe O'Brien, had managed to persuade a huge circle of her Greenwich Village friends to rent houses along Commercial Street near her house in the East End. Most of the artists from *The Masses* had rented spaces, including John and Dolly Sloan, Bob Minor, Boardman Robinson, Art Young, their editor Max Eastman and his wife, Ida Rauh, and Floyd Dell as well. For her second summer, Mabel Dodge rented a large house for her new lover, the young John Reed, only four years out of Harvard but now called "Golden Boy" or "Storm Boy" by his Village "comrades." Dodge also rented a former coast guard boathouse on the remote Atlantic side at Race Point and erected a silken tent in the dune next to the coast guard station in hopes of luring Reed from his habitual womanizing in Provincetown. Reed's new love, Louise Bryant, had left her dentist husband in Oregon to follow Reed east, as had Reed's Harvard classmate the set designer Bobby Jones.

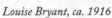

Louise Bryant, ca. 1916   Mabel Dodge, ca. 1914

Provincetown's waterfront had been devastated by the Portland Gale of 1898, which brutally destroyed its fishing industry. The November storm also killed more than 400 people and sank more than 150 boats, including the steamship *Portland* en route from Boston to Portland, Maine, with all 192 aboard. Fifteen years later houses were still for sale or rent for the asking. And with a war beginning between France and Germany, a wave of American "exile" painting families like the L'Engles and Zorachs were returning to both the Village and Provincetown (seeking cheap living quarters). Malcolm Cowley's classic, *Exile's Return*, chronicled this bohemian diaspora.

Neith Boyce (Mrs. Hutchins Hapgood), ca. 1914

Across the street from Vorse lived her friend Hutch Hapgood, anarchist and espouser of free love, and his beautiful wife, Neith Boyce. This was also the second summer for the burly, prematurely white-haired Jig Cook and his new wife, Susan Glaspell, now even more intent on creating a new American theater. The commercial Broadway theater at the time was based on either classic European work or Victorian melodrama. Cook and Glaspell were influenced by four modernist themes—the new politics (socialism), the New Woman (sexually and creatively the equal of men), the new psychology (Freud, Jung, and psychoanalysis), and the new theater taking shape in Europe (Ibsen, Strindberg, Wilde, Shaw, and Synge).

Susan Glaspell   *George Cram "Jig" Cook*

The amateur group Jig and Susan had joined had written, performed, or worked on small one-act plays at the Liberal Club, under Floyd Dell's direction. Many of the group's members had participated in staging the monumentally successful 1913 Paterson Strike Pageant at Madison Square Garden and were planning bigger things this summer. It was decided that Neith Boyce and Hutch Hapgood would allow two of the group's new plays to be performed on the veranda of their cottage after their children were put to bed. On July 15, 1915, they performed Boyce's *Constancy*, a loosely veiled story of a faithless lover based on the stormy relationship of Mabel Dodge and Jack Reed. Then Bobby Jones turned the audience's chairs around so they now faced the parlor instead of the sea for *Suppressed Desires*, a comedy by Cook and Glaspell, who also performed the roles of a young married couple dealing with their respective Freudian psychoanalyses and the sexual feelings they aroused.

The evening was a great success as far as the actors and their guests were concerned, and Neith Boyce wrote to her father, "I made my first appearance on the stage Thursday night! I have been stirring up the people here to write and act some short plays—we began the season with one of mine. Bobby [Jones] staged it on our veranda—the colors were orange and yellow against the sea. . . . I have been mightily complimented on my acting!!!"[1]

For Neith it was a bit of a lark, but for Cook and Glaspell it increasingly became an obsessive quest to capture the classical Greek idea of an elite but amateur group of citizens creating drama for their community or clan without regard to monetary reward and dedicated to the Dionysian celebration of life's joy and to rebellion and visions of a real America.

The Provincetown Players' theater on Mary Heaton Vorse's Lewis Wharf, 1914

The post-premiere excitement led Reed and Cook to seek a larger venue in which to perform, and Mary Vorse offered them the fish house at the end of Lewis Wharf, which she had bought and which extended into the harbor opposite her house on Commercial Street. She was preoccupied with her beloved second husband Joe O'Brien's health, which despite his workman's body was failing rapidly, and she had taken him to New York for an operation. Before she left, she asked Margaret Steele, the painter who had been using the fish house as a studio, to move out. With his famed manic energy, Cook led a group of friends in transforming it to hold a hundred, with a platform candlelit stage. Through the cracks in the floor and the walls, the sound of the waves and the wind created a magical space. In August they were able to restage *Constancy* and *Suppressed Desires* and two new works, Jig Cook's parody *Change Your Style*, tracing the battle raging in Provincetown after the 1913 Armory Show between the new modernist painters and the classical Hawthorne school adherents, and Wilbur Daniel Steele's *Contemporaries*, based on a highly publicized true story of a World War I labor organizer who led a group of homeless men in commandeering a Catholic church as shelter, only to be driven out by the police at the request of the church.

That fall, winter, and spring, Cook labored to further refurbish the wharf fish house theater for the summer of 1916 without the help of the skilled carpenter Joe O'Brien. Sadly, Mary's husband had died of stomach cancer in New York in October 1915. A movable stage and electricity were installed, and circus seats (planks on rows of barrels) were added. When a fire damaged two walls, the painters Bror Nordfeldt and Charles Demuth mixed an ash-gray paint to match the two burned walls, and they were able to open as planned on July 13, 1916. The L'Engles and the Zorachs painted the sets, and John Reed and Jig Cook designed the costumes. The first two new plays were one-acts, a new play by Neith Boyce, *Winter's Night*—in which a young widow is proposed marriage by her brother-in-law immediately after the funeral, and when he is rebuffed, he commits suicide—and *Freedom*, a farce by John Reed based on Victorian romantic sensibilities.

The Game, by Louise Bryant, premiered at Provincetown on July 28, 1916. (from left) John Reed, William Zorach, Helene Freeman, and Judith Lewis. Set by Marguerite Zorach

Then came the revolution: Terry Carlin, a rail thin, long-haired, ravaged but handsome, alcoholic, Irish-born anarchist, and old friend of Boyce and Hapgood's, arrived by ferry from Boston with a former shipmate, the dark, taciturn twenty-seven-year-old Eugene O'Neill. Carlin introduced O'Neill as a playwright with a number of new works. Of course, he came bearing a theater pedigree being the son of James O'Neill, the highly regarded turn-of-the-century melodramatic New York actor famed for his role as the Count of Monte Cristo. Young O'Neill had just completed George Pierce Baker's famous playwriting course at Harvard. He also had a pedigree as a serious binge drinker, the father of an abandoned child, and an experienced tramp steamer deckhand. In sum, a very dangerous and attractive man to both men and women.

Robert Macgowan, Eugene O'Neill, and Bobby Jones,
Provincetown, 1917

The Hapgoods invited Gene to read one of his plays, and he reluctantly selected *Bound East for Cardiff*, the first of a projected three-play cycle based on the lives of the crew of the tramp steamer the SS *Glencairn*. O'Neill, naturally shy when sober, was hesitant to read before the group, and so Friedrich Ebert agreed to read it in the Glaspell parlor while O'Neill sat alone in the dining room. The response was immediate: the play represented just the dark and honest portrayal of the working-class Reed, Vorse, Cook, and the rest had been unable to capture.

Bound East for Cardiff was performed on July 28, 1916, and Susan Glaspell later described that memorable night:

The sea had been good to Eugene O'Neill. It was there for his opening. There was a fog, just as the script demanded, fog bell in the harbor. The tide was in, and it washed under us and around, spraying through the holes in the floor, giving us the rhythm and the flavor of the sea while the big dying sailor talked to his friend Dris of the life he had always wanted deep in the land, where you'd never see a ship or smell the sea.[2]

The cast of that first O'Neill performance is not completely known. O'Neill directed it and played the second mate, who had but one line. The dying sailor, Yank, was played by Jig Cook and his two companions by the experienced actors Teddy Ballantine and Frederic Burt. Jack Reed and Wilbur Daniel Steele played minor roles. The sets were simple, because O'Neill had overruled Bill and Marguerite Zorach's plans for a modernist cubist backdrop.

The audience that opening night included the rising journalist Louise Bryant, with her large violet eyes, soft black hair, and high color in a red cape over a white linen dress (her play *The Game* was on the same bill with O'Neill's), and rumors were already circulating that while she was living with Reed, she was also seeing O'Neill and still not divorced from her husband. Charles Demuth was dressed in a black shirt and purple cummerbund and his companion, Marsden Hartley, in a long blue coat with a gardenia in its buttonhole; the grieving Mary Vorse O'Brien, who had recently lost her husband, Joe, had begun an affair with her neighbor, the architect and set designer Don Corley. John Reed was also in a dark place, having lost his Harvard comrade the poet Alan Seeger in combat at the western front while Reed was covering the Mexican Revolution, where he had been impressed by the religious "miracle plays" performed in remote villages, and he was now facing a dangerous kidney removal.

The seats would be filled night after night that summer by a combined crowd of artists and tourists who flooded the town. In that last year of peace, the Artists' Ball at the town hall drew eight hundred artists and art students in full costume.

Mabel Dodge moped in her newly refurbished coast guard boathouse on the Race Point dunes, slowly losing hope of ever luring Reed back and angry with Mary Vorse for having stolen her Greenwich Village friends from her circle. As Susan Glaspell recalled in her book *The Road to the Temple*, "It was a great summer, we swam from the wharf as well as rehearsed there, we could lie on the beach and talk about plays—everyone writing or acting or producing. Life was all of a piece, work not separated from play."

All, for a moment, forgot their personal lives, entranced by the sound of the waves, the foghorn, and the thrill of being present at the birth of a new American theater.

Marsden Hartley, 1914

O'Neill became close with two new visitors to Provincetown. Marsden Hartley and Charles Demuth were both successful painters and among the returning exiles from Europe; they were gay and made no attempts to disguise it. Hartley was born poor in Maine, the son of English-immigrant mill workers. Nevertheless, he pursued his artistic talent and at twenty-two was studying with William Merritt Chase and had become close friends with Alfred Stieglitz and Georgia O'Keeffe (to whom he left his paintings at his death). He moved to Europe and made a circle of new friends, including Kandinsky, Picasso, and Cézanne. And then found a new world in prewar Berlin, where he was able to dress like a woman and have numerous affairs with dashing Prussian officers. But the war came, and with it the death of several of his officer lovers whose portraits he had lovingly realized.

Returning to America in 1916, Hartley stayed briefly with Mabel Dodge, who had parted from John Reed and was now married to the painter Maurice Sterne, at her new estate, Finney Farm in Croton, just up the Hudson River from New York City, and then moved on to Provincetown at the invitation of John Reed. Reed, flush with cash earned as a journalist covering the Mexican Revolution, had rented a large house for himself and his new lover, Louise Bryant. Eugene O'Neill was boarding across the street, and O'Neill and Hartley became close. Hartley later moved into another house with Charles Demuth, who had also been caught up in the "magic" of the Provincetown Players' season.

Demuth came from a poor family in Lancaster, Pennsylvania, and throughout his wandering life always returned there to live in his mother's house. In Paris before the war, he had met Hartley and they became close. Demuth was a colorful figure with a wicked sense of humor. He dressed flamboyantly and used a cane because of childhood polio and also suffered from diabetes, while Hartley, after Berlin, dressed rather soberly and was known for his reserve with those he did not know. But to friends Hartley was generous; he volunteered to paint the interior of the house Jig Cook and Susan Glaspell had bought in 1914 at 564 Commercial Street.

It was a summer of exploring new painting for both, enhanced by the cauldron of creativity that summer of 1916 brought to all who experienced it. Hartley was said to have suggested the name the Provincetown Players for the group, and he later wrote about that "remarkable and never repeated summer in Provincetown . . . one of really huge import and hugely various satisfaction."[3]

Those who had stayed over that winter to plan the 1916 Provincetown season recognized that they now had a theater company they could bring back with them to Greenwich Village, and at the urging of Cook, Reed, and Bryant they drew up the membership agreement of the Provincetown Players, and it was signed on September 15, 1916, by O'Neill, Glaspell, Hapgood, Reed, Bryant, Steele, the Zorachs, Harry Kemp, and Cook. That October, Cook, staked with $240 (a little over $6,000 in today's money) raised by the founders, had located a space at 139 MacDougal Street, next to the Liberal Club and Polly's Restaurant. The Provincetown Players soon began to draw both a steady audience and major new actors and playwrights, including the rising poet Edna St. Vincent Millay and the author of the notorious novel *Nightwood*, Djuna Barnes.

Jig Cook had been given a key by Jack Reed to his apartment at 43 Washington Square and had immediately started constructing a stage in the old brownstone at 139 MacDougal. Mary Pyne, the beautiful milk-skinned, red-haired actress who had married Harry Kemp and was later to become the lover of Theodore Dreiser, Hutch Hapgood, and Djuna Barnes, wrote to Mary Heaton Vorse, then in Provincetown:

> Jig and Nordfeldt are working like galley slaves—painting, hang-ing beams, sawing wood—Jig Cook awfully tired, he says he hadn't had time to twist his forelocks—the theater is lovely—the benches are lavender—the walls are dark, dull gray with emerald green doors and paneling, the archway over the stage gold squares and purple designs to each side—and the curtain a wonderful royal purple affair with a cerise lamp across it. . . . The Game (Louise Bryant's play) has many gestures in it and two nice girls—Jack Reed rehearses his gestures between courses at meals. Freedom (Reed's play) is going on the next bill. [Harry Kemp] is going to take Jack's part.

She closed by telling Mary Vorse she hadn't seen her new lover, Don Corley, the architect and sometimes set designer for the Provincetown Players.

Jig Cook had said about their new theater, "We exist to cause the writing of the best plays that can be written in the United States and to give each play the best possible start," and indeed it did.

In the winter of 1917, Provincetown was facing record cold at thirteen degrees below zero and heavy snow. O'Neill, now without Louise Bryant, who had joined Reed in Moscow to cover the revolution, had remained in Provincetown working on a number of new plays and was soon pre-sented with an even larger theater when Jig Cook discovered a combined mansion stable and workhouse at 133 MacDougal. The basement was converted to a scene shop and dressing rooms, and the main floor became the theater. On the wall next to the stage, a hitching post hung, a remnant of the building's original use as a stable, and, according to legend, Jack

*The Provincetown Playhouse theater, 133 MacDougal Street,
Greenwich Village, 1916*

Reed had these words painted beneath it: "Here Pegasus was hitched."
Others said it was done by Don Corley.

The second floor, thanks to a gift from the financier Otto Kahn,
a beloved New York patron of the arts, was converted into a restaurant for the theater staff and for sixty cents a dinner to the public as
well. Two part-time actors—Louis Ell and his handsome red-headed,
smudge-faced wife, Christine (who had formerly assisted Polly at her
restaurant)—agreed to run it, and it quickly became, like Polly's, a
meeting place for the bohemians. Both the theater and the restaurant,
already called Christine's, could still remind patrons of its provenance,
because a wet day often brought the clear odor of horse manure. Both
Christine and Polly took their pots and pans to Provincetown in the
summers.

Christine always provided a huge bowl of punch for the cast parties,
and Jig Cook presided like Poseidon over the ladling, particularly generous to his own cup. When accused of being drunk, he roared, "It is for the
good of the Provincetown Players. I am always ready to sacrifice myself
to a cause." In a sense, both O'Neill and Cook did sacrifice themselves to
the cause, and as a result the theater flourished. O'Neill won the Pulitzer
Prize in 1920 for *Beyond the Horizon,* also becoming the only American
playwright to win a Nobel Prize for literature. His play *Anna Christie* was

At Christine's, *by Charles Frederick Ellis. Ellis was also a set painter and actor for the theater and was married to Norma Millay, a sister of Edna St. Vincent Millay. (from left) Two unknowns, Christine, Jig Cook, Eugene O'Neill*

made into a silent film in 1923 and later remade into a talkie in 1930 with Greta Garbo playing Anna.

Cook and O'Neill had never seen eye to eye on the staging of plays. O'Neill had now dedicated his life to the formal study of stagecraft and was no longer bewitched by Jig's philosophy of a group of amateur creators sharing a communal (that is, noncommercial) Dionysian romp. Jig like John Reed had also fallen in love with the new Stanislavsky Russian theater.

O'Neill refused to let Jig direct *Beyond the Horizon*. Cook, already strained by the demanding physical work of building the theater sets, drank even more heavily, feeling that "his" theater was now becoming just a staging ground for O'Neill's plays to move uptown to the commercial Shubert theaters where top tickets cost $2.50. Jig solemnly informed the players, "We promise to let this theater die rather than let it become another voice of mediocrity."

Susan Glaspell and Jig Cook, Greece, 1923

One evening, Susan found him sitting alone on the stage. He turned to her and said, "We are going to Greece." In 1920 they took ship, and Jig once again found the simple agrarian village he always yearned for, filled with friends, drunks, storytelling, and, just four years later, a resting place, under a stone from Apollo's Temple at Delphi, at just fifty.

The L'Engles' version of this parting was colored by their long friendship with Susan Glaspell and her stepchildren, Harl and Nilla Cook. They were sympathetic with the O'Neill-centric version, but in theirs Jig Cook emerges as the flawed but true inspiration for the theater. Certainly, that is the version that Susan Glaspell set forth in her book *The Road to the Temple* about those years in Greece with Jig and his children.

Regardless of whose version of the demise of the Provincetown Players one chooses, indeed here (once) Pegasus was hitched.

5.

THE MASSES

Post–Civil War industrialized America had assembled large groups of mainly immigrant men, women, and children to work in their sprawling manufacturing assembly lines, mines, railroads, and textile mills. Beginning in the 1890s, the radical organization of these workers began in earnest and created a new labor reform movement whose leaders mainly came from the ranks of these working men and women. The women in leadership roles like Mary Heaton Vorse, Emma Goldman, and Elizabeth Gurley Flynn also had another goal: the vote.

While labor unions were already well established in Europe, they were unknown in pre–Civil War America except for craft guilds that banded together to protect their trades from counterfeiting or cheap imports. Suddenly the owners of great enterprises (the Rockefellers, Fricks, and Carnegies) were facing organized labor's demands for shorter days, better wages, and safer working conditions. These powerful owners had the full support of both the politicians they had elected and the judges they had appointed, and they quickly demonized these new labor organizations as "Reds" simply because they marched under red flags as all European labor protesters had long before they were adopted by the communists.

The International Ladies' Garment Workers' Union was founded in

1900 to represent women in the garment trade in New York City, the center of America's dressmaking. The ILGWU consisted almost entirely of women, mainly recruited from the new wave of Jewish immigrants in Greenwich Village. This was the union Emma Goldman first joined when her family emigrated from Lithuania in 1885.

Eugene Debs addressing an antiwar rally, Ohio, 1917

The Industrial Workers of the World, or Wobblies, was founded in Chicago in 1905, and among its founders was the leader of the Socialist Party, Eugene Debs, and "Big Bill" Haywood. Bill's father was a former pony express rider who died when Bill was three, sending him into the mines at ten. The charismatic Haywood, almost six feet tall and large of build, with an eye patch from a childhood injury, could hold audiences transfixed. One of his famous short speeches was "Eight hours of work, eight hours of play, eight hours of sleep—eight hours a day." The IWW, whose members tended to be coal and copper miners, quickly moved away from the American Federation of Labor (AFL), an older alliance of craft unions founded in Columbus, Ohio, by Samuel Gompers in 1886, because the IWW's more radical goal was to overthrow management and give workers control of the enterprises they labored in, in fact the original goal of Lenin's Soviet Union.

Thus the stage was set for Piet Vlag, an eccentric, bearded Dutch socialist who had moved to the Village, to launch a progressive socialist monthly magazine titled *The Masses* in 1911. Piet swiftly gathered an exceptional unpaid staff, including the cartoonists Art Young, George Bellows, John Sloan, and Bob Minor (then the highest-paid cartoonist in

Robert Minor (1884–1952)

America) and radical "muckraking" journalists such as Lincoln Steffens, Susan Glaspell, Upton Sinclair, Mary Heaton Vorse, and John Reed.

The Masses cost five cents, and a year's subscription was one dollar. Its masthead's motto read in part, "This magazine is owned and published cooperatively by its editors. It has no dividends to pay, and nobody is trying to make money out of it. A revolutionary and not a reform magazine; a magazine with a sense of humor and no respect for the respectable." It consisted of twenty-four to thirty pages of articles, book and theater reviews, and exceptional cartoons and drawings.

Lawrence textile strike, a.k.a. the Bread and Roses strike, January 1912

This volunteer staff covered social unrest flaring up around the country, including the mill strikes in the huge textile factories strung along the Merrimack River in northern Massachusetts towns like Lawrence and Lowell (named after the wealthy Bostonian families that had owned the mills for generations). In 1912 the women workers (almost all of whom were young Catholic Irish or Canadians) were striking in Lawrence for better wages. The men joined them, and the owners countered their demands with alleged new "reform wages"—that is, lowering the men's wages to that of women and children. Twenty-three thousand workers abandoned their looms to march under banners that read, "We Want Bread, but We Want Roses Too."

Paterson silk workers' strike leaders. (from left) "Big Bill" Haywood, unknown, Elizabeth Gurley Flynn, Carlo Tresca, unknown

The main organizers of the strike were members of the IWW, including Emma Goldman and her Provincetown friends and fellow Heterodoxy Club member Elizabeth Flynn and Flynn's then lover, the Italian-born socialist and charismatic labor organizer Carlo Tresca, who was also the father of her out-of-wedlock son.

These strikes were shortly followed in 1913 by another huge textile strike in Paterson, New Jersey, where mainly Italian immigrant silk workers were seeking an eight-hour day and improved working conditions. This strike was again organized by the IWW and its leaders, "Big Bill" Haywood, Elizabeth Flynn, and Carlo Tresca (who was immediately embraced by the workers as a fellow Italian). John Reed idolized Bill Haywood, as did his former Village roommate and mentor, Lincoln Steffens, and at Steffens's urging he took the train to Paterson to observe the strike as a reporter. As he watched the thousands of striking workers marching in the rain from a nearby porch, the police suddenly arrested him and several of the workers with whom he stood. Reed was brought before a local magistrate who, when he heard Reed describe his occupation as "poet," sentenced him to twenty days in a filthy Paterson jail.

This seems to be the actual event that transformed Reed from a sympathetic Harvard-educated reporter into a true revolutionary. After he was bailed out by Steffens, he wrote one of the landmark articles on the labor struggle:

> There's a war in Paterson! But it's a curious kind of war. All the violence is the work of one side—the Mill Owners. Their servants, the police, club unresisting men and women and ride down law-abiding crowds on horseback. . . . Their stories brought home to me hard the knowledge that the manufacturers get all they can out of labor, pay as little as they must, and permit the existence of great masses of miserable unemployed in order to keep wages down; that the forces of the State are on the side of property, against the propertyless.[1]

Reed now formally embraced the radical labor movement, and he and Mabel Dodge, soon to be romantically involved, were the two most important organizers of the IWW's Paterson Strike Pageant held in Madison Square Garden on June 7, 1913. The strikers were brought in by train from Paterson to march up Fifth Avenue to Madison Square Garden, where a crowd of 150,000 had assembled. Reed, brandishing a megaphone, had cut a path through the audience for the workers to march to a stage filled with sets of "Dark Satanic Mills" designed by his Harvard classmate Bobby Jones.

These were tumultuous times as Teddy Roosevelt's Square Deal for workers supported by the progressives gave way to William Howard Taft's election in 1912, only to open the door to the Democrat Woodrow Wilson when Teddy created his "Bull Moose" Party and split the Republican vote, scuttling what would have been Taft's second term. Wilson at first appeared to be hearkening to the plight of workers and ran on a ticket opposing foreign wars, which gained the support of many pacifist socialists who failed to vote for their own candidate, Eugene Debs.

Max Eastman (1883–1969)

For reasons unknown, Piet Vlag decided to return to Europe and left *The Masses* to its board of editors. Max Eastman was elected by the board to run *The Masses*. Eastman and his sister, Crystal, the children of radical transcendentalist ministers, were living together in the Village. Crystal was an ardent feminist and an early woman law student at New York University. Claude McKay, a rising Black poet and friend, described her as the loveliest white woman he had ever seen. Crystal introduced Max to a fellow student, Ida Rauh, a striking young Jewish socialist, and their affair led to eventual marriage despite both their pledges to observe free love rather than marriage.

John Sloan's second wife, Dolly, a former prostitute, became the magazine's business manager while her husband made sure that his fellow Ashcan artists Bellows, Young, and Robinson continued to provide a steady stream of drawings. It was Sloan who described the magazine after Vlag's departure: "The *Masses* set a pace and had an influence on all periodicals after [it]. Certainly the *New Yorker*, in a more sophisticated and less liberal way, patterned itself on the early *Masses*." Sloan had run as a Socialist candidate for the New York assembly and, when asked for his credentials, had responded, "I think I know the difference between law and justice."[2]

Eastman was quickly overwhelmed with manuscript submissions and begged the board for an assistant at the then not-unworthy salary of ten dollars per week. With their assent he offered the job to his fellow Liberal Club pal Harry Kemp, who agreed and was given his first manuscript to review. Eastman discovered it the next day on his desk unread, with a note that read, "I must live and die a poet."

Kemp himself remained a contributor with radical poems such as this:

TO KIPLING—

Vile singer of the bloody deeds of empire,
And of the bravery that exploits the poor,
Exalter of subservience to masters,
Bard of the race that bound and robbed the Boer.[3]

Floyd Dell (1887–1969)

Desperate, Eastman sought advice from his volunteer business adviser Berkeley Tobey over lunch. Tobey, an admired bon vivant who married eight times, including for a year to the writer and activist Dorothy Day, was a close friend of Theodore Dreiser's. Tobey glanced out the restaurant window and pointed out a young man to Eastman: "There's your assistant editor." It was the young journalist Floyd Dell, who had recently joined his close friends Jig Cook and Susan Glaspell along with other Chicago intellectuals in the Village and had already submitted several pieces to *The Masses*. When Eastman offered Dell twenty-five dollars per week to review books and articles, he replied yes and, as the only paid employee, believed he "was the luckiest man in the Village." Dell quickly became one of the most respected book reviewers and editors in the country, acquiring national front-page articles like Margaret Sanger's blockbuster piece on birth control, which set off a torrent of government protests, including prohibiting the mailing of the article by the U.S. Postal Service.

Dell's new all-volunteer editorial board met monthly and included John Reed, Mary Heaton Vorse, and William English Walling. Editorial meetings were open to all and usually filled with friends, having become a Village social event. At the high table, Max Eastman kept order behind a pile of drawings and proposed articles; next to him sat the chain-smoking Dell, attired in white pants and an orange scarf hanging from his Byronic open collar, taking charge of presenting the articles and poems, while the lanky John Sloan hoisted the drawings or cartoons for all to examine more closely before casting judgment.

Because they were model bohemians, there was time for play as well. The *Masses* fundraisers in those years were unquestionably the biggest social event in the Village. The *Masses* Costume Ball was started by Floyd Dell after he located the perfect venue, Webster Hall, at 119 East Eleventh Street. The hall was a cavernous, dark space in which the Progressive Labor Party had been created in 1887 and where frequent meetings were led by Emma Goldman for the ILGWU. Webster Hall's owner also owned a connected bar, and when Dell inquired what the rent might be, the owner responded, "Is yours a drinking crowd?" Dell replied, "Hell yes!" and the owner replied, "All right then, you can have it for nothing."

Admission to the ball was one dollar in costume and two dollars without. To avoid total nudity, its tickets read, "There must be some costume." Women came in hula skirts and ballet costumes and as gypsy dancers. There was so much drinking that the owner hired a clutch of huge bouncers who kept the brawling at bay. Among its attendees in 1913 and until *The Masses* closed were Scott and Zelda Fitzgerald, Charles Demuth, Dorothy Day, Marcel Duchamp, and Man Ray.

Mary Heaton Vorse began her annual effort to lure her fellow *Masses* editors to Provincetown for the summer. Floyd Dell went, as did Max Eastman and his lover, Ida Rauh, Crystal Eastman, Boardman Robinson, and Margaret Sanger. Sanger had fallen in love with the Cape, bringing a new lover every summer and even naming her dog "Truro." They all rented near Mary Vorse along Commercial Street. Polly Holladay and Havel had moved Polly's Restaurant to Provincetown for the summers, and all who came quickly embraced the Beachcombers' and Art Association's costume balls as even more elaborate versions of those given by the Liberal Club and *The Masses* in Webster Hall.

Somewhat like the early American Communist Party, *The Masses* was often ridiculed for its lack of real manual laborers as members. One critic wrote, "They draw nude women for the *Masses* / Thick, fat, ungainly lasses—/ How does that help the working classes?"[4]

Slater Brown, a left-wing journalist and Columbia graduate while covering the early years of the American Community Party, reported a conversation at a party rally between two obviously Ivy League men. One congratulated the other on his son's joining the party, but the father replied, "Yes, but it would be nice if some actual working men joined instead!"

The magazine's groundbreaking radical cartoons and drawings were the eventual cause of its governmental woes. One of its most provocative prewar cartoons depicted President Wilson with a group of arms manufacturers and jowly bankers surrounded by piles of munitions. The caption read as follows: Wilson: "But I don't want them, there is no enemy to fight." J. P. Morgan, Schwab, et al.: "You buy these guns and we will get you an enemy!"

John Reed, ca. 1915

Reed was absent the summer of 1915 covering the war in Germany, where millions of young men were struggling through muddy fields of barbed wire directly into machine gun fire and heavy bombardment, leaving thousands dead or maimed each day. Appalled by the slaughter, he returned to the States to lobby against America's possible entrance, only to find a country beginning to shift from "pacifism" to "patriotism." He wrote, "Already in America those citizens who oppose the entrance of their country into the European melee are called *traitors*, and those who protest against the curtailing of our meager rights of free speech are spoken of as *dangerous lunatics*."[5] In his third annual speech to Congress in 1915, Wilson warned, "There are citizens of the United States . . . born under other flags [read Jews] . . . who have poured the poison of disloyalty into the very arteries of our national life . . . Such creatures of passion, disloyalty, and anarchy must be crushed out." At that point, there were 3.4 million Jews in the United States, and more than 250,000 were later to serve in the war.

This was the crisis that faced American socialists, as they observed Wilson fall under the influence of British propaganda created by H. G. Wells and Arthur Conan Doyle, with their tales of the atrocities allegedly being committed by "the Hun" in Belgium—babies hoisted on bayonet points and innocent blond nurses raped. The Socialist Party at the time was not some fringe group but an influential actor in American politics, and its leadership under Eugene Debs was committed to pacifism. Its members, both liberal and radical, were united against intervention.

Despite violent antiwar protests, Wilson persuaded Congress to declare war in April 1917 and with the help of his attorney general he quickly began war on two fronts against external and internal enemies. Oddly, the government's domestic targets were not German sympathizers but loyal Americans who opposed all wars.

Before Wilson obtained Congress's approval for war, he lamented its possible impact on American society to an editor of the New York *World*: "Once lead this people into war, and they'll forget there ever was such a thing as tolerance. To fight you must be brutal and ruthless, and the spirit of ruthless brutality will enter into the very fibre of our national life, infecting Congress, the courts, the policeman on the beat, the man on the street."⁶ Wilson's betrayal made *The Masses* only work harder to oppose U.S. entry, perhaps best represented by Robert Minor's cartoon of a strapping headless conscript being admired by a recruiter who says, "Finally, the perfect soldier," and scathing antiwar articles by John Reed.

Wilson responded with a one-two punch. First he pushed through the Espionage Act of 1917, establishing a twenty-year jail sentence for "disrupting recruiting," then came the Sedition Act of 1918, perhaps the most repressive legislation to date, making it a crime to use "disloyal" language about the government. Three thousand people were prosecuted under these laws, including Eugene Debs, the Socialist Party's candidate for president, for giving a speech opposing the war.

President Wilson had never forgotten *The Masses'* 1917 publication of what he considered treasonable material opposing America's entrance into war in its August issue, and charges were brought against the magazine and its editors, including Eastman, Reed, and Art Young, in April 1918. The first *Masses* trial began in federal court before Judge Learned Hand, a former member of the Progressive Party and a Taft appointee. As "conspirators," the defendants faced fines of ten thousand dollars each and twenty years' imprisonment.

The trial turned into a carnival as only *The Masses* knew how to organize, with constant interruptions and protests from supporters within and outside the courtroom. Edna St. Vincent Millay showed up every day to support her new beau, Floyd Dell, and Ida Rauh came for Max Eastman. Reed was beyond subpoena, being in Russia covering the Russian Revolution. Louis Untermeyer, who covered poetry for *The Masses*, wrote, "As the trial went on it was evident that the indictment was a legal subterfuge and what was really on trial was the issue of a free press."⁷

Despite Hand's charge to the jury that "every man has the right to have . . . opinions as seems to him best whether they be Socialist, anarchist or atheistic," the jury was deeply influenced by the patriotic fervor of the times and was only prevented from reaching a verdict to convict by one holdout whom the jury complained to the judge was a socialist and ought to be lynched. Judge Hand declared a mistrial, but Wilson and his now attorney general, Mitchell Palmer, were not to be thwarted, and in September 1918 new charges of sedition were brought against the same defendants. Reed had now returned from Russia to be a defendant. He and Louise Bryant were now a married couple living in Patchin Place in the Village.

This time the jury included a number of young women who later admitted to having huge crushes on the two most handsome defendants, Floyd Dell and Max Eastman. A majority of the jury voted not guilty. But the final victory belonged to Wilson. *The Masses* had already been prohibited access to the postal service and was now bankrupt, as was the antiwar movement, the target of both the Wilson government and "patriotic" mobs that attacked Socialist Party gatherings with increasing violence. Try as they might to build a community of comrades seeking only truth and creativity, the chaos of the war and the Allies' failure to establish greater democratic models themselves or in Germany, Austria, and Russia were to increasingly affect bohemians' lives.

Edith Hamilton, the classics scholar and author of *The Greek Way*, wrote of the war, "During World War I, a play would have had short shrift here which showed up General Pershing for a coward; ridiculed the Allies' cause; brought in Uncle Sam as a blustering bully; glorified the peace party. But when Athens was fighting for her life, Aristophanes did the exact equivalent of all these things many times over and the Athenians, pro- and anti-war alike, flocked to the theatre. The right of a man to say what he pleased was fundamental in Athens. 'A slave is he who cannot speak his thought,' said Euripides."

In bankrupt Weimar Germany, a disappointed Bavarian army veteran had begun a fascist movement called the National Socialist Party and with his growing followers led a failed takeover, or putsch, against the local government. Sentenced to five years in prison in 1923, Adolf Hitler began writing his Nazi manifesto, *Mein Kampf*, in which Europe's Jews were now charged with the betrayal of Germany in the war and were therefore the enemy of a new restored Aryan Reich.

Across the new post-Versailles Polish border, another leader was also rising to power with Lenin's death in 1924. Joseph Stalin had gained control of the Cheka, the feared Soviet secret police. Emma Goldman, then in exile in Moscow, warned Louise Bryant and other ardent American supporters of Lenin that Stalin's Cheka would be the force that ended any hope of a workers' democracy in Russia. Within two years, Stalin had gained complete control of all of the apparatus of power, and woe betide any who would challenge his right to rule, beginning with Lenin's one-time favorite and presumed successor, Leon Trotsky.

Among the bohemian Left, Stalin's Russia, at least from a distance, seemed to promise a more equitable sharing of the national wealth than what they were experiencing in the United States under Warren Harding, and now Calvin Coolidge. Labor strikes spread from the steel mills of Pittsburgh to the coalfields of Pennsylvania and West Virginia. The miners were now led by a resolute John L. Lewis, head of the United Mine Workers. Many from Provincetown became deeply involved with these strikers, including Mary Vorse and John Dos Passos. The workers' struggle became the headlines for the *New Masses* and *The Daily Worker*, both newspapers increasingly directed from the nineteenth-floor New York headquarters of the Communist Party of the United States of America.

In addition to the bohemian leftists' support for workers' rights, their attention focused on the plight of the southern Blacks, given President Wilson's and his successors' total support for Jim Crow segregation and Congress's refusal to even consider an anti-lynching bill. (Between 1892 and 1968, 3,446 Blacks were lynched, almost all of these in former Confederate states.)

A deep belief in equal treatment for Black Americans had been a central tenet of the Liberal Club's ethos. William English Walling, the white Kentucky aristocrat and Harvard graduate, had co-founded the National Association for the Advancement of Colored People and recruited W. E. B. Du Bois to edit its newspaper. Social interchange was on the rise between white bohemian intellectuals and members of the Harlem Renaissance, including Claude McKay and Langston Hughes, and between political activists of both races. It was a mutual admiration for communism or socialism that brought them together, but it was probably jazz, sex, and romance that cemented the bonds.

O'Neill's 1920 play *The Emperor Jones* was the first Provincetown Players production to feature a Black actor in a leading role. O'Neill had based his play on the Haitian Revolution's descent into terror. The role of the Haitian ruler was first played by Charles Gilpin, who had been recommended to O'Neill as a young actor of talent. The play and Gilpin's depiction of the dictator's final days, haunted by constant jungle drums, drew huge critical praise. John Dos Passos took Adelaide Walker (wife of Edmund Wilson's pal Charlie Walker) to see Gilpin and in a telling diary entry referred to him as "a wonderful coon."

Sadly, Gilpin was in a way as haunted by racism as the emperor he played; feeling unappreciated, he began to drink heavily and refused to audition for O'Neill's next play, which addressed the invidious treatment of Blacks in America. The portrayal of a middle-class Black man married to a white woman scandalized the country and made Paul Robeson, who replaced Gilpin, an international symbol of Black male grace, talent, and fearlessness.

Robeson quickly became a cult figure for the Left, and white women literally lined up to have affairs with this sculpted Black Adonis, a former all-American football star at Rutgers and graduate of Columbia Law School. Jig Cook's teenage daughter, Nilla, just returned from Greece and supposedly under the care of her stepmother, Susan Glaspell, had managed to get a job working on the set and had slept with Robeson, she later confessed to Malcolm Cowley, as did the Provincetown-based painter Niles Spencer's wife, Betty, while Spencer was part of a successful painting exhibition with Charles Demuth.

O'Neill and his new English-born novelist wife, Agnes Boulton, be-came close to Robeson and his wife, Essie, and went clubbing with them in Harlem, setting off a period of binge drinking for O'Neill, who had been on the wagon. In 1925, Frank Shay attempted to engage Robeson to perform in *The Emperor Jones* at his Barnstormers' Theater on Brad-ford Street in Provincetown, but received threats from the Ku Klux Klan, which had branches even in Provincetown, where they had attempted over the years to intimidate Catholic Portuguese immigrants. Neverthe-less, Robeson bravely agreed to come to perform a program of Black spirituals, including "Steal Away" and "Were You There When They Crucified My Lord," and other American folk songs before a sold-out audience. But the constant daily threats and insults finally led the Robesons to move to England, where he became a major success in new presentations of *The Emperor Jones* and *Show Boat* and in a 1930 performance of Shakespeare's *Othello* opposite Peggy Ashcroft as Desdemona. The two stars began a torrid affair that ended only when Robeson's wife returned to America with their son and threatened divorce.

Bartolomeo Vanzetti and Nicola Sacco, 1923

Labor strife and America's treatment of Blacks were not the only national issues consuming the new American Communist Party. A growing battle over immigration standards was brewing while a conservative Congress seemed intent on amending the immigration laws to limit immigrants who were either Jewish or Catholic (Irish or Italian). Nothing brought the Right's aversion to outsiders into such clear focus as the highly contested trial of two Italian immigrants charged with a botched armed robbery and alleged murder of a payroll guard at a Brockton, Massachusetts, shoe factory. The two defendants, Nicola Sacco and Bartolomeo Vanzetti, were admitted political anarchists and thus represented the establishment's greatest fear—a new wave of anarchist immigrants like prewar Emma Goldman and Alexander Berkman. Both defendants pleaded not guilty, and there were other suspects. The Left gathered to their defense others including the infamous mine organizer Ella Reeve "Mother" Bloor, who hitchhiked to the trial from California, and Paula Holladay, the proprietor of Polly's Restaurant, who, in her tousled hair and red rain slicker, walked the 117 miles from her summer restaurant in Provincetown carrying a sign that read AMERICA CANNOT LOOK THE WORLD IN THE FACE IF SACCO AND VANZETTI ARE MURDERED!

Bohemians from across the country arrived in Boston to gather at the

Dedham courthouse where the trial was taking place to support the defendants. The line in front of Governor Alvan Fuller's office was an A-list of socialist and communist supporters, from Edna St. Vincent Millay, Dorothy Day, Mary Heaton Vorse, Susan Glaspell, and other women from the Provincetown Players and the Heterodoxy Club, to John Dos Passos distributing *The Daily Worker*, and Edmund Wilson. George Bernard Shaw, Albert Einstein, Dorothy Parker, John Galsworthy, Robert Benchley, Anatole France, H. G. Wells, Jane Addams, Frank Shay, and Upton Sinclair were all arrested for "loitering," but only Sinclair appealed his ten-dollar fine, on the basis that he was there as a reporter for *The Daily Worker*. They were joined by three-quarters of Harvard's senior class and faculty members, including Felix Frankfurter.

John Dos Passos under arrest, 1923

The trial lasted several months and was frequently interrupted by protests, but finally ended in their conviction and the imposition of the death penalty. For Dos Passos, who was about to publish his well-received war novel *Three Soldiers*, and others, it seemed that the old WASP ascendency was taking its revenge on two naive immigrants. The effort to stay their execution became even more fervent as the doomed men engaged in hunger strikes. Their appeals were ultimately in vain, and after many stays of execution Governor Fuller (who was himself the first Catholic governor of Massachusetts) in August 1927 informed their defense counsel, who had approached him for a further stay while he was playing golf, that he was "playing through!"

Dos Passos was particularly ashamed of the behavior of A. Lawrence Lowell, the deeply conservative president of Harvard and the uncle of his despised commanding officer during the war, Guy Lowell.

The death sentence included these words from the presiding judge, Webster Thayer: "This man [Vanzetti], although he may not actually have committed the crime . . . is the enemy of our existing institutions . . . The defendant's ideals are cognate with crime." (In fairness, Massachusetts, like many states at that time, made any person involved in an armed murder co-responsible with the shooter, although clearly for Judge Thayer being an anarchist was still more criminal than being a murderer.)

Carlo Tresca, Elizabeth Gurley Flynn's lover, had become close to Sacco and Vanzetti as a fellow Italian anarchist and later told Max Eastman in confidence that "Sacco was guilty, but Vanzetti was not."

A host of bohemian intellectuals created articles, novels, and poems based on the trial, and the Lithuanian Jewish immigrant Ben Shahn, who had bought a house in Truro in 1920, created a series of paintings titled *The Passion of Sacco and Vanzetti* as well as a black-and-white etching in 1932 of the two immigrant anarchists that has become their iconic international memorial.

Obsessed by the trial, Dos Passos became an active member of their defense committee together with Mary Vorse. The committee had been organized by Elizabeth Flynn, now being called the "Joan of Arc" of the Left by the press. He also rented a house in Provincetown to work on his piece *Facing the Chair: The Story of the Americanization of Two Foreign-Born Workmen*. He later recorded his anger about American justice in his trilogy, *U.S.A.* (comprising *The 42nd Parallel*, *1919*, and *The Big Money*), in which he depicted the United States as two nations, one for the rich and another for the poor:

> they have clubbed us off the streets   they are stronger   they
> are rich   they hire and fire the politicians the newspapereditors
> the old judges   the small men with reputations the college-

presidents the wardheelers (listen businessmen collegepresidents judges America will not forget her betrayers)   they hire the men with guns   the uniforms the policecars the patrolwagons . . . we stand defeated America.[8]

Sacco and Vanzetti's funeral procession, Boston

6.

THE WAR TO END ALL WARS

Those who had reveled in that last Provincetown summer of 1916, at the peaceful end of the Marconi telegraph cable stretching from Wellfleet to Europe protected by the great Atlantic, slowly began to be drawn to the war, like moths to a flame. First the journalists went. John Reed had been covering the war since it began, returning only as a defendant in the second *Masses* trial, and his consort, Louise Bryant, had joined him as an accredited reporter. Mary Heaton Vorse soon followed, covering the mayhem for a number of papers and, as restless young men have done since warfare began, volunteering to serve in the French Foreign Legion, the French Lafayette Escadrille, and legendary British regiments so as not to be left out of the adventure.

John Roderigo Dos Passos's father, also John Dos Passos, who was half Madeiran Portuguese and a very successful Wall Street corporate lawyer, had refused to marry his mistress, John's mother, until the death of his wife, leaving John to grow up illegitimate until fourteen, when he was adopted and changed his last name to Dos Passos, and launching him on a lifelong search for father figures. At Harvard he had found one in John Reed, who had just graduated a few years earlier and already become a legend for those seeking adventure and rebellion. Dos (as he was to be called for the rest of his life) devoured Reed's latest works—*Insurgent Mexico*

John Dos Passos, 1924

(1914) and *The War in Eastern Europe* (1916). Reed had covered General "Black Jack" Pershing's skirmishes with Pancho Villa's rebel forces on the Arizona border and then moved on to cover the early breakout of the war in Europe, where he was again to meet Pershing as the commander of the American Expedition Forces after Wilson obtained a declaration of war against Germany from Congress on April 6, 1917.

That year, Dos reviewed both books for *The Harvard Monthly* and like many of his fellow seniors reflected on how different from Reed's their lives were: "And what are we fit for when they turn us out of Harvard? We're too intelligent to be successful business men and we haven't the sand or the energy to be anything else."[1]

Upon graduation he followed Reed's path to Greenwich Village and fell in love with the bohemian world, meeting Emma Goldman and her fellow Liberal Club members. Inspired by Reed's pacifist hatred of war but his enchantment with the camaraderie of the men drawn to it, Dos joined the private Norton-Harjes Ambulance Corps, which was based in Paris and assigned to support the French ambulance service. These private ambulance companies were attracting many young Americans, among them the rising writers Ernest Hemingway, Malcolm Cowley, Harry Crosby, and Archibald MacLeish.

Unfortunately for Dos, his commanding officer, Guy Lowell, the nephew of Harvard's then president, A. Lawrence Lowell, and later the architect of Boston's Museum of Fine Arts and Harvard's Emerson Hall, took a very dim view of Dos from the start. In fact, Lowell quickly determined that this obstinate, wire-glasses-wearing stutterer was a most dangerous and unreliable pacifist. Lowell became Dos's constant nemesis as he remained his commanding officer after the private Norton-Harjes Corps was merged into the U.S. Army Ambulance Service and moved to the Italian front, where Dos's soon-to-be-friend Ernest Hemingway was also stationed.

Lowell's judgment was not without foundation. Dos had become a heavy drinker and, given the amount of dead, dismembered, mustard-gassed, and dying young men he had lifted in or out of his blood-spattered ambulance, was probably in shock as well. His war diary reflects his state of mind: "The war is utter damn nonsense—a vast cancer fed by lies and self seeking malignity on the part of those who don't do the fighting." The absurdity was inescapable for Dos: "Of all the things in this world a government is the thing least worth fighting for."[2]

Edmund Wilson, Princeton, 1916

His peers, and soon-to-be-lifelong friends, were transformed by similar experiences. Edmund Wilson, now out of Princeton and knowing his complete unsuitability as a combat soldier, took an assignment as a stretcher bearer at a U.S. Army base hospital in France. Here he lugged

E. E. Cummings, 1930s   Slater Brown, 1917

half-dead boys and men into hospitals and later stacked their bodies in the morgue. Other young men never saw combat but died in their training camps during the Spanish influenza pandemic of 1918, which killed even more than the battlefield. At the armistice in 1919, Edmund Wilson was a much more cynical seeker of causes to believe in.

E. E. Cummings, Dos's friend and classmate at Harvard, had also enlisted in the Norton-Harjes Ambulance Service. On board the *Touraine*, en route to begin his service, he met a fellow Cambridge denizen, Slater Brown, and discovered they had a common cynicism, joie de vivre, and opposition to prevailing mores. These shared qualities led to an incident that dramatically transformed their lives and established Cummings as one of the postwar writers of note. In *The Enormous Room* (1922), Cummings slightly fictionalized their arrest by the French military police for allegedly fomenting treason, that is, writing critically to friends of the weak morale of the French military and their drunken fraternization with French enlisted men. What seemed to them more like college pranks found them interned in the most feared military prison in France, where alleged foreign spies and deserters were held in one enormous room with only buckets for toilets and daily beatings by brutal guards. Almost every morning several prisoners drowned themselves in those buckets rather than face another day.

Fortunately, Cummings's father, a prominent Unitarian minister and former Harvard professor, had friends in the State Department who obtained Cummings's release after several months, but it took many months more before Slater was released, with a mouthful of loose or broken teeth.

They returned to Greenwich Village and rented rooms at 11 Christopher Street, where each attempted a literary career. Cummings focused on his creative work, while Slater stuck with reporting, having gone to Columbia Journalism School, and began writing for radical magazines, such as *Broom* and *The Dial*. They spent their evenings barhopping from McSorley's on Seventh Street to the Hell Hole on Sixth Avenue and its neighbor, the Columbian Tavern, a.k.a. the Working Girl's Home.

Slater Brown, short, rumpled, but brimming with charm, was almost always drunk. One night, as he and Cummings were staggering home under a load of abandoned Christmas trees, a friend sighting them inquired what they were about. Slater responded, "We're planning to do a lot of Wagner." Ironically, shortly thereafter, notwithstanding their voluntary ambulance service, each was drafted, and Cummings returned to France to serve until the armistice. Brown failed to pass the physical due to the missing teeth he had lost during his imprisonment.

Cummings again returned to the Village after the war to live with his new wife at Patchin Place, and he and Brown resumed their drinking. Mrs. Cummings, having seen enough of the effect of Slater Brown on Cummings, forbade him to come to their apartment, but to no avail. Brown would hire a Western Union bicycle telegraph boy to deliver messages to Cummings when she was out as to where they should rendezvous.

Even more direct war experience awaited some young men from Provincetown. Harry Kemp and Frank Shay were avowed socialist pacifists like their close friend John Reed. But for a young man to resist the surging national wave of patriotism or ignore the pointed finger of Uncle Sam in James Montgomery Flagg's ubiquitous "I Want You for

U.S. Army" poster was almost impossible, particularly with the passage of the Espionage Act of 1917, which made draft resistance a crime. Each enlisted and shared their fellow tin-hatted comrades' agony as they tightened their Sam Browne belts and affixed their bayonets in the eerie pause before the shriek of the whistles and the scramble "over the top" of the muddy trench parapet into no-man's-land and the deadly chaos of machine gun and cannon fire. Those who survived never forgot that moment hovering between life and death.

Shay had only recently married his first wife, Fern Forrester (a painter from St. Louis who had gone to the Pennsylvania Academy of the Fine Arts and studied in France and Germany), before serving as a private in the fierce fighting the new American troops encountered at the battles of Saint-Mihiel and the Argonne Forest. Both he and Kemp returned to Provincetown as men who now required a great deal of alcohol to forget.

In contrast, O'Neill had been excused from the draft, having had childhood tuberculosis. In the spring of 1918, his unruly pal Harold de Polo had come down to help him work on a play and would join O'Neill on his regular long walks along the dunes, arousing speculation that they were spying on naval coastal defenses.

Provincetown was now a major submarine base, and there was fear of increasing German U-boat raids on commercial vessels, including the Grand Banks fishing fleet. O'Neill and de Polo were arrested for carrying a suspicious black box on their dune walks. When it turned out to be O'Neill's typewriter, the authorities, embarrassed and also influenced by O'Neill's father's fame, released them. Nevertheless, a detective was assigned to censor O'Neill's mail. They became friends, because both were living in the Atlantic House, and the detective would summarize O'Neill's mail at breakfast. "Well," he would say cheerily, "you got a letter from your mother, Gene, but your girl's forgot you today, but someone's sent you a knitted tie just the same."[3]

On the eleventh hour of the eleventh day of November 1918, the guns suddenly fell silent across the hundreds of miles of the western front. The additional two million U.S. expeditionary troops had tipped the balance in the Second Battle of the Marne, and the kaiser's government realized they could no longer sustain their line, and despite the pleas of the German General Staff surrender was ordered and the armistice signed. The Allies, ignoring President Wilson's plea to create a new and more equitable world at the Versailles Peace Conference, were determined to punish Germany and in turn reward themselves by returning Alsace and the Rhine to France and dividing Germany's African colonies among them and, even more damaging, burdening the new Weimar Republic with such enormous war debt payments that Germany almost immediately became bankrupt.

Now it was over, the greatest killing cycle in modern history, and what were the journalists, ambulance drivers, soldiers, and sailors to do with the rest of their lives?

John Reed, 1919

John Reed had become obsessed with the Russian Revolution as Lenin's Bolshevik supporters battled in the streets of St. Petersburg with Menshevik and czarist forces while the Russian front crumbled with starving, deserting soldiers ignoring their officers' orders. On March 3, 1918, the Lenin forces, now in power, negotiated the Treaty of Brest-Litovsk with Germany and its allies, leaving the infant Soviet Union at peace but having ceded czarist Poland and the Baltic territories to Germany.

Reed became an active supporter of Lenin's most radical measures but in doing so also aroused the suspicion of many of Lenin's advisers

Louise Bryant at John Reed's state funeral, Moscow, October 1920

that he was actually an American counterrevolutionary. He was perhaps purposefully sent by the Communist International (Comintern) to cover affairs in a typhus-infested region in the South and returned to Moscow violently ill and died with Louise Bryant beside him on October 17, 1920, at thirty-two. Lenin gave him a massive funeral celebration, attended by Emma Goldman, and he was buried in the Kremlin necropolis, the first American to be so honored. He left behind his classic work, *Ten Days That Shook the World* (1919), his eyewitness account of the revolution, later the basis of Sergei Eisenstein's silent film *October* (and the 1981 Warren Beatty film *Reds*, in which Beatty played Reed). Shortly after his death John Reed Clubs were organized across the United States by communist supporters, adopting "Art is a weapon of the class struggle" as their motto. At its height there were clubs in twelve major cities, and their members included Whittaker Chambers, John Dos Passos, Langston Hughes, Granville Hicks, and Richard Wright.

Louise Bryant's end was equally tragic. After Reed's death she fell into a deep depression but continued to cover Soviet and European news from her now dedicated leftist perspectives. In 1924 she married a man about as different from Reed as possible. William Bullitt was a wealthy Philadelphia-born diplomat who had advised Wilson at Versailles to recognize the Soviets. Bullitt also struggled with depression and was one of Sigmund Freud's first male patients and helped him escape to London from the Nazis in June 1938. As time passed, he became a dedicated opponent of Stalin's Russia both as FDR's first ambassador to the Soviet Union in 1933 and for the remainder of his life (he also wrote a book on Freud).

They led a torrid social life in Paris, and Louise, who had never been interested in drink, became an alcoholic as she grew disillusioned with Bullitt and the world he represented. They parted, but Bullitt, using his boyhood Philadelphia friend Francis Biddle as his attorney, obtained custody of their daughter by claiming Louise was an unfit mother. Louise drifted into a desperate condition in Paris, where Dos Passos encountered her with horror, going from bar to bar drunken and bloated with elephantiasis. She died alone in 1936, her funeral paid for by soldiers from the bars she frequented.

In the years immediately after the war, and amid the explosion of unlicensed alcohol birthed by the Volstead Act, a.k.a. Prohibition, in 1920, Cummings finished his *Enormous Room* in 1922. Slater Brown was now an active contributor to *The Dial* and *The New Republic*, edited by his fellow ambulance driver Malcolm Cowley. Under Cowley, *The New Republic* also attracted others from Flanders Field as contributors, including Edmund Wilson and Dos Passos. The desire to somehow make sense of, or at least come to terms with, the horror and loss of innocence resulted in a torrent of some of the best writing on combat since Stephen Crane's Civil War masterpiece, *The Red Badge of Courage*, and Ambrose Bierce's "Occurrence at Owl Creek Bridge." Dos Passos published his novel *Three Soldiers*, closely modeled on his own experience during the war and afterward in Paris. Edmund Wilson addressed war twice, first in his 1922 collaboration with his Princeton classmate and later Cape neighbor John Peale Bishop, in *The Undertaker's Garland*, a chilling collection of their war experiences, and later, in old age, in *Patriotic Gore* (1962), an examination of the horror of the Civil War.

Henry Beston, an ambulance driver for the French at the nightmare of Verdun, returned to America in a state of shock. He rented a one-room shack on the outer beach not far from Mabel Dodge's abandoned coast guard house, where he described the vast ocean's healing powers in his

1928 classic, *The Outermost House*. "In that hollow of space and bright-ness, in that ceaseless travail of wind and sand and ocean, the world one sees is still the world unharassed of man, a place of the instancy and eter-nity of creation and the noble ritual of the burning year."

Hemingway's *A Farewell to Arms* and Wilson's Princeton pal Scott Fitzgerald's *The Great Gatsby* framed a generation's disillusionment and their new identity as members of the "Lost Generation."

Soldiers returning from World War I, 1919

7.

REDS!

Vladimir Lenin addressing Red Army troops, Moscow, 1920

The socialists and anarchists who had constituted the antiwar fringe continued their fight even after the war ended. Labor strikes sprang up across the country. A new vision of a worker's model country now existed in the Soviet Union, born of the chaos of czarist Russia's withdrawal from the war in 1917 and the resulting revolution. While Woodrow Wilson lay incapacitated by a deadly stroke, members of the IWW, the American Civil Liberties Union, and the Socialist Party, led by Elizabeth Gurley Flynn and others, formed a new party, the Communist Party of the United States of America, on May Day 1919; it soon claimed more than fifty thousand members.

Attorney General A. Mitchell Palmer was more convinced than ever that the country was riddled with socialists and anarchists who opposed both the government and the capitalist system, and as in the past these "radicals" turned out to be mainly immigrant labor leaders and, of course, Jews!

Palmer intensified his raids on radicals despite the war's end, and the radicals returned the favor. Palmer elevated a twenty-five-year-old clerk in the General Intelligence Division of the Justice Department to head up a new surveillance unit to arrest radicals, and by the end of President Wilson's second term J. Edgar Hoover had identified 450,000 radical leaders and created detailed files on 60,000. From April to June 1919 no fewer than three dozen bombs were mailed or attempted to be mailed to the radicals' most prominent targets, including Justice Oliver Wendell Holmes, John D. Rockefeller, and of course Attorney General Palmer, one of which exploded on the front porch of his home. Fortunately, he had gone upstairs, but his neighbor, FDR, then assistant secretary of the navy, ran to assist. On September 16, 1920, a horse-drawn carriage pulled up in front of J. P. Morgan's downtown New York offices and exploded, sending shrapnel through the adjacent building and injuring hundreds on their lunch break. Morgan was abroad, and his partners were luckily meeting in a room at the back of the building. The stock exchange windows were blown out, and trading was suspended.

Palmer, now armed with Hoover's list of radicals, began his famous "Palmer" or "Red" raids from November 1919 to January 1920. The first "Bolshevik" suspects were 400 pro-communist laborers, most foreign-born, and 249 were deported to Russia. Another 4,000 were arrested in thirty-three cities and denied lawyers. Four hundred were deported, including Emma Goldman and her lover Alexander Berkman (Berkman had earlier been imprisoned for his attempt to assassinate the steel magnate Henry Clay Frick, who had ordered his armed Pinkerton mercenaries to shoot unarmed miners and their families during the Homestead steel strikes). They with other czarist-born immigrants were deported to the now Soviet Union on the USS *Buford*, dubbed by the press the "Red Ark."

In the Senate the Overman Committee increased its investigations as the war ended. Those who volunteered to testify were of course universally opposed to Lenin's new government, but few had any real knowledge of Russia. They provided imagined horrendous "evidence" of rape and slaughter by the Soviets, causing both John Reed and Louise Bryant, who had now published extensively on their experience in the new Soviet Union, to volunteer to testify before the committee. On February 2, 1919, Bryant, glamorous in a dark suit and gunmetal stockings, was asked even before the oath was administered whether she believed in God. Smiling, she replied, "I thought I was here to talk about Russia?" The inquiring senator then suggested that if she didn't believe in God, then she didn't attach any significance to an oath. Unflustered, she replied, "I understand. Let the record show there is a God."

Senators immediately raised her background as a student radical at the University of Nevada and her opposition to the war while two of her brothers were fighting in Europe. This indeed was a painful fact for Louise, as it had been for Jack Reed, whose mother threatened suicide over his opposition to the war while his brother was fighting. Finally, Bryant was asked the critical question: "Do you wish to see a Bolshevik government set up in the United States?"

After a pause she replied, "Revolutions, sir, are not like commodities that are exported from one country to another. They are created by conditions within a country. The Russian Czars made the Bolshevik Revolution possible. If there is ever a revolution in this my country, it will not be created by the Wobblies or the anarchists or anyone else. It will be the result of the sort of repression now sweeping this country and by those of this country's leaders who want to see the repression go on." The resulting headlines varied from "Ravishing Beauty a Bolshevik Dupe" to "Louise Bryant Proves Match for Investigators." But Jack had cast their fate with Russia, and she was soon to join him on their final journey.

The year 1919 ended badly for all. Wilson's League of Nations was scorned by a conservative Republican Congress. The Palmer "Red Raids" continued with thousands arrested but fewer than five convic-

William "Big Bill" Haywood (1869–1928)

tions as the country grew suspicious of the government's tactics much as they later did of McCarthy's. Huge strikes exploded across the nation, from the violent Boston Police Strike, in which rank-and-file officers attempted to join the AFL, to a vast series of equally violent steel strikes in which the striking unions permitted their governing committee to be co-chaired by William Z. Foster, later to be head of the CPUSA. These strikes gave the owners the basis to claim these unions were communist-led and bring in Black and Italian immigrant scabs to set off fights with the all-white strikers. The violence and hatred between large corporate owners and radical unions split the country. Reed's hero Big Bill Haywood, on bail while he appealed a charge of murder, fled to Russia, where he died and was interred next to Reed in the Kremlin in 1928.

Phoenix-like, a successor to *The Masses* arose, *The Liberator*, founded in March 1918, named after William Lloyd Garrison's abolitionist paper, and run by many formerly involved in *The Masses*, including Floyd Dell and Max Eastman. Max, after divorcing Ida Rauh and abandoning their son, moved to Russia from 1922 to 1927. Eastman's sister, Crystal, was a co-founder but resigned in 1922 to pursue other, more radical publications with Bob Minor and Boardman Robinson.

The Liberator's first issue set forth its principles: "[*The Liberator*] will fight in the struggle of labor. It will fight for the ownership and control of industry by the workers and will present vivid and accurate news of the labor and socialist movements in all parts of the world." Its cover depicted a Russian peasant sowing wheat and featured an article by John Reed titled "The Story of the Bolshevik Revolution." While *The Masses'* second trial was in process, *The Liberator's* circulation rose to sixty thousand (twice that of *The Masses*), but somehow its articles seemed less relevant in a world at war, and its drawings and cartoons lacked the savage bite of the original *Masses*.

Before she departed *The Liberator*, Crystal Eastman wrote a piece on feminists in the December 1920 issue that reminds us just how active women were in politics on the Left. It read in part, "Many feminists are socialists, many are communists, not a few are active leaders in these movements. But the true feminist, no matter how far to the left she may be in the revolutionary movement, sees the woman's battle as distinct in its objects and different in its methods from the workers' battle for industrial freedom."

In 1922 with Max in Russia and Crystal now blacklisted as a radical from her job as a labor researcher, management was turned over to Bob Minor and Mike Gold (Gold had changed his name from Itzok Granich to confuse the police during the Palmer Raids), both of whom were members of the CPUSA. Gold and Minor transitioned the new magazine's editorial position to absolute support of the party. Gradually the magazine became a pawn of the CPUSA, and in 1926 its assets were merged into the *New Masses*, which Gold edited from 1928 to 1934. This split between those who wrote primarily for the communist-controlled *New Masses* or *The Daily Worker* and those who wrote for *The New Republic* and *The Nation*, like Dos Passos and Edmund Wilson, now divided bohemian writers who followed the party line and those who still identified with the Left but were increasingly suspicious of Stalin's Russia.

This same division among Stalinists, communists, and Marxists was playing out in Provincetown, where those now dedicated to the Stalinist-controlled CPUSA, including Bob Minor and Boardman Robinson, moved their summer abodes to Croton-on-Hudson in Westchester County. Still, each group remained in constant touch through parties, love affairs, and their common opposition to capitalism's growing suppression of organized labor, Jim Crow, and the right of dissent.

8.

THE JAZZ AGE

Prohibition repeal, 1933. A scene at a bar in Greenwich Village

Enormous crowds madly cheered the returning troops as they marched down New York's Fifth Avenue beneath a cascade of ticker tape and colored paper, flanked by huge American, British, and French flags hung from three triumphal arches built and decorated by volunteer artists. Eight hundred Barnard College students snake-danced through the onlookers, many of whom took a moment to step into the nearest bar to toast the "Boys" while the military bands brayed "I'm a Yankee Doodle Dandy" and "Over There."

It would have seemed an auspicious debut for the new decade, but for those who had experienced war firsthand, their belief in beliefs had ended. Malcolm Cowley, on returning from France, spoke for many of the young bohemians who had fought, driven ambulances, worked in hospitals, or covered the carnage as journalists:

> "They" had been rebels, full of proud illusions. They made demands on life itself, that it furnish them with beautiful adventures, honest friendships, love freely given and returned in an appropriate setting . . .
>
> We believed that we had fought for an empty cause, that the Germans were no worse than the Allies, . . . that the world consisted of fools and scoundrels ruled by scoundrels and fools . . . But it was fun all the same. We were content to build our modest happiness in the wreck of "their" lost illusions, a cottage in the ruins of a palace.

For many the road back to a cottage in the ruins led to Provincetown. The Village was now filled with frantic postwar pleasure seekers and tourists, whom Cowley called "Half Villagers," eager to associate with bohemians whom they viewed as even greater seekers of pleasure, living in a haze of promiscuous young women, alcohol, and drugs.

In 1920, to the amazement of Mary Heaton Vorse, Crystal Eastman, Ida Rauh, Emma Goldman, and Margaret Sanger, their work for suffrage garnered the support of every state and the vote was finally theirs. But another, very different group of dedicated women, the Anti-Saloon League and the Woman's Christian Temperance Union, cared less about the vote than about the abolition of alcohol and had won the support of the states even earlier that year. So even as the Heterodoxy feminists celebrated the Nineteenth Amendment they had marched and been jailed for, the Eighteenth Amendment, known as the Volstead Act, now banned the sale or consumption of alcohol, preventing them from raising a glass in public to their victory. "The Jazz Age" had begun. After Scott Fitzgerald's death in 1940, his friend and classmate Edmund Wilson collected his essays and letters, which were published in 1945 by New Directions. In one, Fitzgerald referred to the New Age as follows: "The restlessness . . . approached hysteria. The parties were bigger . . . the pace was faster . . . the shows were broader, the buildings were higher, the morals were looser." Those who before the war had come to Provincetown in the summer to write or paint with Charles Hawthorne now bought or rented the empty houses along Commercial Street, or even larger and less expensive old farms in Truro and Wellfleet, uninterested in the tawdry corrupt world of the Harding administration and Teapot Dome Scandal, stock market speculators, and the sudden proliferation of cheap goods and even cheaper entertainment. In the postwar workplace corporations had swiftly reestablished their dominance, being no longer bound by wartime wage restrictions. They set about busting unions—whose members they once again branded as Reds, Bolsheviks, and communists—with the full support of Congress and the Supreme Court. After Harding's death in 1923, his vice president, Calvin Coolidge, who succeeded him, announced, "The business of America is business!" The postwar bohemians seemed to have more and more reasons to feel alienated.

Like their predecessors, they dreamed of being within a car, train, or boat ride of New York, which would always remain the epicenter of publishing, galleries, theaters, and politics, and was home to old haunts like the Hotel Brevoort and Romany Marie's, the restaurant run for years by "Romany" Marie Marchand, a faux-gypsy Jewish Romanian immigrant, particularly favored by artists like John Sloan, Isamu Noguchi, and Buckminster Fuller.

Now a new state highway, named for the Civil War veterans' association the Grand Army of the Republic, stretched the entire length of the Cape.

Mary Heaton Vorse had left her children with an English nanny during the war to work tirelessly as leader of the International Women's Peace Congress, sailing through German minefields to The Hague. She returned to Provincetown and to her first love, the labor movement, covering strikes for the *New Masses* and *The New Republic* and was never without a new lover. In 1920, she married Bob Minor, no longer just a cartoonist but a rising leader of the CPUSA who had met with Lenin and been arrested by the FBI. Her Provincetown was now much changed because the armistice brought closure to the naval base and the dispersal of the sailors and the brothels that had followed them.

Her older children, Heaton and Mary Ellen, were suddenly teenagers and fascinated by a new lifestyle that was also transforming their peers who were listening to jazz (or "race music," as it was called by those who resented what they saw as Black intrusion into white culture) on the Victrola and dancing to Fats Waller's "Blue Black Bottom" and "I'm Always Chasing Rainbows." They ignored their parents' requests to be home early, and the teenage girls were smoking cigarettes and wearing makeup, long silk stockings turned down below their knees, "flapper" braless short dresses, and bobbed hair. Their "boyfriends" were driving Model Ts with a door only on the driver's side and under the seat a flask of "hooch" as they headed to remote farmhouses, or "roadhouses," where booze and dancing were to be found and where "necking" and more dangerous sport took place in the dark parking lots.

It wasn't just the fast young women of the Vorse circle. Almost all women were now wearing wristwatches, smoking in public, attending cocktail parties with men, and suddenly spending more time away from domestic life as households acquired coast-to-coast telephones, GE refrigerators, vacuum cleaners, and canned food.

At the Golden Swan *(a.k.a.* Hell Hole*), 1919, by Charles Demuth*

Eugene O'Neill had never really left Provincetown during the war and after the Provincetown Playhouse's move to MacDougal Street. He and his new wife, Agnes Boulton, whom he had met in the Golden Swan, a.k.a. the Hell Hole, where he mistook her for Louise Bryant, who had made her choice to break their love triangle, marry Jack Reed, and accompany him to Russia. Agnes, a pre-Raphaelite beauty, was a good deal more sophisticated than Louise was when she first accompanied Jack Reed to Provincetown, having already been married and had a child. Her English painter father, Edward, had assisted Thomas Eakins with Walt Whitman's death mask, and her well-read American mother ran a barely functioning dairy farm in Connecticut. Agnes had begun a career as a writer of short pulp fiction, having left her three-year-old daughter with her parents and moved to the Village. She had already made friends with many of the Provincetown Players, including Mary Pyne, who with her new husband, Harry Kemp, was now dividing time between the Village and a shack on the Race Point dunes near the former Dodge coast guard house. Mary had warned Agnes about Gene's drinking and depressions, but that failed to deter Agnes, who had fallen deeply in love.

Agnes Boulton,
ca. 1919

Agnes Boulton,
ca. 1920s

Agnes in many ways was a flapper. As she wrote, it took one to know what these New Women were thinking: "In effect, the woman of the Post-war Decade said to man, 'You are tired and disillusioned, you do not want the cares of a family or the companionship of mature wisdom, you want exciting play, you want the thrills of sex without their fruition, and I will give them to you.' And to herself she added, 'But I will be free.'"[1]

Gene had rented a flat in town for them from John Francis, the dig-

Charles Demuth and Eugene O'Neill, Provincetown, early 1920s

nified half-Portuguese, half-Irish owner of the local market on Commercial Street. Francis was beloved by writers and artists alike for his generous extension of credit on groceries and his willingness to take paintings instead of cash and was also the local real estate agent of choice for bohemians. He was also probably the only member of the Portuguese community to vote the communist ticket. He had grown particularly close to O'Neill and seemed to understand his wild mood swings and binge drinking better than anyone.

Eugene O'Neill celebrates his 1920 Pulitzer Prize
for Beyond the Horizon.

After O'Neill won the Pulitzer Prize for *Beyond the Horizon* in 1920, as a celebratory gift both for the prize and for the birth of his first grandchild, Shane, James O'Neill had bought the old Peaked Hill Bars coast guard boathouse from Mabel Dodge, who had decorated it for Jack Reed. Its large main room, which once held long coast guard rescue dories suspended from chains in the ceiling, was cleared and now shone with many coats of blue and white paint. Dodge had furnished it with two huge couches from Isadora Duncan's Croton house and lovely pieces from her Italian villa, including ceramics based on marine life. All were left in place. From that point the O'Neills led a life divided between New York in the winters and the coast guard house in the summers but keeping Gene's Francis flat in town for serious writing or attending parties and the summer dances at the Art Association or Beachcombers' costume balls.

Their marriage brought O'Neill the most peace he had thus far been able to find. The empty great ocean beach at his doorway provided him license to tan to a dark mahogany and swim at will in the dangerous Race Point currents until he struggled ashore, half drowned but exorcised for the moment of the black dog that was always awaiting him. Usually he discouraged visitors from making the one-hour walk from town through the dunes. If he chose to go into town, he could leave their new son, Shane, with their nurse or Agnes.

While O'Neill ricocheted from drunk to sober, from hours of swimming amid tremendous waves to long days of intense solitary writing,

*Eugene O'Neill and Agnes Boulton with their son, Shane,
coast guard house, Provincetown*

there was also a social beast within who loved to dance and party. He and Agnes often held dance parties to jazz records at the coast guard house. O'Neill was an eager but unskilled dancer, pumping his arms enthusiastically, and among their favorite songs was "Yes, We Have No Bananas." These parties could suddenly turn ugly. At the 1922 Art Association Costume Ball, a Black jazz band played songs like "Black Bottom," and the deeply tanned O'Neill appeared in a loincloth and bright red wig. When a female Boston reporter attempted to touch his tanned body with a handkerchief, assuming it was makeup, she suddenly found herself flying across the room. Later Gene furiously turned on Agnes, dragging her out of their friend Eben Given's open touring car on their way to an after-party and, leaving Agnes sprawled on the ground, vanished into the night.

Just in case O'Neill might remain sober and productive for too long, his old Village drinking comrade Harry Kemp had already located his dune shack close by. O'Neill had always admired Kemp, a former tramp (his 1922 autobiography, *Tramping on Life*, was a bestseller), well-read poet, former prizefighter, and at that point still a strikingly handsome womanizer (he had run off with his best friend Sinclair Lewis's wife). Upon his return from the war, Kemp had somehow lured the beautiful nineteen-year-old actress and journalist Mary Pyne to marry him and share his primitive life in the dunes with occasional trips to the Village during the Provincetown Players' theater season. No matter the weather, he and O'Neill swam every morning beneath the circling gulls. Kemp believed the saltwater helped his eyesight.

Provincetown had now closed its liquor stores, but Kemp had no difficulty finding bootleggers, and his shack often served as a reunion site for O'Neill with his old tramp steamer companion Terry Carlin, who had first brought O'Neill to Provincetown. It was Carlin who often rescued O'Neill from his many depressions by reminding him, "Cheer up, Gene, the worst is yet to come." Carlin, Kemp, and O'Neill could drink until the liquor was all gone and somehow arise early for a long swim and another day beneath the vast blue sky and the blazing sun. Sometimes Kemp would exceed the loose bounds of drunken friendship, knocking on O'Neill's door at 3:00 a.m. to read him the greatest poem ever written, his blond hair decorated with beach roses. O'Neill's response: "Go to hell!"

The Cape provided O'Neill with inspiration and was the one place where he found moments of joy and fierce physical relief, but the sense of sanctuary was receding like the tide outside his coast guard house. The marriage to Agnes had never been an easy one, with Gene's alcoholic binges, rages, and insistence on putting his work above family. Agnes had encouraged O'Neill to rent an estate in Connecticut for the winters, which Gene saw as her attempt to lead a "Social Register" life with maids and nurses for the children. He longed instead for his old drinking crew of Carlin, Frank Shay, and Harold de Polo.

The summer of 1924 was to be his last in the coast guard house. O'Neill was having a rough time balancing drinking and writing. He was extremely pleased by Frank Shay's revival of the *Glencairn* cycle in Provincetown that summer, admitting it made him long for the "homeless and single life" of a tramp sailor not trapped in the "property game," as he now referred to the commercial theater. This was the summer the sea provided him with a ten-gallon barrel of pure alcohol that washed up on the beach, probably from a rumrunner. It soon was empty. Agnes gave birth to their daughter, Oona, while they were vacationing in Bermuda, and then Agnes and the children returned to Connecticut. Gene stayed on until October, convinced his work done on the Cape in the fall, while he could still swim, was always his best.

In November 1924, *Desire Under the Elms* opened at the Greenwich Village Theatre. Bobby Jones, O'Neill's favorite director, cast an unknown forty-year-old Canadian vaudeville actor named Walter Huston as the Yankee patriarch farmer, Ephraim Cabot. This was a career-changing role for Huston and also for Jones, who later married Huston's sister.

In 1925, for the first time since 1916, O'Neill did not return to Provincetown. He moved with the family from a winter in Bermuda to a summer on Nantucket but actually spent much of the time apart from them, drinking heavily in the Village or with Paul Robeson in Harlem at Smalls Paradise, Connie's Inn, or the Cotton Club.

In 1926, Gene was finally able to stop drinking, realizing 1925 had been a lost year. His marriage was over, and he was now in love with the actress Carlotta Monterey, who intended to bring him to California and forever away from his old haunts. That April he confided to Kenneth Macgowan, who had directed *The Emperor Jones* for O'Neill, and Macgowan's Harvard classmate Bobby Jones that he would never return to Provincetown, saying, "The old truth is no longer true," and confessed that if he wanted to remain sober, he could not be surrounded by old friends like Carlin and Shay.[2] He moved to California with Carlotta, leaving his beloved coast guard house to his son, Eugene junior, whom he had rarely seen and who promptly rented it to Jimmy Light, who in turn rented it to Edmund Wilson and his new wife, Margaret Canby. In 1927, Wilson, like O'Neill, found it fully furnished with everything Mabel Dodge had left when she sold it to Gene's father.

Somehow, John Dos Passos had never met Wilson, either in France during the war or in Provincetown or the Village. When Malcolm Cowley had become managing editor of *The New Republic* in 1922, he had hired both Wilson and Dos Passos as editors, and Dos was introduced to his new co-editor at the offices of *Vanity Fair*, where Wilson was also an editor. Dos described him as "a slight, sandy-haired, young man with a handsome profile. He wore a formal dark business suit." But what truly began their lifelong friendship was that while waiting for the elevator, "Bunny," with a completely straight face, suddenly turned a somersault! Shortly they were seeing each other constantly in the Village and had given each other nicknames—Wilson was Anti-Christ and Dos was Emfish—which they used in correspondence for the rest of their lives. Dos was living alone, working on *Manhattan Transfer*, his history of New York City from the Gilded Age to the Jazz Age. He was also a gifted artist and unique among the writers of his time, with the exception of Cummings, for painting throughout his writing career.

Both were appalled by the corruption of Wall Street and the condition of American workers. Dos had joined the board of the *New Masses* with the leading Communist Party members Joe Freeman and Mike Gold, although he considered himself a radical socialist (he voted for Debs in the 1920 election in which Debs got 3.5 percent of the vote while in prison). Wilson also shared Dos's admiration for the Soviet experiment, as did many of their friends in the Village and Provincetown.

Edna St. Vincent Millay (1892–1950)

Wilson had spent his first summer in Provincetown, pursuing Edna St. Vincent Millay to Truro, where her mother had rented a house on Longnook Road near the L'Engles and Susan Glaspell. His short affair with Edna ended there in almost comic romantic failure (their one coupling was abruptly ended by mosquitoes), but he continued to carry a torch for her until her death. Wilson became increasingly fond of Provincetown, its bohemian residents, and its unique beauty, which he chronicled in his diaries for forty years. Although he was a shy, if eager, observer of women after Princeton, the 1920s and bachelorhood seem to have addicted him to prostitutes, who were everywhere in the Village after the war during Prohibition. So, it was a surprise to his friends when he married one of the Provincetown Players' lead actresses, Mary Blair, on February 23, 1923, and seven months later was the father of a daughter, Rosalind.

Mary was, at first meeting, rather unassuming but gifted with an indescribable presence that makes all great actresses glow. Slim and, like

Millay, with an extremely deep and flexible voice, she had a reputation for playing her role differently each night. She had become a legend for her brave insistence on continuing to play Robeson's wife in *All God's Chillun Got Wings* despite multiple daily death threats from the Ku Klux Klan. Mary was a member of the uniquely gifted class of students at Peabody High School in Pittsburgh that included Malcolm Cowley, Wilson's new boss at *The New Republic*; the critic Kenneth Burke; Jimmy Light, who had quickly made a reputation after Harvard as a brilliant theatrical producer; and Light's first wife, Susan Jenkins, a pretty, wild, and gifted labor writer who later left Light for Slater Brown.

Their marriage was not meant to last. Mary's acting schedule kept her away, and in her absences Wilson ramped up his drinking and whoring. However, in 1924 Wilson wrote a play for her, *The Crime in the Whistler Room*, which premiered at the Provincetown Players' theater that October. They divorced but remained friends, and Wilson undertook to be the main custodian of their daughter, Rosalind. Wilson began his custom of renting various houses in Provincetown for them during the summers. Like his friend Scotty Fitzgerald, who was at work on *The Great Gatsby*, Wilson was wrestling with the effect of class on American behavior. Both men were also attempting to care for their daughters, when they remembered they had them.

Bunny was not in good shape. He was still depressed about the failure of his marriage, and he had even made a will leaving his estate one-third to Mary and two-thirds to Rosalind, and his library to Charlie Walker, the labor scholar Gilbert Seldes, and Edna St. Vincent Millay. Despite his despair, he was beginning to be recognized and feared as one of America's most able literary critics. Wilson understood that the job of critic could negatively affect his relationship with writers and friends like Fitzgerald, Dos Passos, and Cummings, and it did. He wrote, "For a worker in ideas, it is dangerous, it may prove fatal to one's effectiveness, to betray that one's feelings have been hurt. The critic must remain invulnerable."[3]

Dos had first met Katy Smith in 1928 while she and her brother Bill Smith were staying with Hemingway in Key West. Dos Passos quickly realized he had finally met the woman with whom he wanted to share his life. He pursued her from Key West back to her communal cottage, the

The Smooley, ca. 1925. (back row, from left) Pat Foley and Bill Smith;
(front row, from left) Katy Smith and Edy Foley

Smooley (a contraction of "Smith" and "Foley," the Smooley was a house
rented by Katy and her brother Bill Smith and the two Foley sisters),
in Provincetown, where he pitched a tent on its lawn. The Smooley was
originally the Arequipa Cottage, named after the ship *Arequipa*, whose
hull was incorporated into the house that Katy eventually bought from
its owner, Mary Vorse. Katharine Foster Smith, nicknamed Possum, and
her brother Bill had grown up with the Hemingway family in Oak Park,
Illinois. She was four years older than Dos but looked much younger than
he, with his bald head and thick glasses. Bill Smith was one of Hemingway's closest friends and fishing companions. Hemingway had once proposed to Katy, before marrying her friend and former classmate Hadley
Richardson. Dos and Bill Smith became lifelong friends, Katy became
his lifelong love, and Hemingway, their mutual sidekick. They were to
remain close until the Spanish Civil War destroyed their friendship.

From that summer until it slowly slid over the eroded dune in a powerful storm in 1930, the O'Neill house was a place where Wilson entertained regularly and even forced his well-rounded torso to exertions such
as lugging ice, liquor, and food on the long trek through the woods from
town. Wilson even took to swimming in the ocean's rough waves rather
than the still glacial ponds. Those he entertained regularly included E. E.
Cummings and his then wife, Anne Barton. They had married in New
York City that year at All Souls at Twentieth Street and Fourth Avenue,

which was affectionately known as the Church of the Holy Zebra for its striped black-and-white architectural interior design. Dos was Cummings's best man, and they had begun drinking well before the ceremony, leading Dos to later say, "I was a little besotted—just a bid sodden."[4] Wilson had first met Cummings through Dos in the Village in 1925, although he had long admired his poetry. He described Cummings as having a "spirited crest of hair and . . . narrow self-regarding eyes." From town Wilson also invited the Dos Passoses, Susan Glaspell and her lover, Norman Matson, Hutch Hapgood and Neith Boyce, and his next-door ocean neighbor, the young and attractive Hazel Hawthorne, whom he "encouraged" in her writing. Uninvited, some of Gene's old drinking friends like Harry Kemp would often appear at the door.

Kemp was despondent. His beautiful Mary Pyne had left him, in part to pursue poetry and acting in the Village, but also to explore other love interests, including an affair with Hutch Hapgood (often using Agnes O'Neill's family's Connecticut farm for their rendezvous) and with the writer Djuna Barnes, a fellow Provincetown Players devotee. When Mary developed TB, it was Djuna who supported her financially and nursed her until her death.

Wilson was once again happy with his second wife, Margaret Canby, but both of them felt guilty about how little time they spent with their children. Margaret returned to California, where she could be with friends and her son. This left Wilson to drink and whore in New York and to continue his long affair with Elizabeth, the beautiful blond, highly neurotic wife of Coulton Waugh, a painter and illustrator like his father, Wizard Waugh. Wilson featured her as the Princess with the Golden Hair in his *Memoirs of Hecate County*. The Waughs ran a respected modelship and hooked-rug store in Provincetown and in New York in the winter, which Wilson frequented when Elizabeth's husband was away. Bunny often expressed his contempt for gay men, or, as he called them, "fairies," in his diary of that period. A particular target was Peter Hunt, the colorful gay proprietor of Peter Hunt's Peasant Village store adjacent to the Waughs' hooked-rug shop that featured old furniture repainted with colorful European peasant decorations by Peter and a host of young daughters of prominent Provincetown painters.

Still, as always, throughout his alcoholism and depressions, Wilson was hard at work at *The New Republic* and on both *Axel's Castle*, perhaps his greatest work of literary criticism, and *I Thought of Daisy*, one of his rare works of fiction, based on the obsessive love of an older man for a pubescent girl. The book was ultimately to be one of the causes of the end of his friendship with Vladimir Nabokov after the latter's publication of *Lolita*, which Wilson believed plagiarized *Daisy*.

The year 1929 opened with a new president, Herbert Hoover, who had decisively beaten America's first Irish Catholic candidate for the presidency, Al Smith, the popular and respected four-term governor of New York, who was succeeded as governor by FDR. It was the year that Bunny Wilson finally had the nervous breakdown he had been courting. Margaret Canby had tragically died from a fall at a house party in California. Within minutes of receiving the news, Wilson broke into sobs, the only time his daughter, Rosalind, had ever seen him cry. Wilson, like Fitzgerald and others, was also depressed that he was not equipped by either class or education to survive the postwar Jazz Age.

While recuperating, he made a list of his favorite people to have at a party: Gilbert and Alice Seldes; Tom Matthews, a Princeton friend and Henry Luce's right hand at *Time*; Dorothy Parker of the Algonquin Hotel's Round Table and fellow heavy drinker, who always answered her phone by inquiring, "What fresh hell is this?"; the writer and humorist Robert Benchley, another Round Table veteran; Scott and Zelda Fitzgerald; Allen Tate (the poet who was later to spend summers in Wellfleet), E. E. Cummings and Anne Barton; Dos; and Edna St. Vincent Millay.

Another exile returning to Provincetown was Susan Glaspell, now a widow after Jig Cook's death in Greece in 1924. She had been renting their Commercial Street house to friends, including Bunny Wilson and his daughter, Rosalind, but had also retained their old farmhouse on Longnook Road in Truro. Susan was eager to begin a new life after those turbulent years with Jig, but first she knew she must exorcise his powerful and essential presence. She had found some peace in completing her memoir, in which O'Neill appears very much the bad guy for driving

Jig from the theater he had created and so loved to his early death. To O'Neill's credit, he established a new relationship with Susan soon after her return. O'Neill had always admired Susan for her own theatrical skills, ranging from directing and acting to writing, and had often sought her counsel when his own plays were not going well. Their rapprochement led to O'Neill's commissioning a large plaque to be mounted on the Provincetown Playhouse in Greenwich Village honoring Jig as its founder. Susan had also assumed an active stepmother's role for Jig's two children, Harl and Nilla, now teenagers, who often spent the summers with her in Truro after growing up in Athens.

While Jig would always be the man who most inspired her work, during a stay in New York she met a young film writer named Norman Matson who seemed to bring her alive after those last years with Jig so ill and drunk. Matson joined her in Truro, where they presented to the world as a married couple, although there is no record of their ever marrying. Susan always regretted her inability to have children, the result of an early miscarriage that she felt had negatively affected both her marriage to Jig and her relationship with the younger Matson.

Nevertheless, despite her heavy drinking, these were productive years for Glaspell. She had always been a disciplined morning writer, and now happy with Norman, she produced a bestselling novel, *Brook Evans*, and her crown jewel, a play titled *Alison's House*, based on Emily Dickinson's cloistered life. In 1931, *Alison's House* won her the Pulitzer Prize for Drama. She was the first woman to win it, and she became the toast of all her women friends at the Heterodoxy Club, which she always attended when in New York. O'Neill also much admired the play, which further cemented their renewed friendship. Matson, also a heavy drinker, was somewhat threatened by Susan's success, given his less successful career as a writer mainly of pulp fiction and film scripts. However, they did collaborate on a play in 1927 called *The Comic Artist*, which had a successful Broadway run.

After the war, Frank Shay had resumed control of his once thriving bookstore publishing operations, but his marriage to Fern Forrester was not a success. They had married in 1918, just before he shipped out to France. He saw serious combat and lingered for a year in Paris acquainting himself with French publishing. On his return to their Village apartment they had a daughter, the curly-haired, fiery-tempered, and willful Jean (she was to have been a he and named after his pal Gene O'Neill).

Before he closed his Village bookstore, the Parnassus, and moved full-time to Provincetown, Shay left several legacies: the first, the thickly inscribed door to his 4 Christopher Street bookstore, which is now in the Harry Ransom Center at the University of Texas. It bears the signatures of 242 writers, poets, playwrights, and postwar luminaries, including Sherwood Anderson, Floyd Dell, John Dos Passos, Theodore Dreiser, Susan Glaspell, Josephine Herbst, Harry Kemp, Sinclair Lewis, Robert Nathan, Upton Sinclair, John Sloan, Mary Heaton Vorse, and William Zorach. Another legacy was his 1922 publication of the young Edna St. Vincent Millay's *Ballad of the Harp-Weaver*, illustrated by his wife, Fern Forrester, which earned Millay the Pulitzer Prize. And finally, in 1925, a rented wooden-sided station wagon filled with the store's remaining stock to sell in Provincetown and adjacent towns. The car's journey was launched with a bottle of champagne wielded by Christopher Morley. The station wagon now bore the painted logo "Parnassus on Wheels." (Jig Cook apparently was not the only bohemian with an urge to return to classical Greece!)

Shay, when not brawling, was now driving his bookstore truck through local towns when he could start it, but often, when it would finally start, he was too drunk to drive. One of Shay's favorite drinking combatants was the tall and sturdy Polly Holladay.

He and Fern began to spend long summers in a rented house in Provincetown, where she attempted to resume her career as a painter and Frank resumed his heavy drinking with O'Neill and Harry Kemp. Mary Vorse recalled seeing both O'Neill and Shay drag their protesting wives by the hair from wild parties at the Art Association or the Beachcombers'. One night a drunken Shay kicked in all of Fern's paintings that were lined against the wall. Another night Vorse recalls trying to break up a drunken brawl, only to have Shay break her nose for her troubles. They embraced, and the party continued. One evening while Frank was babysitting Jean and drinking with O'Neill, he became enraged at Jean's crying and began to break the crockery. O'Neill quickly joined him until the cupboards' contents lay in a broken pile of shards on the apartment floor. Fern had finally had enough and left, letting Jean remain with Frank (a very unwise choice).

Now a bachelor with a small daughter, Shay became a central figure in Provincetown social life, creating a small theater in a barn he rented, which he modeled closely on Mary Vorse's original fish house/theater on the water. Here he presented a number of summer performances of O'Neill's work. Frank began an affair with the popular magazine and novel writer Phyllis Duganne, who had separated from her first husband, Austin Parker, a decorated Lafayette Escadrille fighter pilot who after the war continued to fly for the French in the fight with the Riffs, who had revolted against their French colonial masters in Morocco. Parker later married the movie star Miriam Hopkins and became a noted screenwriter.

Duganne, a lanky, blond, blue-eyed woman of temper, was every inch a match for Shay. One night at a party at the Smooley, Shay passed out on the floor, and Edy Foley knelt down beside him and exclaimed, "He's brave and he's beautiful." The swashbuckling Duganne had always dismissed Edy as a "prissy Wellesley girl," but before long Edy and Frank were engaged and married and remained so for the remainder of their tempestuous lives. Duganne quickly found a new husband and father for her young daughter in Eben Given, a wealthy painter and friend of O'Neill's who was living in an antiques-filled house in Provincetown with his mother and sister, Thelma, an internationally celebrated violinist.

Given, considered by many the most handsome man in Provincetown, moved with Phyllis to Truro near the L'Engles and Susan Glaspell. Phyllis insisted they include her mother, Maude Emma, famed as one of the last people of Indigenous descent on the Cape. The Givens became serious party givers, and no matter how drunken the dancing and trysting, Phyllis remained in command. Eben said of her that you could look right through her triangular blue eyes on a clear day. When he complained of her heavy drinking, she replied, "Then get yourself another General!"—a reference to President Lincoln's response to Grant's critics that he only wished he could give his other generals whatever it was Grant drank.

Phyllis, like Susan Glaspell, was always able to combine her drinking with writing and sold many stories to *The Saturday Evening Post* and other leading magazines on a schedule that had her at her desk every morning, hungover or not. She remained committed to radical politics and feminism, having grown up in the summers on the Cape with her aunt Inez Haynes Irwin, Radcliffe graduate and leader of the National Women's Party. Edmund Wilson recalled being enchanted by Ms. Irwin at a party at the Givens', where she sat ensconced on Phyllis's huge blue velvet sofa, which had once been the casting couch of Jed Harris, the Broadway producer.

Optimistic songs kept pouring out of Tin Pan Alley—"My Heart Stood Still," "My Blue Heaven," "Ol' Man River" (from the musical *Show Boat*), and, perhaps the most prescient, "Button Up Your Overcoat," for on October 29, now known as Black Tuesday, the bottom fell out of the stock market. It lost 12 percent of its value in hours, and by 1933 half of the nation's banks had failed and 30 percent of the American workforce had no jobs.

PART II

SUMMER

9.

BOUND BROOK ISLAND

The 1930s brought another defining moment of radicalization for the bohemians. Stalin's purge of the heroes of the revolution was at its height, and Leon Trotsky had fled to Mexico City. Hitler's Condor Legion of new German-designed dive-bombers was obliterating the Republican forces in Spain. If you had work, life might have seemed almost reasonable with a four-course dinner for fifty cents, a new Kodak Brownie for twenty-five cents, or a postcard stamp for a penny. But how could there be a basis for any optimism when any thinking person humming "Brother, Can You Spare a Dime?" knew that more than 25 percent of white men were without work and the unemployment rate was far worse for Blacks and women? Restless Americans were either despairing or demonstrating. President Hoover ordered General Douglas MacArthur to use the cavalry to drive twelve thousand World War I veterans seeking their service bonuses from the Capitol grounds.

Radical solutions seemed called for, and Roosevelt's election in 1932 was not supported by most bohemians, who viewed him as a patrician capitalist in sheep's clothing. How could a president of such moderate views possibly rescue the nation from the deep pit it was in? But he began to gather more bohemian adherents by his actions against banks and with his new public welfare programs, and by his 1936 reelection many took special note of his inaugural speech: "I see one-third of a nation ill-housed, ill-clad, ill-nourished." FDR soon raised the income tax rate to 63 percent on the top bracket, gaining more bohemians' respect.

John Hughes Hall, Princeton, 1935

In 1937, John Hughes Hall, known as Jack, a tall, dark, and angry graduate of Princeton in his prime and just beginning to discover the new world of radical American culture and politics, married a Martha Graham dancer (in fact, they had met at a dance to raise funds for the Spanish Republic) and violinist, Camille L'Engle, known as Cammie, the twenty-year-old daughter of Brownie and Bill L'Engle. Jack was the only son of his father's second marriage to an admiral's spinster daughter and felt estranged from his much older half siblings from his father's first marriage. Jack's father was the wealthy owner of a phar-maceutical company, and Jack had grown up in a vast Manhattan town house and a country estate at St. James on Long Island. Lonely and des-perate to escape the clutches of his Victorian mother, he had happily gone to all the right schools of his class—St. Bernard's, St. Paul's, and Princeton, where he was a member of the polo team and first began to drink heavily.

L'Engle family portrait, by Bill L'Engle.
(back row, from left) Bill and Lucy; (front row, from left) Madeleine and Cammie

Their wedding at the L'Engles' Truro house was savagely mocked by Edmund Wilson in his diaries, published in *The Thirties*, as an upper-class marriage between a rich non-bohemian and the daughter of the Truro painters Bill and Brownie L'Engle (whom Dos Passos called "the Duchess of All the Truros"). Wilson's devastating portrait of their wedding was actually based on a letter he had received from Katy Dos Passos, who had attended it while Wilson was pursuing Mary McCarthy. Ironically, Katy profited from her attendance because she had been ordered by Dos to sell the abandoned farm she had bought while Dos was in Spain and Brownie L'Engle persuaded the new couple to buy it from Katy.

Wilson wrote,

The L'Engles' daughter's wedding in Truro, which had taken place before I was wed [to Mary McCarthy]: The Provincetown people, who had knocked together what old ceremonious clothes they could find, were confronted when they arrived by much smarter guests! The L'Engles' Long Island friends in morning coats and striped trousers. People reflected that it was the only wedding they had ever been to where it was easy to see what was going on. They realized that "Brownie" (Mrs. L'Engle) had turned it around so that the bride and groom were facing the audience and the minister talked into space, to which he directed his "dearly beloveds." But worse realizations came when the bride and groom disappeared and instead of the general drink and refreshments—they had promised champagne—which usually takes place after the ceremony, the Provincetown guests seemed abandoned and were presently brought big, thick, locally made sandwiches with mousetrap cheese—tough cheese and pink jelly and with crusts on and a freezer full of orange sherbet into which was poured with feeble popping corks a few bottles of California champagne. Presently, Betty Spencer [wife of the painter Niles Spencer] became aware that something was going on in the studio and when she tried to investigate it she found "Brownie" L'Engle with her foot in the door saying, "This is only for family,"—Bill L'Engle reached out a glass of champagne saying, "Try this—Pol Roger Vingt et un," but she yelped, "No, Bill! I don't want it! I'm beyond the pale! I don't want it!"—All the people with morning coats were inside clustered around canapés, caviar, buckets of champagne, etc. The Provincetown guests soon went home. On the way back, Charles Kaeselau (a respected painter who was renting the Dos Passos's Truro house) said, "I never saw such a separation between the sheep and the goats! It makes me want to vomit." The sheep and the goats were separated along the lines of the rich and the poor— so that the impoverished Princess Chavchavadze (the late Czar's niece) ate mousetrap cheese.

Not long after their wedding, Jack and Cammie drove slowly and without speaking through the spring morning to their newly purchased home, smoking through the open windows. They paused at the now silted Herring River, which was completely surrounded by clumps of large white blossoms; the shad bushes were in bloom. The old Cape Codders called it a shad "blow," from the old Gloucestershire word for "blossom." The Indigenous people had taught the first settlers that the "blow" meant

The Captain David Baker House, Bound Brook Island, ca. 1937

the shad or alewives, a saltwater herring, were running from the sea up the rivers and brooks to lay their eggs in the deep, cool glacial kettle ponds. The Indigenous people netted them to fertilize their corn mounds.

Their silence barely masked the wound that would not heal: Cammie's affair with Jack's best friend on their honeymoon. It had been Jack's idea to bring his new bride on a honeymoon cruise aboard the rented seventy-foot *So Long*, just built in Hong Kong by the father of his old St. Paul's and Princeton pal Bobby Baker, and, unwisely, also his idea to invite the charming Bobby to join them.

Bound Brook was the largest of a chain of islands bordering Wellfleet Bay on the Truro border. The island had been cut off from the mainland by high tide until the 1880s. It was formed by the Herring River on one side and a tidal brook on the other that at high tide "bound" it into an island. They turned up the island's narrow sand road, which followed the original cart path to Duck Harbor. As it cut through hog cranberry moors overlooking the bay, the prospects from the car were vast. Like the mainland, the island had been farmed and deforested over the years, first the great oaks and red pine for use as naval masts and spars and later for lumber and furniture for its houses and farms. It had slowly reverted to its original postglacial state, the hog cranberries barely covering its sandy hills and valleys. The road ended at the now silted-in Duck Harbor, which had been transformed into a dune-ridged beach that stretched from Wellfleet Harbor on the left to Provincetown on the right, whose hills and Pilgrim Monument could be seen on a clear day.

The harbor was encircled by three bayside tidal islands: Bound Brook, Myrick's, and Griffith's. From the late seventeenth until the early nineteenth century, each island had a whale tower from which to watch for right or humpback whales, which fed close to the shore in those days, and small settlements had grown up on each island around the towers. Bound Brook, the largest island, had its own schoolhouse, smallpox cemetery, and at its peak more houses than the town of Wellfleet.

Jack later described the island's many advantages for its early seventeenth-century settlers in an unpublished history of the island: "[The] attractions were plentiful: hard woods for buildings, salt marshes providing nutritious hays for cows and horses, rich tidal shellfish beds (clams, oysters, mussels, and scallops), fin fish and plenty of rabbits, grouse, deer, and ducks."

They reached Katy's house, which had not been occupied for forty years. She had bought it, and the surrounding 180 acres, for three thousand dollars at a tax lien sale in the Wellfleet Town Hall two years earlier, while Dos was covering the civil war in Spain. The Dos Passoses already had a house in Provincetown and one farther down the bay beach in South Truro, and Dos by 1937 was between books and reduced to cadging loans from friends. Katy had yet to spend a night there but had had a picket fence built around the houses and outbuildings.

They had not spoken on the ride, and it hadn't helped that the radio had just played "The Lady Is a Tramp." They pulled off the road near the crest of the island and turned in to the crushed-clamshell driveway of what the locals still called the Captain David Baker House. It stood alone in a large, sloping field, its clapboard devoid of paint and its shingled roof salt-dried to a silver gray. Two derelict barns were nearby amid a small locust grove; otherwise, not a tree or shrub was to be seen. They got out, scrunched their Lucky Strikes in the sand, and made their way to the front door. The doorframe pilasters bore carvings of stars and moons, and there were just five windowpanes above the door. All Bound Brook houses built before 1750 had only five windows, and old-timers could thus identify former Bound Brook houses in Wellfleet and Provincetown that had been "flaked" (each beam and board removed and carefully chalked with a Roman numeral) and then moved by oxen or boat in the hope of finding a better living off the island, now bereft of trees and topsoil and with a silted harbor.

No one had lived in the Baker homestead since Captain David Baker's grandson, Captain Lorenzo Dow Baker, had left it for a much larger house in Wellfleet where he could supervise his thriving tropical fruit import business, soon to be called the United Fruit Company. In 1850, at age ten, he had shipped from the island as a cabin boy and at twenty-one, with his captain's papers, entered the West Indies trade on his schooner, the *Telegraph*. Baker was a devout Methodist who kept an organ on board for hymns and neither smoked nor drank nor fished on Sundays. In 1870, having taken a group of gold miners and their equipment to the Orinoco River basin in Venezuela, he found himself with an empty hold for the return. Pulling in to Port Antonio, Jamaica, he decided to take aboard a cargo of coconuts, bamboo, and bananas for the journey to New England. The bananas ripened and the crew enjoyed them, but the remainder were mostly rotten seventeen days later when they docked. After several more attempts on borrowed money, he got the knack of it, buying the bananas very green, or "thin," and making the return voyage in less than two weeks. Baker's fleet grew, and his company became the greatest provider of tropical fruit in America. (Baker died before his company destabilized Central America in its search for more land for bananas.) His docks, his yacht the *Bound Brook*, warehouses, U.S. customhouse, Jamaican boys' orphanage, and sixty-two-room hotel, the Chequesset Inn, had transformed sleepy pre–Civil War Wellfleet, and the remnants of that boom time still dominated the waterfront when the bohemians discovered it in 1910.

Because they had both heard the Baker tale before, Cammie broke the silence by suddenly singing the new radio advertisement for Chiquita bananas. They walked through the empty rooms together, their voices echoing off the horsehair-plastered walls and white painted wood paneling. Was there a chance for them to put things back together here? Cammie was unsure of what she wanted and felt more at home in the vibrant social world of her family in Truro and Manhattan. The L'Engles and many of their friends had fled the increasingly thronged streets of Provincetown for Wellfleet and Truro in the early 1920s. Also joining the exodus were Edwin Dickinson and his wife, Pat, and her sister Edy and her husband, Frank

Shay, the Dos Passoses, Edmund Wilson, Jig Cook, and Susan Glaspell, all of whom had bought old farms in Truro and Wellfleet's hills and hollows. It was still the height of the Depression on the Outer Cape, and the old Yankee families were fleeing north to larger towns and cities, seeking work and eager to sell. The newcomers were after a simpler life, a woodpile for fall and winter, a garden, some gear or a boat to fish, clam, or oyster.

The Baker homestead had the feel of abandonment, which seems to invest houses once actively lived in, and had no electricity, toilets, or running water, although there was a well. Neither Jack nor Cammie was used to "roughing it," both having grown up with servants in all their houses. Her mother, Brownie, was not called "the Duchess of All the Truros" for nothing on her estate on Longnook Road in Truro. Brownie's brother, Lathrop Brown, had been FDR's roommate at Groton, and FDR supposedly had proposed to Brownie before Eleanor.

Portrait of Jack Hall by his new father-in-law, Bill L'Engle, ca. 1937

They settled in, furnishing the place with gifts from their families— Oriental rugs, silver, and mahogany tables. Jack connected the well to a kitchen sink hand pump and installed a generator for electricity and lights (electric and telephone wires did not reach Truro until 1949). There was no furnace, but there were fireplaces in the living room and every bedroom. He dressed in wool shirts and work pants and was clean shaven with a full head of thick black hair when he posed for his portrait by his father-in-law, Bill L'Engle. For a few months, they almost forgot their grievances as they painted, cleaned, repaired, and planned new gardens. They had paid Katy the three thousand dollars, and Dos Passos was happy again with Katy, whom he always referred to as Possum.

While they did not present as farming material, Jack was bent on learning carpentry, repairing the house and barns for his horses and two old Rolls-Royces, and learning how to farm while he wrote a novel. A large vegetable garden took shape in the damp plot below the front of the house, and Jack repaired enclosures to house a cow and some sheep, pigs, and chickens. Cammie was more intent on repairing their marriage and continuing her music career. Both wished to escape convention and live a creative life not governed anymore by money or class and based on the land, not the city.

Jack and Cammie, Bound Brook Island, ca. 1937

At dusk, the last of the spring peepers could be heard in the watery cow pasture across the road, while deer, still unused to cars, leaped into the brush. As it grew dark, the peepers, now joined by whip-poor-wills, serenaded a panoply of stars, all against the muffled roar of the incoming tide attacking the dune by moonlight.

When the generator was working, they had a radio and avidly followed FDR's New Deal as it rolled out after his 1936 reelection. Jack,

Nina Chavchavadze, Lucy L'Engle, and Madeleine L'Engle

now flirting with communism, had reluctantly voted for Roosevelt and kept moving further to the Left as he got to know the L'Engles' circle of friends, particularly Dos Passos, who had just published *The Big Money* (1936) and was now railing against FDR's refusal to assist the Spanish Republic in its civil war. FDR had proclaimed at his renomination, "This generation of Americans has a rendezvous with destiny," and so they did.

Madeleine L'Engle and Thelma Given, Manhattan, 1938,
by William L'Engle

At parties in Truro, at Eben Given and Phyllis Duganne's or the L'Engles', and in Provincetown, they danced to records. Cammie, having studied with Martha Graham, was by far the best dancer on the floor. That year, Fred Astaire's voice seemed to capture the jaunty feeling of a country making a comeback, at least for those with top hats and tails. They drove to New York to see productions of Clifford Odets's *Golden Boy* and Steinbeck's *Of Mice and Men*. Jack, not yet interested in painting, was taken by Cammie to see works on exhibit by her parents' friends: Ben Shahn's *West Virginia*, Edwin Dickinson's *Still Life*, and Bill Zorach's statue of Ben Franklin. Bill Zorach and his wife, Marguerite, old friends of the L'Engles', were later to rent the Delight studio on Bound Brook from Jack and Cammie.

Jack, as a lonely child, had become an early and voracious reader and, despite his heavy drinking at Princeton, graduated with honors and had already begun to accumulate a substantial library. In 1937 he added work by new Cape acquaintances: Waldo Frank's *In the American Jungle, 1925–1936*, Allen Tate's *Mediterranean, and Other Poems*, Archibald MacLeish's *Fall of the City*, and Edna St. Vincent Millay's *Conversations at Midnight*.

But Cammie was young and restless, and Jack was always one for long periods of dark moods in which his grudges and grievances gathered momentum. It did not help that the bohemian world he had now married into was fond of cocktails, beach parties, and long, boisterous dinners, all liberally fueled by alcohol. They made one last attempt in the fall of 1937 when Cammie became a fellow at the new artist residency in Cummington, Massachusetts, in the Berkshires. There, she studied violin and Jack began a novel. But the wound would not heal, and upon their return they separated, Cammie taking her belongings, and her spaniel Cello, back to Truro and New York and Jack buying out her portion of the Dos Passos purchase price.

Jack, now alone on Bound Brook Island at twenty-nine, had found the life he had always sought, surrounded by writers, painters, and political activists. While he failed to maintain friendly ties with subsequent wives, he always maintained close ties with the L'Engles and later in-laws, who provided him with a network of future friends from Provincetown to Wellfleet. This included one young man who was to become his closest friend, Jack Phillips, who was now living across the narrow Cape on the ocean side, in a duck-hunting camp he had inherited from an uncle by marriage. Unlike most bohemians, the two men had much in common: upper-class backgrounds, independent incomes, and time to explore whatever creative or romantic roads they chose.

10.

THE POPULAR FRONT

Jack Hall stood at the edge of his clamshell driveway on Bound Brook Island admiring the sign he had just nailed on the tree shading his vegetable stand; on it was painted NO TROTSKYITES! The unfinished business of World War I and the worldwide depression were having profound effects on both Russia and Germany. After Lenin died in 1924, the troika of Stalin, Lev Kamenev, and Grigory Zinoviev that Lenin had wickedly designated to replace him were at each other's throats. Lenin's death had left radical bohemians and members of the CPUSA (which rarely rose above fifteen thousand after his death, with membership usually abandoned after less than two years) who espoused the Soviet model of governing badly divided. Some, particularly those who were intellectuals or Jewish, supported Leon Trotsky as Lenin's rightful heir. Born Lev Bronstein, he had adopted, while imprisoned as a revolutionary, the name of a brutal czarist interrogator. Others backed Stalin, the violent Georgian enforcer and bank robber for Lenin's rising Bolshevik Party. He had adopted the sobriquet Stalin (Russian for "steel") and now controlled the Cheka, the Bolshevik secret police. A few very sophisticated adherents backed Grigory Zinoviev, the leader of the Comintern, Russia's extremely successful espionage and foreign recruiting organization.

Geoffrey Wheatcroft, the English journalist, has wittily observed, "In the 1930's, New York was the most interesting part of Soviet Russia, it's been said, since it was the only place where the conflict between Stalinism and Trotskyism could be played out in the open without one side simply killing the other."[1]

As those in the final days of the Roman Republic had watched in fear at its gradual replacement by a triumvirate and then its end when Julius Caesar seized power for himself, American party members watched as Stalin crudely but effectively ended the Marxian dream of rule by a collective of organized workers as he systematically tried, convicted, exiled, or executed any who would challenge him. By 1929, he held the reins of unchecked power in his bloodied hands, and the word "comrade" no longer connoted equality, as the word "citizen" had in the French Revolution, but instead an acknowledgment of which speaker was closer at the moment to Stalin. In 1933, the CPUSA was still 70 percent foreign-born,[2] not that the American presidential troika of Harding, Coolidge, and Hoover inspired confidence in its American-born members.

Many of the bohemians who visited Moscow after 1919, whether CPUSA members or not, came away deeply impressed. Of course, their travel was often limited to Moscow and St. Petersburg, and they were allowed to see only what Lenin or Stalin wished them to see. Like Jack Reed and Louise Bryant, they saw enough to confirm their belief in communism, as did later visitors like Theodore Dreiser, Mike Gold, William English Walling, and his wife, Anna Strunsky.

But others began to have doubts as they traveled outside the two cities or interviewed more widely. Over the course of their years there, Emma Goldman and Max Eastman changed their minds as they saw the workings of the secret police and the growing inability of citizens to express dissent without dire consequences. Both Dos Passos and Edmund Wilson, outspoken enthusiasts for communism in the late 1920s and early 1930s as a cure for the slough of America's depression and capitalist system, gradually began to change their minds as the 1930s proceeded. Wilson had gone to Russia in 1935 to research his book *To the Finland Station* (1940), about its transformation from socialism to Marxian communism, and had begun to feel he might have been misled.

Some returned dazzled by Stanislavsky's Moscow Art Theatre, groundbreaking modernist paintings of the Russian futurists Natalia Goncharova and Kazimir Malevich, or the films of Sergei Eisenstein, such as *Battleship Potemkin* (1925) and *October: Ten Days That Shook the World* (1927). When FDR's Works Progress Administration (WPA) began government support of the arts in programs such as the Federal Art Project (FAP), directed under the Truro resident George Biddle, FDR's college classmate, or the Federal Theatre Project (FTP) under Hallie Flanagan, it quickly became apparent to the press that both had been deeply influenced by their exposure to the Soviets' successful attempt to include both politics and culture in the creative process. This enthusiasm encouraged the House Un-American Activities Committee (HUAC) to renew gathering the names of party members.

Former friends in the three towns were now divided into hostile groups: anarchists, Stalinists, Trotskyites, or socialists. Jack Hall and Truro bohemians, including Polly and Bud Boyden, Joan Colebrook, and Mary Heaton Vorse, despite growing rumors of Stalin's purging of the heroes of the revolution, continued to believe he was Lenin's rightful successor. Other former friends supported Trotsky's claims. In 1929, Stalin had exiled Trotsky but permitted him to take refuge on the Isle of Princes off the Turkish coast. Generations of the Ottoman emperors' male children or siblings had been imprisoned in luxury on the island, but often later blinded or murdered to remove them as possible threats to the emperor. Hasan Özbekhan, a charming professor at the University of Pennsylvania and founder of the Club of Rome, summered in Wellfleet for many years with his wife, Ann, who was the former wife of Paul Rand, the graphic designer who created the IBM logo. Hasan was the last descendant of these hereditary khans who governed the Isle of Princes for the Ottomans.

Trotsky's continued criticisms of Stalin and his creation of an international opposition to Stalin's rule in the form of the Socialist Workers Party finally exhausted Stalin's patience, and he ordered his secret police, now renamed the NKVD, to end his life. Trotsky fled Turkey with his family for New York, but found America lacking in revolutionary potential, and moved to a safe house in Mexico City, where he was welcomed by Mexican communists, including Frida Kahlo and Diego Rivera, and other Mexican artists, among them Miguel Covarrubias.

Leon Trotsky, ca. 1920s

The Truro neighbors Waldo Frank and Adelaide and Charles Walker, who had worked together in raising support for striking miners in Harlan County, Kentucky, visited Trotsky in his fortified house in Mexico City, where he was now carrying on an open affair with Kahlo. Frank was appalled by Stalin's murder of many of the Jewish heroes of the revolution and had left the party in 1937. Adelaide and her husband had been joined on their trip to Mexico by a group from the Cape including Katy Dos Passos and her brother Bill Smith and Gwenyth Clymer (one of the painter Wizard Waugh's daughters). They stayed with Adelaide's wealthy mother, also a Trotsky supporter, in her rented house in Mexico City to attend the hearings before a commission established to investigate the truth of the charges Stalin had brought against Trotsky and many others in the infamous secret purge trials of 1936 that they were actually fascist supporters of Hitler and "Enemies of the People!" The commission had been established by Dos Passos, Sidney Hook, the famous religious scholar Reinhold Niebuhr, Edmund Wilson, and the perennial Socialist presidential candidate Norman Thomas, among others. They selected

John Dewey, America's most distinguished academic, as chair. Among those also on the commission were Carlo Tresca, now the lover of the wealthy Margaret DeSilver, who had given Dos Passos and Hemingway the money to make their film on the Spanish Civil War. The committee found Trotsky innocent of Stalin's charges, which caused worldwide headlines but led Stalin to harden his determination to have Trotsky killed.

S. Osborne "Ozzie" Ball was a Stalinist and heir to more than a thousand acres of ocean beach in Truro, where his family had built a well-known seaside resort, the Balls' Town Colony. Ozzie was a colorful lawyer who signed his papers "S.O.B." and loathed Trotskyites, in particular Adelaide and Charlie Walker, who he knew used his private road to swim at his Ballston Beach. Ozzie disguised an "elephant pit" dug in the road just to disable their car.

Dwight and Nancy Macdonald, another wealthy Truro couple, were to become devout anarchists during the Spanish Civil War, but earlier had been attracted to Trotsky (although Dwight voted for Earl Browder, the CPUSA candidate for president, in the 1936 election). Dwight, when just a few years out of Yale, had been hired by Henry Luce at *Fortune*, where, much to Luce's displeasure, Macdonald began organizing its employees to join the Newspaper Guild, which was closely allied with the CPUSA. They, too, visited Trotsky, but it did not end well, because the egocentric and outspoken Dwight soon angered Trotsky, who later is al-

Dwight Macdonald (1906–1982)

leged to have remarked, "Every man has a right to be stupid on occasion but Comrade Macdonald abuses it."[3]

Some remained true to the socialist vision of Gene Debs, like Gardner and Ruth Jencks and Shelby Shackelford and Richard Cox. Shelby had left the Maryland Institute College of Art for Provincetown in 1921 to study with Marguerite Zorach and also had become friends with Jack Tworkov and his third wife, Wally, and Jack's sister Biala, named after the Russian Pale village the Tworkovs had fled. The Tworkovs were both gifted painters and Marxists. Jack was later to become a famous, much sought-after teacher at Yale and spent as much time as possible at their Provincetown house. Biala later lived with Ford Madox Ford, whom she had met during the years he lived in the Village, and moved with him to London.

Shelby's husband, Richard Cox, a nuclear scientist who taught at New York University, was recruited by the Manhattan Project after war was declared. In 1940, they bought land next to the only other houses on Chipman's Cove on Wellfleet's upper harbor, which belonged to their fellow socialists Edwin and Pat Dickinson and John and Mary Fraser. (The two families had earlier lived near each other in Provincetown, where Ed and John painted and taught.) The cove was isolated, and the land was cheap. Dickinson would teach at the Art Students League in the winter and Fraser at the Rhode Island School of Design, where he later became director. All three families would move into their studios in the summers in order to rent their houses to friends. The Dickinsons usually rented to fellow bohemians like Dwight and Nancy Macdonald, the writer Bob Hatch and the painter Ruth Hatch, and the English socialist artist Clare Leighton, who later built an adjacent house.

All shared a belief in socialism and could not accept the tenets of either Stalin's or Trotsky's communism, which clashed with their deep belief in pacifism. They represented the Left's "middle way" that many bohemians continued to adhere to amid the battle for loyalty demanded by Trotskyites and Stalinists. That belief later led to Richard Cox's opposition to the bombing of Hiroshima and his prohibition from participation in any government nuclear research.

The *Provincetown Advocate* reported that on September 4, 1936, the

Board of Selectmen refused to rent the town hall to the Massachusetts Communist Party for a rally; they had earlier turned down its rental for a production of Clifford Odets's 1935 striking labor workers' play *Waiting for Lefty*, which they deemed a "Communist show." (They were probably right.)

These (at least for Americans) arcane schisms of the Left suddenly seemed to find a common enemy: fascism. In 1931, the Spanish Republic had been formed by popular vote and King Alfonso forced into exile; however, the monarchy, the church, and surprisingly the peasants who remained loyal to both continued to resist the republic's new poorly equipped army made up of women, intellectuals, and forty thousand "volunteer" anarchists and socialists from all over Europe. This motley group became known as the Popular Front.

America, like all signatories to the 1928 Kellogg-Briand Pact except Nazi Germany and Stalinist Russia, continued to enforce the pact's strictures against permitting the sale of arms or their citizens participating in "internal foreign conflicts." For a brief time, the civil war in Spain was a stalemate with the monarchy supported by Germany's new modern weaponry—the Condor Legion's Stuka attack planes piloted by German pilots—and the republic by Russia's more primitive planes and tanks and feared NKVD police. Stalin had demanded that agents of his police force be attached to all-volunteer international brigades, which included the American volunteers' Lincoln Brigade and the much larger International Brigades, consisting mainly of European anarchist volunteers known as the POUM (the Spanish acronym for the Workers' Party of Marxist Unification) with their fist-to-forehead salute. The International Brigades had attracted George Orwell and many other European intellectuals.

Both Hitler, now in total power after his stunning victory in the democratic Weimar election of 1933, and Stalin viewed Spain as the final campaign to persuade socialists who still made up the majority of the Left to become fascists or communists as well as a chance to test out their own new weaponry. The former *Masses* cartoonist Bob Minor had joined the Party in 1920 shortly before marrying Mary Heaton Vorse and had risen through its hierarchy until he was sent to Spain to "advise" the

Lincoln Brigade on the importance of following Stalin's NKVD officers rather than those of the anarchists or socialists.

Republican volunteers on a commandeered bus, Barcelona, July 1936

The tide of civil war had dramatically turned against the republic in 1936 when General Francisco Franco invaded Spain at the head of a large North African army composed mainly of troops from Spain's African colonies, which had remained loyal to the king. The Republican forces were driven back to Catalonia and its capital, Barcelona. Despite the Republican forces' plight, Stalin's NKVD police continued to weed out socialist and anarchist leaders as Stalin was to do again in World War II even as the Germans threatened Leningrad.

Orwell left the legion in disgust and returned to England to write his devastating picture of Russia's sinister behavior in *Animal Farm* (1945).

Dos Passos and his old friend Ernest Hemingway had determined to make a propaganda film in support of the Republicans' desperate position. Hemingway had always enjoyed bullying the stuttering, bookish, and balding Dos Passos, but they had remained friends, even after Dos had stolen Katy Smith from Hemingway. Dos was also now a bit of a figure himself, having been on the cover of *Time* in 1936 after the publication of his last book, *The Big Money*.

Hemingway was also going to Spain as a reporter with his new mistress, the alluring journalist Martha Gellhorn, which troubled Dos Passos, because Hemingway's current wife, Pauline Pfeiffer, was an old friend of both his and Katy's.

Dos was also looking forward to a reunion with another old friend, the Spanish aristocrat and academic José Robles, who he hoped would help them with the film. Robles had spent considerable time in the States teaching at Johns Hopkins. He and Dos Passos had first met in Spain in 1916, and Dos Passos had invited the Robles family to Provincetown one summer, where Edmund Wilson also got to know and respect him. Robles had been on vacation in Spain when the civil war broke out and had volunteered to act as a translator for the Russian "advisers" to the Republican Ministry of War. Unfortunately, this had given him access to both the suppressed details of Stalin's secret purge trials and his orders to "eliminate" certain anarchist or socialist leaders in the Republican forces. Dos arrived in Valencia in April 1937, only to learn from Robles's distraught wife that he had been taken at night by special police some months before. She had been informed he was alive and that the matter would be cleared up shortly. Both Hemingway and Josephine Herbst, who was the first woman to report on the war, had already learned that it was the NKVD who had arrested Robles and, like many others to follow, had executed him as "an enemy of the people." Hemingway cruelly told Dos Passos the truth, suggesting that Dos Passos grow up and realize this was a war that could be won only with Russian assistance and to stop seeking answers that would lead only to trouble.

Robles's murder, and its causes, ultimately led to the end of the long friendship between Dos Passos and Hemingway. Hem's flaunting of his relationship with Gellhorn certainly alienated Katy, but most probably it was that Hemingway had become an increasingly unbearable macho war lover and braggart. Dos decided to leave Spain, turning over his material on the film project that had brought them there to Hemingway, who later finished the now pro-Russian documentary *The Spanish Earth*.

Katy had sailed to Paris to meet Dos, and on the eve of their return to the States, Hemingway suddenly appeared and demanded Dos write nothing disparaging about Robles's death, threatening that to do so would ruin his career. Katy furiously responded, "Why Ernest I never heard of anything so despicably opportunistic in my life!"[4] On the voyage home, Katy confessed she had purchased an abandoned farm on Bound Brook Island. Dos Passos, now broke, demanded she sell it upon their return to Provincetown.

In fairness, soon after the civil war ended with the defeat of the Republican forces, Hemingway also began to be suspicious of Stalin, enough so that his young admirer Mike Gold, now a co-editor of the new *Partisan Review* and part of a group trying to align it with the CPUSA, branded him a "renegade"—that is, a traitor. In typical Hemingway fashion, he responded, "Go tell Mike Gold, Ernest Hemingway says to go fuck yourself."[5]

Edmund Wilson, now living full-time in Wellfleet and remarried to the glamorous Mary McCarthy, had also joined Dos Passos's growing skepticism of the Communist Party and also viewed Hemingway as a poseur. Wilson once did a hilarious imitation for Dos and Katy of Hemingway shooting a helpless animal, then cradling its head in his lap and moaning, "It looks at me with so much love," a performance that Edmund used extensively thereafter.[6]

Katherine Anne Porter, a "fellow traveler," as party sympathizers were called, wrote to her close friend the active party member Josephine Herbst in April 1938, "Josie—you knew well the original aim, its Russian Revolution was the best thing that had happened to the minds of men . . . the real revolutionists are betrayed and kicked out or killed by the dictator . . . or the Party . . . Stalin, who was a henchman of Lenin, will not rest until he has wiped out every trace of Lenin in the Revolution . . . I think he, if dared, that madman would have Lenin's corpse shot and tried as a traitor."[7]

In December of that same year, Dos Passos wrote from Provincetown to an old friend who was considering rejoining the party's struggle: "I have come to believe that the Communist Party is fundamentally opposed to our democracy as I see it and that Marxism, although an important basis for the unborn sociological sciences, if held as a dogma, is a reactionary force and impediment to progress. Fascism is nothing but Marxism inside out and of course a worse impediment."[8]

The final brutal act of the civil war was the introduction of the new German tactic of blitzkrieg. It captured the world's attention when a small Basque village was initially struck by German incendiary bombs and then its fleeing citizens were slaughtered from the air by machine gun fire, leaving sixteen hundred dead and inspiring one of the world's iconic paintings of the horror of war, Picasso's *Guernica*.

In America, the Spanish Civil War had serious implications. In 1937 a large group of editors at the *New Masses* led by Philip Rahv, a Russian-born intellectual, broke away, disaffected with Stalin and the CPUSA's total control of both the *New Masses* and *The Daily Worker*, to start the *Partisan Review*.

The *New Masses'* anger with the founding of the *Partisan Review* ran along class and ethnic lines. Alfred Kazin observed in his memoir *Starting Out in the Thirties* (1965) that the political writers of the 1920s came from socially secure families—Dos Passos, Wilson, E. E. Cummings, Malcolm Cowley—while those of the 1930s tended to come from "pleb" families—either poor, immigrant, or Jewish—like Mike Gold, James T. Farrell, Robert Cantwell, Clifford Odets, and Elia Kazan, all of whom had worked as physical laborers when young.

The "Traitors," as Gold referred to those who abandoned the *New Masses*, were led by Rahv, also Mary McCarthy's lover before, during, and after her marriage to Wilson, and William Phillips (born William Litvinsky), who also later lived in Wellfleet. The Stalinist core of the *New Masses*—Joe Freeman, Gold, and Granville Hicks—attacked them as "Trotskyite thieves," but when Freeman sought legal help to sue them for stealing the *New Masses'* mailing lists, they were warned that legal discovery in such a suit could expose Hicks, Freeman, and Gold's intimate connection to Stalin. Rahv later bragged that he and William Phillips were "the only people who had the courage to take a magazine away from Joe Stalin."

Mary McCarthy was not atypical of those bohemians who longed for a transformative political belief. She recalled it was almost three years after her graduation from Vassar, when she was just starting her new career as a book reviewer for *The New Republic*, that she realized she had become part of the "anti-Communist movement." While she scorned "business-men," she was equally unimpressed by Stalinists. Nevertheless, she and her first husband, an actor, had many friends in the party and joined them to march in the May Day parades singing Spanish Civil War songs like "Bandiera Rossa" and "The Internationale." She attended their cocktail parties and could usually be found in a corner in a black dress with her hair in a bun, one high-heeled leg extended, cigarette and drink in each hand, both charming and offending the men who surrounded her. "For me, the Communist Party was *the* party, and even though I did not join it, I prided myself on knowing that it was the pinnacle," she wrote in *On the Contrary*.

The Popular Front that might have united socialists, anarchists, and communists into a formidable fascist opposition had failed, and in October 1939 the Molotov-Ribbentrop Pact was signed by Hitler and Stalin in a mockery of the Popular Front to dismember the newly formed democracies of Poland, Danzig, the Baltic countries, and Czechoslovakia. The pact read in part, "The two contracting parties obligate themselves to refrain from every act of force, every aggressive action, and every attack against one another." Even the most devout American communists were stunned when Stalin's order was read to them from the CPUSA offices on the nineteenth floor of the party's New York City headquarters, forbidding members to criticize Hitler or any fascist activities, such as Lindbergh's America First movement, which now had eight hundred thousand members and 450 chapters. Party members were ordered to vote for FDR in the upcoming 1940 election, rather than their own party's candidate, Earl Browder. Stalin ordered that to do otherwise was to be labeled a "premature antifascist" and suffer party discipline. This was particularly astounding to Jewish members who were hopelessly following the Nazis' increasingly barbaric treatment of German Jews. Even the Russians were confused as Stalin ordered Sergei Eisenstein's popular anti-Nazi film *Alexander Nevsky* pulled from the theaters, only to be re-released after Hitler's invasion the next year.

Suddenly the world seemed filled with jagged propaganda posters depicting handsome young Slavs or blond Teutons brandishing previously unknown weapons of mass destruction. Stalin finally had his revenge on Trotsky, the man whom Stalin had labeled a fascist! On August 21, 1940, a special NKVD agent who had begun an affair with Trotsky's secretary was able to gain entry to Trotsky's well-guarded house and bloodily murder him with an ice pick.

Now seemingly free from his last opponent, Stalin lowered his guard, and on June 22, 1941, Hitler launched Operation Barbarossa penetrating deep into Russia in just a few weeks.

The Popular Front was dead, but a new popular front against fascism was waiting to be born.

II.

DODIE

Dorothy "Dodie" Merwin, ca. 1929

Dorothy "Dodie" Merwin was born in 1914 at Pickwick Farm on Mount Airy Road high above the Hudson River in the Hessian Hills section of Croton, New York. During the Revolution, the British had barracked their mercenary Hessian forces here to prevent Washington from gaining control of the river, and some were said to have deserted and married local girls.

By 1914, Croton, and particularly Mount Airy Road, had become another outpost of Greenwich Village, many of whose denizens maintained close ties with Provincetown, either having lived there year-round or continuing to have strong summer attachments. The townspeople referred to it as Red Hill because among its leading figures were John Reed and Louise Bryant and Mabel Dodge and Reed's replacement, the painter Maurice Sterne. Many editors of *The Masses* and the *New Masses* also had homes there, including Floyd Dell and Ida Rauh, Boardman Robinson, Max and Crystal Eastman, Robert Minor, and Wilbur Steele. They had been joined by many painters, including George Biddle, Peggy Bacon and Alexander Brook, and Rockwell Kent, whose illustrations of *Moby-Dick* had become instant classics.

The dancer Isadora Duncan had built an outdoor dance platform at her Croton Finney Farm estate before her tragic death in 1927 when her trailing scarf became caught in the spokes of her car. There she gave performances Dodie attended and where she first admired the slim and attractive Crystal Eastman and the actress Ida Rauh in the audience.

Dodie's mother, Margaret Leary, was an angular, dour woman whose parents had emigrated from Ireland to Michigan's Upper Peninsula, where Margaret's father had found work as a supervisor in the huge Calumet iron mines. In some ways a pioneer in the newly enfranchised working woman culture that spawned the passage of the Nineteenth Amendment, granting women the right to vote, she had come east, acquired a nursing degree in the first class to admit women at Columbia University's Bellevue Hospital, become a highly valued private nurse for wealthy clients, and fallen in with the bohemian set in Greenwich Village and Croton. She married an upper-class charmer and amateur painter named Francis Horace Bloodgood Merwin, called "Frank," whose stepfather was the famous turn-of-the-century stage actor William Faversham, "Brutus" to his friends after his most famous role. He was a theatrical contemporary of Eugene O'Neill's father, James.

Pickwick Farm was probably beyond their means because it was a large, old Dutch farm with extensive grounds. With Margaret's nursing jobs their sole means of support, they proceeded to have two daughters, Billie and Dorothy, soon called only "Dodie." They also drank and entertained constantly to avoid what both realized was a poor match. Shortly after Dodie's birth, Frank began to spend increasing time in New York City until, by the time Dodie was three, her mother rarely heard from him anymore.

Margaret took up with a raffish crowd and regularly entertained gentlemen who spent the night and whom Dodie often found sitting on the edge of her bed as she grew older. Margaret first sent the girls to live in

Michigan with her parents, who soon discovered they were really too old to assume this role. Eventually, their mother placed them in the hands of a strict order of nuns at Holy Angels Academy for Girls in Fort Lee, New Jersey, where, except for vacations in Croton, Dodie remained from age five through sixteen. Her mother visited sporadically; her father, never.

In 1932, almost a quarter of the country was unemployed, wages were down 60 percent from 1929, and most people were humming Bing Crosby's hit "Brother, Can You Spare a Dime?" Dodie soon realized that whatever life she would have would be based solely on her good looks, charm, and work ethic, all of which were abundant. She began working for the gentry of Croton in the summers and during vacations, including two of Roosevelt's "Brain Trust," the economic adviser and member of the Federal Trade Commission Stuart Chase and Henry Hunt, one of FDR's legal counsel and the first socialist reform mayor of Cincinnati, and his young beautiful wife, Eleanor Phelps Hunt, on their estate, Edge Hill Farm. Eleanor took a great fancy to Dodie and often brought her to New York City and Washington during the heady first days of FDR's presidency.

The Hunts ran a large model dairy herd at Edge Hill Farm, where they were among the first to experiment with adding vitamin A to milk. Eleanor had two young boys, whom she gladly left in Dodie's care as she pursued an extensive number of affairs with both men, including George Biddle, and women. This atmosphere of country living—hot days deep in the fields and cold nights amid a bohemian life of sexual exploration—was to be a key theme in Dodie's life. In 1934, the Hunts took her in to live with them in Washington, D.C. Eleanor found Dodie a job in Henry Wallace's Agriculture Department working on vitamin A research. The Agriculture Department under Wallace's leadership was being penetrated by communist adherents, including Joe Freeman, Alger Hiss, and Josie Herbst's husband, John Herrmann (Josie was to remain a lifelong friend of Dodie's). Herrmann, an active party member, was later to take credit for persuading Hiss to copy secret documents for Whittaker Chambers, then an active communist.

With a narrow waist, swelling breasts, strong legs, clear blue eyes, and silver-blond hair, Dodie began modeling for George Biddle, Edward

Hopper, and the Greenland explorer and avowed communist Rockwell Kent, whom she remembered as satyr-like, chasing her about his studio. She also started her lifelong profession of working in gardens and with children. All these jobs exposed her to arguments after Lenin's death between adherents of Stalin and Trotsky among her various employers. Elizabeth Moos, the founder of Hessian Hills School, where most Croton bohemians sent their children and where Dodie later worked, was a devout Trotskyite but remained a loyal communist after his murder and was targeted by the House Un-American Activities Committee and forced to resign. Stuart Chase was also a Trotsky supporter and constantly battled with his Stalinist neighbors Floyd Dell, Boardman Robinson, Robert Minor, and Josie Herbst.

Dodie began to work summers at the North Country School's Camp Treetops near Lake Placid, New York, beneath the surrounding Adirondack Mountains. The camp and the school were among the first to accept both boy and girl boarders and had quickly become a favored school for diplomats' children and wealthy bohemian families who wished to pursue their careers unencumbered by children. There, aside from her ever-present male admirers, she made two close women friends, Meg Barden, a Croton neighbor, and Jean Taylor, a gay flour heiress from St. Paul. All were to remain passionate friends for life.

The summer of 1933 found her modeling for the tall, stooped, and aristocratic George Biddle and doing live-in cleaning for his second wife, Jane Belo, the daughter of Texas newspaper barons, in the vast Croton house they had purchased from the movie star Gloria Swanson, with its abandoned swimming pool filled with poison ivy. One hot day, while Dodie was swimming in the Croton reservoir, three handsome young men appeared: Menalkas Duncan, the nephew of Isadora Duncan; Roger Rilleau, his best friend and fellow sandal maker; and a tall, slender, tanned body with an unruly lock of dark hair over one eye, like his father, George "Jig" Cook. Harl Cook had lived much of his early life with his mother in Iowa after his father had remarried Susan Glaspell, but later had been brought to Greece by them with his sister, Nilla, when Jig stormed out of the Provincetown theater, never to return. Harl and Nilla had learned to speak both modern and classical Greek as well as practice ancient crafts like leatherwork and spinning yarn while living in the country village that Jig had transformed. Harl had left Harvard after only three days and at twenty-two already had a job writing "Bill and Betty" episodes for *True Stories*, a popular monthly magazine where his stepfather, Bill Rapp, was editor. He was earning the then-princely sum of two hundred dollars per month (forty-five of which went for rent on his Barrow Street apartment in the Village).

Harl had lived a much more sophisticated life than Dodie and was enormously attractive to both women and men. He was also already a hopeless alcoholic. For Harl, the end of Prohibition was also the end of any inhibitions about drinking. His sister, Nilla, while living with Jig and Susan, had married a Greek officer and had a son, Topie, but sent him to the States to live with his step-grandmother, Susan Glaspell, in Truro. She later left Greece, taking her spinning wheel, to join Mahatma Gandhi in his campaign for Indian independence.

Harl and Dodie immediately fell in love, and later that day he proposed she join them on their road trip to Truro to visit his stepmother. Dodie had never been to the Cape, and Provincetown and Truro soon cast their spell. The L'Engle house, where Cammie had married Jack Hall, was almost across the road from the Glaspell house. As chance would have it, Dodie would later meet Cammie in 1933 with Harl in Truro, and they later double-dated in New York after Cammie left Jack and was seeing Wally Astor.

On that first trip with Harl, Dodie was welcomed by Susan, who was still recovering from her much younger lover, Norman Matson, having run off with the pregnant eighteen-year-old Anna Walling. Her Truro kitchen floor still bore the painted checkerboard she and Norman had painted, on which they used cups and plates as checkers. Despite her continued drinking, she was famed for her disciplined writing schedule. Sinclair Lewis, who often stayed with her, later admitted to stealing her definition of writing: "Apply the seat of your pants to the seat of your chair!" Susan's old-world Portuguese housekeeper, Isabella, was disgusted with Harl and Dodie being unmarried yet sleeping in the same bed, but Susan ignored her.

Susan finally found new "comfort" in the Provincetown-based primi-

Susan Glaspell at her house in Provincetown, 1936.
Photograph by Carl Van Vechten

tive painter Mary "Bubs" Hackett's thirty-six-year-old brother, Langston Moffett, a handsome alcoholic who had separated from his wife and was staying with Bubs and her husband, Chauncey. Langston had left Dartmouth early to work in Hollywood with their father, Cleveland Moffett, the well-known magazine editor, and later in Paris for the *Paris Herald*. There, he had become friends with Hemingway, Fitzgerald, and Janet Flanner. Perhaps influenced by Bubs and his new membership in the Beachcombers, on a dare he decided to become an artist and painted his first work in Provincetown in one sitting, which was immediately shown by the Art Association and acquired by the Whitney Museum (he never painted again until the 1970s).

Langston would depart Provincetown in his swanky open touring car, pick up Susan in Truro, and return to town, where they would stop at the Vorses', the Givens', the Frederick Waughs', or the Dos Passoses', with Susan ringing a hand bell to announce their availability for cocktails. When Langston finally returned to his wife and family, Dodie remembered Susan drunkenly ascending to the second floor of her Truro house to play "Nearer, My God, to Thee" on a small organ she had placed there.

At that first glorious summer's end, Dodie followed Harl back to the Village and under his guidance quickly learned her way around its environs from Romany Marie's to the Hotel Brevoort, the favorite rendezvous of all Cape bohemians. Harl seemed to know every bar from Sammy Schwartz's, Jimmy Savoy's, Tony's, and Bleek's to Techno's and its resident Russian jazz singer, Spivy. Spivy, who had already become a favorite of the Provincetown crowd, appeared in Bill L'Engle's paintings and often stayed with the Wellfleet Russian émigrés the Chavchavadzes and sang at Cape beach parties. For many years, she ran her own gay club, Spivy's Roof, on Fifty-Seventh Street in New York.

That fall, Dodie took childhood education classes for two terms at the progressive Bank Street College while working at the Little Red School House in the Village, whose name was a double entendre because most of its parents were communist adherents. The Little Red School House had been founded as a public school by Elisabeth Irwin, a famed social worker and education reformer who agreed with John Dewey that children learned best by doing and by structured play, not solely by memorization of facts. It became a private school in 1937.

With her move to the Village, two themes that were to dominate her life emerged: a constant search for a place in the country she could call home, and for love from a man, which she had never received as a child. These quests constantly appear in her lifelong correspondence with her younger Croton and Treetops friend Meg Barden. Meg's parents had lived on Isadora Duncan's former estate, Finney Farm, with its stone dance platform and multiple dwellings. Meg's loathed stepfather, a charismatic German "businessman," left the family for a "visit" to the homeland just as war broke out and never returned. It later emerged that he was a senior Nazi intelligence agent. Meg, like Dodie, was never quite satisfied with the man in her life but loved children and country work. She became the confidante of Dodie's adventures in the 1930s and the early 1940s and often came to stay on Bound Brook after Dodie's marriage to Jack Hall.

Sadly, most jobs for Dodie ended abruptly. Her zeal and independence eventually alienated her employers, and she was soon off with her small suitcase in search of another. The only constants in those years were being a summer counselor at Camp Treetops and caring for the children of the wealthy. Treetops was a dream realized for Dodie, because it was situated on a large farm where all the children were required to learn to plant and harvest, ride horseback, hike, feed the pigs and chickens, and milk the cows. Of all the places in her life that were lodestars, Treetops and Provincetown remained at the top of her list. However, as usual, Leo Clark, the wife of the director of the camp, took a strong dislike to Dodie, probably because Dodie seemed to be the center of all male desire from the teenage counselors to the married senior staff.

There was no real work to be had on the Outer Cape or Croton at the height of the Depression, and Dodie kept returning to New York City, where she held several short-lived jobs: sales clerk at Wanamaker's at seventeen dollars per week and Saturdays off; babysitter for the radical heiress Margaret DeSilver's daughter. Margaret's late husband, Albert, had been a co-founder of the ACLU with Roger Baldwin, and Margaret was now the lover of the radical labor leader Carlo Tresca, who by the 1930s had become the publisher of a leading Italian-language antifascist paper, *Il Martello* (The Hammer), in New York.

Perhaps Dodie's favorite job during those wander years was telephone operator/receptionist and manuscript reader at the newly formed publisher Simon & Schuster. She became close to its co-founder Dick Simon and his wife and often babysat their elder daughter. It was, as usual for Dodie, a glamorous but short-lived job. Dodie bid adieu to Dick and the other writers who haunted the main office to flirt with her, including her short-time beau the suave *New Yorker* cartoonist Peter Arno. Arno's September 19, 1936, *New Yorker* cartoon of a group of well-dressed New Yorkers urging some friends, "Come along. We're going to the Trans-Lux to hiss Roosevelt," had become a classic.

There were other lovers besides Harl Cook, including the young writer John Cheever, with whom she lived in a Village cold-water flat along with the budding photographer Walker Evans, who used their bathtub to develop his film. Both Cheever and Evans had spent time in Province-town. Walker was then working with James Agee on what would turn out to be the classic work of lyrical journalism, *Let Us Now Praise Famous Men* (1941), in which they documented the lives of three Alabama farm families at the height of the Depression. Whether Dodie was aware that Cheever and Evans were also having an affair is not clear.

In Blake Bailey's biography of Cheever, he quoted an entry in Chee-ver's 1979 journal: "the face of a girl, young, very fresh and healthy. It could be Dodie when we first met. There is nothing so portentous as Deja-vu but there is that sense of thrilling juxtaposed dimension on meeting a girl one desires." Cheever had taken Dodie to visit the writer's colony Yaddo when he was a fellow, and there she re-met her Croton neighbor and Agriculture Department colleague Josie Herbst. Yaddo had been conceived by Aaron Copland as a fellowship open to writers and musicians, in particular gay people who might not be admitted to other colonies. Dodie found Cheever a passive lover, but they eventually re-sumed a friendship after he married.

In 1939, Harl again lured her to Truro, but she had fallen in love with someone else and was recovering from an abortion and Harl had begun an affair with the sculptor Leonora "Leo" Coleman, whom he later mar-ried and after whom one of Dodie's daughters with Jack Hall was named. At loose ends in Truro, broke and determined to never again be a servant for the rich and as always lured by country life, Dodie was introduced to Jack Hall by Susan's Truro neighbors the L'Engles.

Jack had finished and abandoned the novels he'd begun while married to Cammie and was now seriously farming on Bound Brook with a large vegetable garden beneath his NO TROTSKYITES! sign. He was still binge drinking, and his latest farmworker, Marvin Waldman, an alcoholic but a gifted musician, had just left to play the piano at the Flagship restau-rant in Provincetown. Jutting on pilings into the harbor across the street from the Art Association, the Flagship was Provincetown's favorite des-tination for painters and writers. There Marvin could continue his affair with Mary Grand, one of the most notorious nymphs of bohemia. A statuesque blond Smith graduate and a descendant of William Lloyd Garrison's, Mary had first come to Provincetown in the late 1920s with her lifelong friend Agnes Boulton, after her marriage to O'Neill. She remained a major figure in the life of Provincetown and the Village, famed for her many lovers and cocktails. To protect her and Sylvia Plath's beloved Smith teacher, the famed American Melville scholar Newton Arvin, from dismissal for circulating gay photographs, she married him. Their sad marriage lasted eight years, although Arvin spent several of these in residence at Yaddo, where he began a two-year affair with the young Truman Capote, whom he referred to as "Precious Spooky." In 1948, Truman Capote dedicated *Other Voices, Other Rooms* to Arvin, about whom he later said, "Newton was my Harvard." Mary's many lovers included the abstract expressionist Franz Kline, who had come to Provincetown to work with Hans Hofmann. Franz remained loyal to her for years, and her chaotic later life was somewhat stabilized by the sale of a large painting he had given her at the height of his fame.

Jack was desperate for help, and finally one night at a party at the L'Engles' the writer Polly Boyden again urged him to hire Dodie. On her first day it became instantly clear that Dodie not only liked farming but was a deeply experienced gardener (as well as extremely attractive to a man living alone on isolated Bound Brook). She had moved into the small two-room studio next to the main house called the Delight for a sign carved with that name that Jack had found in Provincetown and hung above its

Dodie and Jack, Bound Brook Island, 1941

door (allegedly, it had once advertised one of Provincetown's most famous brothels). The Delight later became the summer residence of the sculptor and painter Chaim Gross and his wife, Renee, lifelong friends of Jack's. Chaim had given Jack and Cammie as a wedding gift a model ebony figure for a major work he had sold to the Museum of Modern Art.

Dodie later confessed to her children that she had had no real romantic feeling about the self-absorbed farm owner or sympathy with his deep political beliefs and intellectualism, but she did fall quickly under the spell of Bound Brook Island and its isolated hog-cranberry-covered hills; marshes; long, empty shoreline; and stunning view of Provincetown's Pilgrim Monument across the bay.

She was a demon worker, and while she might have never read a novel in her life, she was an avid, though indiscriminate, reader of nonfiction and was totally devoted to the cult of Nature and a "universal spirit" as a lifelong follower of Henry David Thoreau. (She treasured his journals of his walking trips to Cape Cod in 1849 and 1855 and had devotedly traced every step.)

The sole spiritual figure in her life was Ralph Waldo Emerson—"Mr. Emerson," as she always referred to him. She lived her life guided by his favorite maxim, "Do not go where the path may lead, go instead where there is no path and leave a trail." Her friend Meg Barden often reminded her that she had said, "I want to be a farmer, not the farmer's wife."

Indeed, she had found the farmwork congenial, and Jack, uxorious by nature, having always found women much more attractive than men as friends, with the possible exception of Jack Phillips, soon began to see Dodie as other than the "hired girl." Of course, they had immediately discovered a number of friends in common, many from Dodie's youth in Croton, such as George Biddle, who now lived nearby in an old house in Truro, and her original host, Susan Glaspell, and Susan's lover Norman Matson, who was now living with Anna Walling in the Wellfleet woods on Jack Phillips's road in an old farmhouse owned by Lorenzo Dow "L. D." Baker. Anna had been followed to the Cape by her charismatic brother, Hayden English Walling, who quickly found a job working with Jack Phillips and Jack Hall on their building projects. Both Wallings had been educated in the progressive Edgewood School in Connecticut, founded by the nature writer Ernest Thompson Seton and his Native American wife.

Because Harl had so many friends, Dodie actually knew more Cape bohemians than Jack. In Provincetown, Harl had introduced her to Mary Heaton Vorse and her children, Heaton and Mary Ellen, the latter a former girlfriend of Harl's. She also met Fritz Bultman, not yet married and continuing his study with Hans Hofmann, and the Portuguese fishing heroes Manny Zora, already a Cape legend, and Francis "Khaki" Captiva, his protégé. Khaki took in Dodie's attractiveness at a glance and flirted with her in the fisherman bars—including Mike's, where Manny's pictures covered the walls. It was also in these bars that Dodie first met Rhodes Hall, who was in Provincetown trying to organize a fishermen's union, and his wife, Martha ("Mardi"), in her Brooks Brothers sweater set and destined to be Jack Hall's last wife.

Bubs and Chauncey Hackett were, of course, old friends of Harl's stepmother, and Bubs had a considerable crush on the handsome Harl. The Hapgoods' daughter-in-law Tamsin would become a lifelong Provincetown friend of Dodie's. Both disdained creature comforts, favoring privies over toilets, preferring hunting for blueberries or mussels to deep discussions of modern art and public transit to cars.

Harl had also introduced Dodie to two couples who would become lifelong friends. First were Tiny and John Worthington. John had just moved from Trinidad, where he had been working in the oil business, back to old family land in North Truro. Tiny was a six-foot English blond beauty who had served as a volunteer ambulance driver as a teenager in World War I, when worshipping Tommies hung the nickname on her. She had come to the States to be an actress but then decided to attend nursing school. John had been a World War I pilot and adventurer but had grown up on the Cape fishing with all the contemporary Portuguese legends. Tiny opened a store in 1936, hiring local Truro women to knit fishnet shawls, jackets, and handbags. The store immediately became a supplier to Bonwit's and other Manhattan women's fancy stores and was featured in *Vogue* with the Duchess of Kent modeling a fishnet hat. Tiny spent a great deal of time in New York marketing her fishnet fashions but also mixing with the theater and gay worlds. She was said to have had a child with Paul Robeson as well as love affairs with both sexes. Her Greta Garbo look and straightforward charm seduced many, including Harl Cook's first wife, Leo Coleman, who left Harl after their affair.

John was a handsome, calm Yankee who seemed able to ignore Tiny's other life and concentrate on their children and manage the first local cold-storage plant in North Truro, which he had bought to hold the Provincetown catch for the market in Boston, rather than force the fishermen to sell it cheap off the dock to dealers no matter what the market price.

The second couple were Paul and Nina Chavchavadze. Paul was a youthfully slim, charming Georgian prince. One of his uncles had been Prince Stroganov, the czar's ambassador to the Court of St. James's who is credited as the creator of the beef and cream dish that bears his name. His mother's brother, Mikhail Rodzianko, had been a czarist cavalryman and statesman and in the family was referred to as "Uncle Horse." Paul

"Tiny" Worthington at her Fish Net Store, Truro, ca. 1960s

Princess Nina Romanov,   *Prince Paul Chavchavadze,*
London, 1920   *London, 1929*

himself had been a young cadet in the Imperial Cavalry Academy when the revolution broke out. Ordered to mount up, they were led south from St. Petersburg to join General Yuri Danilov's "White" Army in defense of the czar. They passed through his father's estates in Georgia, where Paul discovered his father had been shot by the Reds. He kept riding.

Nina, known as "the Princess of All the Russias," was the czar's niece. Her father, Grand Duke George, had been assassinated by the Bolsheviks. She and her mother, the grand duchess, whose sister was the queen of Greece, had also fled to their estates in the south and were rescued in 1914 by a British destroyer in the Black Sea with nothing but their jewelry. (Nina's mother was also the sister of the Duchess of Kent, which meant they were connected to the British royal family.)

Nina and Paul first met in London, both penniless. They married there in 1922 and sailed to New York to work, he as a translator and Nina as a portrait painter of apartment interiors. One might ask why in 1934 they chose the bohemian Cape to move to at the height of the Depression. Perhaps because they found there just what they had imagined about America, a beautiful and unspoiled country with a mix of fellow penniless bohemians and working-class locals to charm and amuse them. A dinner party at Nina's might well consist of the plumber, a visiting czarist émigré noble, Edmund Wilson, Adelaide Walker, and Spivy, the lesbian jazz chanteuse who was spending the weekend from New York. In an astounding turn of history, when Stalin's daughter, Svetlana, sought refuge in the United States in 1967, she requested an invitation to stay with the Chavchavadzes in Wellfleet while Paul translated her memoir, *Only One Year* (1969). It was Harl who asked Dodie to accompany him in 1934 together with a bottle of bootleg whiskey to take to Princess Nina for her first driving test, which she failed. On the drive back the whiskey was passed around, and when he hit a bump, Dodie banged the bottle into her tooth, which she needed to have capped.

Back on Bound Brook, Jack and Dodie eventually began an affair. She slept no longer in the Delight but in Jack's larger bed in the Baker house, and he soon proposed, but she was full of doubts about her ability to love him. Just as she was about to board the train in Provincetown for another summer at Camp Treetops, he proposed one final time, and she, desperate for the security she had never known, accepted. They were wed on June 5, 1940, in the West End Protestant church in Provincetown with no family present. A small wedding reception was hosted by Susan Glaspell and Harl and his new wife, Leo, at the L'Engles' Truro house. Brownie L'Engle gave Dodie a bouquet of bridal wreath. Cammie did not attend.

In so many ways they were an unlikely pair. Dodie was of the old Left, still dedicated to progressive socialist goals, including pacifism, and an ardent supporter of labor and the New Woman, expecting equal sexual experiences and enjoyment and embracing women who led their own independent work lives. Her friendships included many from the Cape's working class, wives of Portuguese and Yankee fishing and farming families upon whom those who lived on the Outer Cape depended. She particularly admired women whose independent careers inspired her—Bubs Hackett's unique paintings, Susan Glaspell's writing, Tiny Worthington's fishnet fashion industry, and the Australian journalist Joan Colebrook's husbands-and-children-be-damned attitude.

Jack had trouble relating to the working class or the seemingly unsophisticated or politically uncommitted. He elected to be with the artists and architects who shared both his aesthetic and his Stalinist views. Not that he didn't have a growing respect for the daring Provincetown fishermen he had come to know.

12.

COUNTRY LIFE

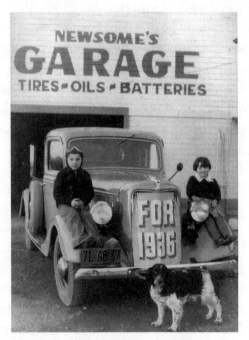

Newsome's Garage, Truro, 1936

Jack and Dodie, like so many couples in 1940, were supporting Roosevelt in what seemed a time of peril, with the Depression still affecting most lives and Europe and Asia in chaos. Germany had invaded Poland unopposed. The Japanese had likewise moved brutally into northern China.

New neighbors were settling on Bound Brook. Sonia Brown, her children grown, had sold the old harbormaster's house to Robert Loesser and his dog-raising wife. A young couple, Ted and Joan Clark, with strong family Cape connections, were now living in the old Atwood house farther down on their road, opposite another abandoned Atwood house that Jack was later to buy. There were other new neighbors as well; in 1934 the composer Gardner Jencks and his wife, Ruth, had purchased the town's picnic ground on the height of the island, much to the dismay of Wellfleet. Gardner's relative Phillip Wren, a painter, had first introduced them to Wellfleet and led them to Bound Brook Island.

Gardner Jencks had grown up in a distinguished Baltimore family and showed early musical gifts. He attended the Hotchkiss School, where he became lifelong friends with Varian Fry, whose France-based rescue network made him one of the heroes of World War II refugee work. Among those Fry aided in escaping the Nazis were Max Ernst and Wassily Kandinsky. Fry often stayed with the Jenckses on Bound Brook. Prior to World War II, Gardner gave several acclaimed piano concerts at New York City's famed Town Hall at 123 West 43rd Street but turned to composition and became a contemporary of Aaron Copland and Elliott Carter, who also summered nearby. His Bound Brook studio contained two grand pianos back-to-back. His wife, Ruth, was an amateur painter and his most devoted fan. They both voted Socialist for Norman Thomas as pacifists suspicious of Stalin.

Jack and Dodie were becoming increasing involved in Provincetown, both with its fishing community and with the artists who had come to study or work under Hans Hofmann. Nearer by, their social lives revolved around parties at Jack Phillips's "Back Woods" across the new state highway in Truro. Jack was now Jack Hall's closest male friend and remained so throughout their intertwined lives. They had begun to work together in designing or reconstructing various summer cabins on Phillips's extensive landholdings. Phillips's great-great-grandfather of the same name had been the first mayor of Boston. His memory is honored by Phillips Street, which runs parallel to Boston's old Charles River waterfront at the base of Beacon Hill. The street name was bestowed somewhat sardonically, because this was the location of Boston's roughest bars and brothels during his mayoralty. Another ancestor was the abolitionist Wendell

Phillips. Phillips had graduated from Harvard in 1930, having attended Phillips Academy in Andover, which, like its sister school, Phillips Exeter Academy, had been founded by an ancestor and namesake. At Harvard, he studied fine arts and was a member of the Fly Club, of which FDR and his attorney general Francis Biddle were also members. He was pre-ternaturally handsome and charming, and women found him irresistible, although all but the last of his five wives abandoned the marriage. He was tall, with black hair, aquiline features, and high color, and was said to have posed, with requisite eye patch, for one of the "Tetley Tea Man" ads. An outdoorsman by birthright, he grew up on Wenham Lake, north of Boston, where his father, also John Phillips, an avid sportsman and amateur ornithologist, had written the still authoritative *Natural History of the Ducks*.

Jack Phillips, Horseleech Pond, ca. 1962

In his senior year at Harvard, his uncle by marriage had left him a seeming small bequest in his will: "My duck hunting camp in Truro." The uncle, Dr. William H. Rollins, had come from a much less elite back-ground than the Phillipses but had turned out to be a superb investor and creator of patents—with no children. Rollins, an avid sportsman, had become fascinated with the undeveloped ocean side of the Outer Cape from Truro to Eastham and began a lifelong contest with Captain L. D. Baker, whose family homestead Jack Hall now owned, to acquire as much of the moors, kettle ponds, and oceanfront as the desperately poor Yan-kee and Portuguese farmers would sell. The "duck hunting camp" turned out to be more than eight hundred acres of abandoned farm pasture and wooded lots viewed then as valueless and mosquito-ridden. Today, Rollins's kettle ponds and dunes are considered one of the most pristine and unique landscapes remaining on the Cape and the crown jewel of the Cape Cod National Seashore.

Fernand Léger's painting class, Paris, 1932.
Elizabeth "Libby" Blair is in the far right foreground.

Thus, Jack Phillips was perfectly set up to live a charmed bohemian life on the Outer Cape. Jack's duck-hunting camp on Horseleech Pond had become the hub of Cape bohemian social life. The two beautiful kettle ponds, Horseleech and Slough, nestled behind the great dunes of Newcomb Hollow Beach (soon to be known to all his friends as "Jack Phillips's beach") on the pounding Atlantic, seemed indeed like Eden to the New Yorkers who were lured there by Phillips's social and personal magnetism and his willingness to sell land to friends. After Harvard, Jack had studied painting in Paris with Fernand Léger and had also fallen under the spell of the Bauhaus and its new approach to architecture and design. Phillips had met Elizabeth "Libby" Blair when they were both in Paris studying painting and had married her. They had two daughters,

Blair, named after her mother, and Hayden, named after Hayden Walling, and with a nurse for the children both were able to concentrate on
their painting. Jack Hall once said of Phillips, "I wish I were Jack Phillips.
He was born without guilt." And Phillips replied, "I was born with a gilt
spoon in my mouth." When accused of sleeping with Mary Grand he
replied, "We were only colleagues."

Gathering at Jack Phillips's Horseleech Pond cabin, ca. 1961

It was Jack Phillips's conceit to celebrate the mid-August Perseid
meteor shower by hosting a large beach party to view the Swift-Tuttle
Comet's trail of debris in all its splendor under a totally dark sky. Jack Hall
and Dodie packed up their Ford Beach Wagon with the requisite bathing suits (which Jack rarely wore) and sweaters for the late evening on-
shore wind, Lucky Strikes, and scotch with a jar of ice. Dodie, never one
for heavy drinking but a lover of beach cooking, threw in some Bound
Brook corn, baked potatoes wrapped in foil, and a fresh-caught bluefish.

After several years of renting, the Chavchavadzes had purchased the
old sea captain's house on Blackfish Creek in 1939 using money from the
sale of Nina's brooch, a wedding present from her maternal grandmother,
Queen Olga of Greece). Paul and their teenage son, David (sometimes
called Prince David), packed their guitars. Both were justly famous for
their sophisticated and bawdy repertoire of songs in French, Russian, German, and English. Tonight, they had additional vocal help from Spivy,
who was staying with them that weekend and whose repertoire was even
bawdier.

Edmund Wilson's closest Wellfleet friend, Charles Walker, the Greek scholar and Yale labor lawyer, and his wife, Adelaide, the former lover of Harry Crosby, founder of the Black Sun Press, and their two teen-age sons, Charles and Danny, the latter no mean beach party singer and storyteller, also packed their car. Charles was desperately hoping Adelaide would not talk about her recent visits to Mexico City to attend the Trotsky Commission, because he knew Jack Hall was a Stalinist and the Chavchavadzes were no admirers of either, having both lost many members of their families in the revolution.

Anna Walling, now married to Norman Matson, was wrapping her famous watercress sandwiches, the cress picked from the brook that ran at the foot of their old house in a secluded hollow on the road to Jack Phillips's beach, which they had bought from the L. D. Baker estate. Norman was nineteen years older than Anna. He had first met her when her parents, William English Walling and Anna Strunsky, were writing for *The Masses* and summering in Provincetown. Their fatal meeting was on Ballston Beach in Truro, where her parents were renting a house in 1929. Anna was seventeen, beautiful, and sitting alone reading Hemingway's *The Sun Also Rises*, when Norman encountered her. He sat down and asked her how she liked it. She replied, "Not very much, so far." He confessed he, too, had not really liked it, and they fell deep into conversation about books. Anna recalled it as the first time an adult had treated her like a peer and developed a secret crush on Norman. Two years later, they met by total chance in France. Anna, now at Swarthmore, was traveling with her family, and it was she who pursued him until they began the affair that led him to leave Susan and marry her.[1] They were also bringing Anna's brother Hayden and their son Peter, now at school with the Walkers' son Danny. Peter was later to become a respected literary agent, working in his uncle Harold Matson's agency before he started his own.

In North Truro, on the bay, the Worthingtons packed up some freshly filleted striped bass and a bottle of Johnnie Walker with a bottle of ice cubes. Liquor was no stranger to Tiny, who often brought a flask of coffee to her fishnet store that rarely contained coffee. Of all those heading for Jack's beach, probably John knew it best, having grown up in Truro, where his family had long summered. (His father had been the clerk of court in Dedham during the Sacco and Vanzetti trial.)

One by one they parked their cars along Jack Phillips's sand road in the Back Woods and staggered with their baskets down the steep dune to the beach. The sun was just beginning its descent, and there was still plenty of light in which to dig a fire pit, gather driftwood, spread the blankets, unpack the liquor closet, and have a drink or two before donning swim clothes or not. Libby Blair, Jack Phillips's wife, was quite beautiful and well aware of it and famed for removing her bathing suit at the first sight of a man.

Ati Gropius, the daughter of Walter and Ise Gropius, then a young, strikingly beautiful student at the newly formed Black Mountain College, recalled those long-ago beach parties:

> The only people on the beach at Newcomb [Jack Phillips's Newcomb Hollow Beach] were the people who lived in the woods—there was no "public." So, every Saturday night, different families like the Chermayeffs would have a big bonfire and . . . there was singing and roasting and several girls going down the beach, and it was very, very nice. . . . Jack Hall would be there with children from one marriage or another [actually all his children were with Dodie] and one wife or another . . . that's where, I think, all the great love affairs sprung from . . . people went off on starlit nights.[2]

Another Bauhaus child, Tamas Breuer, recalled Jack Hall singing "I'm Popeye the Sailor Man" in a deep voice, to everyone's delight.

Drying off, the women began to assemble a communal meal from their collective hampers, and, as always, there was enough to make up for the Chavchavadzes' habitual failure to bring anything. As the night grew darker, the ghosts of the figures who haunted their lives began to occupy their conversation and songs: Roosevelt, Stalin, Hitler, and Freud.

Sigmund Freud had begun to influence the lives of bohemians in 1910 as German intellectuals transported his theories to the Village. They were received with both fascination and humor and showed up as themes in the early plays of the Provincetown Players. But as amusing as psychiatry and psychiatrists could be, they had now insinuated themselves deeply into the bohemian psyche and influenced their approach to sex, families, and culture. Suddenly there were psychiatrists actually mingling with them, some deeply respected, like Erik Erikson. Erikson, a German-born child psychologist, created the "identity crisis" theory and was the author of the classic *Childhood and Society* (1950). Erikson began to hold professional conferences on the Cape that drew many serious practitioners and others less esteemed but perhaps more influential in the lives of the bohemians. Of the latter, Sandor Rado, a Hungarian and Jewish psychiatrist who had met Freud in 1915 but diverged from some of his theories, had moved to the United States and co-founded the Center for Psychoanalytic Training and Research at Columbia. Rado created a devoted following among what he termed "schizotypes" in New York and Provincetown, including Mary McCarthy. Rado seemed to take a nonprofessional interest both in young attractive women and in being accepted by Provincetown's bohemian elite. He rented a summerhouse near Katy and John Dos Passos and begged McCarthy to introduce him, but unfortunately the Dos Passoses had never taken to Mary and particularly loathed Rado, which might have had some anti-Semitic roots but was more likely based on Rado's pursuit of the teenage Rosalind Wilson, whom the Dos Passoses adored. The emotional lives of a great many even around the fire were now partially in the hands of their psychiatrists, and the terrifying month of August, when psychiatrists traditionally abandoned their patients for vacation, became increasingly less stressful as they found their shrinks now neighbors on the beach and at cocktail parties.

With drink their spirits rose, and weekend guests and lovers joined in passionate song by the driftwood fire, ranging from homages to Joe Hill, antiwar songs, and labor movement ballads, such as "Hard Travelin'," to the more sophisticated bawdy songs of Cole Porter and Black songs from the Jim Crow South as rendered by Lead Belly and Marian Anderson. A new assortment of communist songs had been learned by the Cape's "Red Diaper" babies, like the young painter Paul Resika, who had been sent to party-run summer camps in the Catskills and at the Jersey Shore. Many dealt with the Spanish Civil War or Stalin's recently imposed "premature antifascism," such as "Eleanor Roosevelt, Don't Send Our Boys to War."

Martin Dies, the Texas congressman who chaired the House Committee on Un-American Activities, had recently accused Eleanor Roosevelt of being a communist in his 1940 book, *The Trojan Horse in America.* To mock Dies, they struck up songs by Woody Guthrie, Pete Seeger, Burl Ives, and the Weavers, all soon to be placed on the FBI's list of "dangerous persons."

When the comfort and alcohol level was high enough, those seated around the fire began to share their own or their friends' or families' explorations of the party. Sadly, for those who had fought in Spain, that service alone could put your name on the list. A certain justifiable pride was shared by those who themselves had been targeted by HUAC as suspected Communist Party members or sympathizers or knew someone who had. But it was no game for those who had been forced to testify or had refused to sign a loyalty oath and had to face the consequent loss of their teaching position or other professional standing and now had an FBI dossier that ensured they would probably have trouble with employment, government clearance, or travel.

The meteor shower ended, and it was growing cold with both the firewood and the liquor finished, so the couples rose, shook the sand off their blankets, extinguished the fire's embers, and bade each other good night, never to forget the comet and their ephemeral comradeship.

Mary McCarthy at her typewriter, 1944

There were some bohemians who loathed beach parties, and certainly Edmund Wilson would have been near the top of that list. Wilson had met Mary McCarthy, now a young widow, at a party in New York and was smitten. He invited her to stay at Margaret DeSilver's country estate, which he was house-sitting. Edmund was always vulnerable, and Mary was already a skilled seductress. Soon she wrote to Wilson, "You know the delight of speaking the name of someone with whom one is privately intimate to a third person to whom the name is just like any other one mentions? It's wonderful. Such conversations have a kind of pleasing dramatic irony."[3]

They married in 1938, and their son, Reuel, was born that December. Rosalind, Edmund's daughter with his first wife, Mary Blair, was fourteen when she met Mary. She had hoped her father would marry his old friend and fellow writer Dawn Powell, whom she found more sympathetic. After their marriage, Wilson rented various houses, including the Dos Passoses' in Provincetown and the Boydens' in Truro, until he finally persuaded his mother to give him the money to buy an old captain's house on Money Hill, just off the new highway into Wellfleet center.

During the interval between alcohol-fueled rages and occasional physical brawls, Wilson paused to reflect on his love for his much younger, beautiful, and talented wife. This is a section of a poem he wrote for her thirtieth birthday:

Mary, this morning when sunrise
First met your green and lighting eyes
In debt and dèche the way I live,
I have no other gift to give—
Nothing to guard our flickering foyer
Against Judge Otis, paranoia,
Tovarishch Stalin's dark apostles,
The envious reviews of hostiles,
Against the rank and shallow weeds . . .

Their marriage was also based on a strong intellectual bond, and it was Edmund who encouraged Mary to move from nonfiction to fiction,

Dodie Hall (center), Wellfleet Fair, 1941

but ultimately it ended in an ugly divorce in which Mary's character witness, Adelaide Walker, the wife of his oldest Wellfleet friend, confirmed Edmund's physical assaults. It was several years before Edmund and the Walkers were able to socialize.

Jack and Dodie continued to improve their farm. Tiny Worthington helped Dodie rub a mixture of paint and turpentine into the old plaster walls, leaving them a glowing Umbrian orange. Jack Hall's soon-to-be next father-in-law, Frank Shay, and his wife, Edy, had moved to Wellfleet from Provincetown, and Frank had organized the first Wellfleet Agricultural Fair in 1940, at which Dodie exhibited some of her vegetables. Shay had created an appealing poster for the fair with the words "Well, well, Wellfleet!" In digging the garden, they had discovered a cache of trade items exchanged by the early European cod fishermen and the Pamet people: pipe stems, coins, and arrowheads, which they buried under the millstone step to the front door. They also bought an iron-wheeled tractor that they dubbed "Babe the Blue Ox."

They were not alone. Since 1910, many bohemians had been attracted to the Cape by the opportunity to once again have a garden and feel closer to the rural landscape many had grown up in before coming to New York. It was a joy to once again dress as they had as young men, in khaki shirts, dungarees, and old army boots. In Provincetown, Jig Cook and Dos Passos were famed for their kitchen vegetable gardens, as were Robert Nathan and Frank Shay in Truro and Wellfleet. Their mutual friend Malcolm Cowley, now living part of the time in rural Roxbury, Connecticut, where he farmed, wrote, "We were most of us countrymen . . . We were radicals in literature and sometimes in politics, but conservative in our other aspirations, looking back for ideals to the country we had known in childhood. I supposed we were the last generation in which those country tastes could be taken for granted."[4]

Roosevelt's Works Progress Administration and its Federal Art Project were providing a working wage for many painters who in the years before the war were able to spend the summers in Provincetown studying with Hans Hofmann. Both Jack Phillips and Jack Hall were increasingly torn between the world of architecture, as they discovered the modern design being proselytized by the Bauhaus refugees beginning to settle around Jack Phillips's ponds, and the thrilling world of abstract painting espoused by Hofmann.

Jack Hall, always reluctant to turn to his widowed mother for financial support, and with the farm producing little income, had also become fascinated with the colorful, virile life of the Provincetown Portuguese fishermen he had come to admire. He determined to enter the trade and began plans to commission the building of a fishing vessel, hopefully to be captained by the charismatic Khaki Captiva. Khaki was the son of a respected mainland Portuguese captain who had come to Provincetown at the turn of the century. Khaki had fished, as a boy, with his father and uncle on five-masted schooners off Newfoundland's dangerous and foggy Grand Banks, giving him deep roots in the Portuguese community. He had gone to Provincetown High School in the 1930s with young Joe O'Brien Jr., the son of Mary Heaton Vorse and Joe O'Brien. The Vorse house on Commercial Street was a haven for Provincetown's teenagers and a center of its bohemian life. Khaki, with his pockmarked face alight with a roguish smile, enormous virility, and daring, was a hero to both sexes and had just married a local Portuguese girl and had a child when Jack raised the idea of a boat. Upon their first meeting, Khaki had grasped both Dodie's sexuality and her lack of deep connection to Jack.

This was to have dire consequences after he agreed to captain Jack's boat once built.

Meanwhile, back at the farm, other adventures were unfolding. Jack had bought a used fire engine from the Wellfleet Fire Department, and it caught fire while he was fueling it in the barn. Because they had no telephone, he saddled his thirty-three-year-old horse, Dapple, and headed for the nearest telephone to call the Truro and Wellfleet Fire Departments. Meanwhile, Dodie was keeping the fire at bay with the garden hose. (Jack always left her role out after their divorce.) The town fire trucks arrived, and while they lost the barn, the two adjacent structures were saved. The couple finally gave in and bought a telephone and were listed in the Outer Cape directory as "Mr. and Mrs. John Hughes Hall, Bound Brook Island," and had stationery printed and engraved with "Island Farm-Wellfleet, Massachusetts."

When Hitler finally invaded Poland and exposed Chamberlain's "Peace for our time" as nothing more than a "piece of paper," Americans began to accept that the oncoming clash between the Axis powers and England and Russia would ultimately bring war to all. This approaching storm made it almost inevitable that Roosevelt would break the long-standing presidential rule of two terms and seek a third in 1940.

Provincetown Interior, *by Mary "Bubs" Hackett*

13

WORLD WAR II

The disillusionment over Stalin's 1939 pact with Hitler and his "premature antifascist" policies was suddenly forgotten on June 22, 1941, when Hitler launched his fatal folly, the blitzkrieg invasion code-named Barbarossa, against his new ally, the Soviet Union, seeking to attain his long-held goal of *Lebensraum* (living space for an expanded Germany). It seemed inevitable to Hitler, as Tolstoy chronicles Napoleon's belief that the world's most experienced and well-armed land force would swiftly overwhelm the poorly armed and badly trained Russian troops, and indeed by late fall Hitler had transferred half of his armies to a front that stretched from Finland through Ukraine and Georgia to the Black Sea. Opposition to the Nazis now seemed hopeless. Arthur Koestler, now a refugee in England, wrote *Darkness at Noon*.

Roosevelt was at first blocked by an isolationist Congress from doing anything but amending the Kellogg-Briand Pact, which had embargoed arms in the Spanish Civil War, to permit some arms aid under the disguise of the "lend-lease" of old destroyers to France and England. But the Soviets' surprising resistance gave hope that England, itself badly damaged by Dunkirk and the blitz, might both survive and make it worthy of U.S. entry into the war. Suddenly Stalin and communism were again palatablc to the U.S. legal authorities as allies in the oncoming Armageddon with fascism.

Mary Vorse had gone to Europe in 1939 to cover Hitler's invasion of the Sudetenland in Czechoslovakia and had returned to find Provincetown in uneasy peace, knitting socks for English soldiers (nicknamed Bundles for Britain) and also slowly realizing that Chamberlain might have badly misdiagnosed Hitler's intentions. Cape newspapers were full of new civil defense and evacuation plans for women and children on its one highway to Boston.

Charles "Lucky Lindy" Lindbergh addressing an America First rally,
Madison Square Garden, 1941

Led by Charles "Lucky Lindy" Lindbergh, the America First pro-Nazi movement had grown from a small group into a major isolationist force in American politics fueled by the belief that Hitler was the only answer to the growing international communist and Jewish influence. On May 23, 1941, twenty-two thousand New Yorkers filled Madison Square Garden to hear Lindbergh urge Americans to ignore Germany's brutal bombing attacks on England and remain neutral, threatening that "the three most important groups which have been leading the country toward war are the British, the Jewish and the Roosevelt administration." Few on the Cape listened to him.

Jack Hall's Truro neighbor and fellow ardent Stalinist Polly Boyden was in a movie theater in Manhattan on Sunday, December 7, 1941, when a loudspeaker interrupted the film to announce the Japanese attack on the vast Pearl Harbor naval base in Hawaii and request that all servicemen immediately report to their units. She rushed home to inform her then roommate and fellow Stalinist, Josie Herbst. Soon everyone on the Cape was gathered around their radios as FDR requested Congress to declare war on Japan. The vote was passed in the House 410–1. The single vote against the declaration came from the first woman to be elected to Congress, Jeannette Rankin, the Montana Republican feminist firebrand. She had also voted no in 1917. Again in 1941, as a pacifist and feminist, she said, "As a woman I cannot go to war, and I refuse to send anyone else." To the ninety million Americans who breathlessly listened, Roosevelt promised, "In the future days, which we seek to make secure, we look forward to a world founded upon four essential human freedoms . . . speech . . . worship . . . freedom from want . . . freedom from fear."

The other Axis powers, Germany and Italy, as required under their mutual treaty, immediately declared war on the United States, and in embassy courtyards around the world fires began to burn as staffs destroyed diplomatic records.

On Bound Brook Island, things were moving fast as well. Dodie, as a progressive pacifist and socialist, had always believed all wars were criminal and had particularly opposed World War I's draft. She was even more disturbed with the announcement in late December 1941 of a new one. All men between eighteen and sixty-five now had to register, and those between twenty and forty-four were immediately eligible for call-up. She had stood clear of the turbulent politics of the 1930s, although her heart was always with the working class, be they nurses, teachers, farmers, or fishermen. She had attended lectures by Earl Browder and had known many of those with strong Communist Party ties in Wallace's Agriculture Department, such as John Herrmann and Josie Herbst, but she could never subscribe to the rigid discipline and loyalty demanded of the party by Stalin and knew her beloved Mr. Emerson would never have approved.

For Dodie, the individual was always far more important than the group and the group's authority figures.

It was quite a different story for Jack. He was now the father of two children, Darius and Noa, and Katrina was soon to be born, and he was fully aware of the growing suspicions of his fellow townsmen toward him and Jack Phillips, as wealthy young eccentrics who were neither in uniform nor seemingly likely to be so.

In numbers, the American armed forces ranked seventeenth in the world in 1939, between Portugal and Bulgaria. In 1941, Hitler had launched 2 million highly trained soldiers into Russia—and this was less than half his forces—while the United States had fewer than 175,000, many ill-trained and armed with World War I weaponry. It was only the third time in American history that a draft had been imposed, but unlike those of the Civil War and World War I there was little opposition. FDR began a "blitzkrieg" of his own and to the astonishment of Hitler and the Axis powers swiftly created the largest armaments program in history, spewing out tanks, jeeps, submarines, and bombers twenty-four hours a day. As it became clear that indeed America might be the country that could be the difference in the winning of the war and emerge unscathed and immensely powerful, Henry Luce's *Time* began to use the phrase the "American Century."

Many of the original bohemians were too old to serve in combat, and those who volunteered or were drafted were often assigned to specialty services such as the arts, culture, or military design. From the Cape's bohemian world came a few professional soldiers, like Admiral Chester Nimitz, married into the old Wellfleet Freeman family, one of whose houses Edmund Wilson had just purchased for four thousand dollars.

George Biddle had served with distinction in World War I as a second lieutenant in the trenches and returned, like so many, totally disillusioned. Now living partly in Truro and still licking his wounds from being accused by the Dies Committee of making his Federal Art Project a communist "front," he nevertheless again approached his Groton and Harvard friend FDR for a role in the war. Roosevelt approved him to be the head of the Art Advisory Board for the War Department to recruit artists to record the war and create propaganda.

Biddle gathered an impressive group of artists, just as he had for the Federal Art Project, and followed the war in person with the Third Infantry Division in North Africa and Italy, often in combat. Among his recruits were a number of bohemians, including Ben Wolf, a student of Hans Hofmann's and neighbor of Mary McCarthy's and her new husband, Bowden Broadwater, a friend of Jack and Dodie's. Wolf became a combat artist for the coast guard.

Lee Falk (born Leon Gross), the creator of the *Mandrake the Magician* and *The Phantom* comic strips, which had more than a hundred million daily readers, was the owner of an estate in Truro called Xanadu, complete with tennis court. He became head of the radio foreign-language division in the Office of War Information. Falk was a multi-married, dashing figure who was once quoted as saying, "My only politics is up with democracy and down with dictatorships." While working on propaganda in the War Office, he was instrumental in disseminating the unexpurgated translation of Hitler's *Mein Kampf* with all its anti-Semitic vitriol rather than the sanitized version the Germans had been distributing in the West.

Sidney Simon sketching in the jungle, World War II

Others who served as military artists were Sidney Simon and his friend Henry Varnum Poor. Both had spent time in Provincetown before the war. Simon ended up on MacArthur's staff and was ordered to portray the Japanese surrender aboard the USS *Missouri* in 1945. Poor and Simon with two fellow war artists founded Maine's Skowhegan School of Painting and Sculpture in 1946. Both returned to Provincetown and Truro, where Simon became a lifelong friend of Dodie's.

Of course, everyone had some connection with the war, be it a relative in the service or a job in the home-front services. Chauncey Hackett, who had served as a captain in World War I, volunteered as a bus scheduler. Phyllis Duganne wrote a screenplay that became the film *Nice Girl?*, starring Deanna Durbin, Franchot Tone, and Robert Benchley. Universal Pictures released it in February 1941, and it became a huge hit in wartime Britain, where Durbin was a popular star. The English version added a final scene with Durbin singing "There'll Always Be an England," which turned out to be true: its English release came in the afterglow of the Battle of Britain, in which the "few" RAF pilots thwarted the German Luftwaffe's attempt to bomb England into submission.

Others who were writers suspended their books to take on writing assignments as journalists. Edmund Wilson replaced Ring Lardner's son David at *The New Yorker* after he had been killed in the war. John Dos Passos, after covering the war in the South Pacific, attended the Nuremberg trials in November 1945, where he observed the trial judge Francis Biddle's open affair with the English journalist Rebecca West. Wilson and Philip Hamburger, later married to Anna Matson, were both sent by *The New Yorker* to Europe to report on the war's astounding human and cultural devastation (the total military and civilian casualties in World War I were seventeen million, and in World War II they were fifty million).

The two Jacks' collective first encounter with the new American patriotic vigilantism occurred as they were riding in Phillips's station wagon, whose backseat was covered by a Navajo blanket, and were stopped by the Wellfleet police. Apparently, others had reported that they were two of the few men who wore beards (much favored by the crews of German U-boats that were haunting the Cape shore for prey) and were often seen drawing on the beach for obviously treasonous purposes. But the definitive proof was the ancient symbolic swastika that was woven into the blanket on the back seat.

Sadly, this was not a unique experience in bohemia. Edwin Dickinson also wore a beard, painted, and drew alone on the beach in Wellfleet, where his two young children attended public school. The children began to be taunted as Nazi supporters and threatened with physical harm. Ed, warned to act quickly in his family's defense, because they lived in such a remote section of town, went to the VFW post in Provincetown, from whence he had joined the U.S. Navy and served aboard the *Nantucket* lightship, dangerous duty during World War I. He met with an unsympathetic VFW committee who by a bare majority agreed to write a letter confirming his loyalty. Nevertheless, military police soon appeared at his primitive cabin and studio on Chipman's Cove and threatened to shoot his dog while accusing him of being a Nazi collaborator on the basis of two 1936 German propaganda magazines that his close friend John Dos Passos had brought back from Europe during his coverage of the Spanish Civil War.

The Chilean painter Roberto Matta had rented Jack Phillips's Paper Palace beach house in 1942 to both paint and continue his affair with his friend Arshile Gorky's widow, Agnes (called "Mougouch") soon to be Jack Phillips's wife. Matta had also invited Robert Motherwell and Peggy Guggenheim's new husband, Max Ernst, to stay. Peggy had married Ernst to enable him, with the assistance of Varian Fry, to escape Nazi Germany. One day, while Peggy was in New York and Motherwell in Provincetown, Matta and Ernst decided to burn some trash in the dune and were suddenly surrounded by armed naval police and arrested. Ernst spoke little English and proffered a Nazi passport, ironically marked "Juden." Unbeknownst to him, it was now a crime for a German national to be within fifteen miles of the coast without formal government permission. Matta, as a Chilean national, was considered a co-conspirator, and their smoky fire was assumed to be a signal to a nearby German U-boat. Fortunately, Peggy returned to find the house empty and traced them to a Boston jail, where her high-priced New York lawyers soon obtained their release.

Paul Chavchavadze, Wellfleet, ca. 1960

One by one the freshly painted list of names of the men who had joined the service in the Wellfleet Town Hall grew until the two Jacks were almost the only eligible males not in service. The list now even included a number of older men and their sons, including Jack Hall's Princeton classmate Durand Echeverria and his son, Charles, and Paul Chavchavadze, who had joined the Red Cross in Europe, having last seen service as a cadet at the Imperial Cavalry Academy in St. Petersburg. Paul later became the Third Army's liaison with the Russian forces. His young son, Prince David, had left Yale to enlist in army intelligence. Given his flawless Russian and youthful service in the elite New York cadet corps, the Knickerbocker Greys, he was quickly recruited by the OSS and would become a lifelong CIA operative. Others, like Jack's older Bound Brook Island neighbor Gardner Jencks, the modernist composer, went to work on the production line in a radar company.

Jack Hall was also deeply affected by his nephew Stuart Bartle's war. Stuart was the son of Jack's older and beloved half sibling, Alice Bartle Dowling. She and Stuart often stayed with Jack and Dodie on Bound Brook while he was at Harvard before he enlisted in his sophomore year. Stuart had been severely wounded at Normandy and after his recovery spent his summers in Wellfleet as a part of Jack's extended family.

The pressure to serve was just too great. Jack Phillips moved to New York to join a camouflage painting unit in the Brooklyn Navy Yard but after a short stay returned to his camp on Horseleech Pond and, together with Hayden Walling (a Quaker and conscientious objector), began to raise turkeys, a draft-exempt occupation, in a series of small houses they erected along the pond's shore. The turkeys shortly died, but the "turkey houses" became prized summer retreats for Phillips's many offspring and the scene for his granddaughter Miranda Heller's novel, *The Paper Palace* (2021).

Manny Zora and Jack Hall aboard the Pilhasca, *ca. 1943*

Jack Hall decided to join the crew of the *Pilhasca*, the fishing boat he had commissioned to be co-captained with Khaki Captiva. The dragger was named for Khaki's Portuguese father, who was nicknamed Pilhasca, which, roughly translated, means "Que sera, sera": "Whatever the hell happens, will happen." Edmund Wilson wrote to his new wife, Mary McCarthy, about attending its launching in early 1944: "We went over to Provincetown Monday with the Geismars and found the town full of exhilarated friends who were celebrating the christening of a magnificent new fishing boat, which Jack Hall had had built for himself and which he is going to operate with a Portuguese crew. Matson, Bubs Hackett,

Joan Colebrook, Harl Cook, the Portuguese crew and many others all on board drinking various kinds of liquor."[1]

But fishing was not going to get your name painted on the town hall wall, and Jack finally gave into his feelings of guilt and joined the army as a private. He was sent to an all-white infantry battalion at Fort Bragg, North Carolina, for training. Dodie had begged him to at least let her remain on the farm with the children, but Jack felt that with nothing but a generator for electricity and being the only year-round family on the island, it was just too dangerous and demanded she move into Province-town, despite its wartime "blackouts" and German submarine raiders, to become the pay mistress for the *Pilhasca*. Khaki Captiva was younger and certainly more fit for service than Jack but had continued to take advantage, as many Portuguese fishermen did, of being exempt from the draft by working in a protected wartime industry.

Dodie's resistance to leaving Bound Brook was not just based on her desire to remain on the island, for she had fallen under Khaki's spell as she and Jack spent more time in Provincetown near or on the boat. She had always loved the sea and the dashing Portuguese fishermen who surrounded Khaki and Manny Zora. They were her kind of uncomplicated, adventurous, and highly sexed men.

Dodie knew what was coming and determined to blame Jack for abandoning her to become Khaki's mistress. When he returned for his first furlough after six months at Fort Bragg, she announced she could not sleep with him because she was now with Khaki. World War II might have ended in 1945, but the war between the Halls for the loyalty of friends, custody of their children, and monetary support was just beginning and would not end until their respective deaths.

In a letter to her father, who was in Reno with his next wife-to-be, Elena Mumm Thornton, who was waiting for her divorce, Rosalind Wilson wrote, "We attended a rather wild party at the Cooks [Harl and his new wife, Leo] where all sorts of scandals occurred. Polly Boyden kept turning to me and saying, 'I despise Edmund Wilson. He has got to choose between George Orwell and me. . . .' Polly and Cappy [Khaki] Captiva made violent love until Dodie Hall threw a pail of water on them. She was rather upset as she and Cappy were getting married the next day, but not so upset she postponed the ceremony. Polly left for California the next day and isn't coming back until Spring."[2] (Polly's son Bill had joined the air force and had been shot down over Germany; he survived, but his face and body were horribly burned.)

The world forever changed in August 1945 with the atomic bombing of the Japanese cities of Hiroshima and Nagasaki, bringing World War II to an abrupt end. Jack was now again alone on Bound Brook Island, brooding but sober, perhaps reflecting that boats had led to the demise of both his marriages. His three children were living with Dodie in North Truro in a house Khaki had rented in Sladeville, the rustic neighborhood created by a group of artists that surrounded Jerry Farnsworth's School of Art. During the period Khaki and Dodie lived there, Farnsworth painted portraits of both Dodie and Noa. There was increasingly bad blood between the Halls over Dodie having won custody, and Khaki didn't help by openly complaining about Jack's irregular child support and, most important, his sale of the *Pilhasca* to Khaki's best friend, Manny Zora, thus divesting Khaki of the ship that provided his income and that had brought Dodie into his arms.

Jack's marriage was not the only postwar trauma that befell the community. In 1947 while driving to New York, Dos Passos crashed into the rear of a parked cranberry truck, instantly killing Katy and leaving Dos blind in his right eye. Wilson returned and recorded her burial in his diary. She was placed in the Givens' plot in the old Truro cemetery above the Pamet River. His entry recalled their early days of bohemian intimacy:

> The little cemetery looked light, clear and dry—with its millstone and its old-fashioned tombstones, up there, along with the bold town-square characters, above what had once been the seafaring community. I had tried more or less to disassociate myself from them as Dos had done first, but when we had been living there, dining together, struggling with the Native traders and work-

men . . . I thought how they had lived on that—and in spite of all that was frivolous and "escapist"; childish and futile, in our lives, we had derived something from it and belonged to it—and Katy's death for the moment had given the whole thing dignity. I felt as I had not done before, that we (Givens, Shays, Chavchavadzes, Walkers, Dos Passos, Matsons, Vorses, ourselves) had all become a group, a community, more closely bound up together than we had realized or perhaps wanted to be. It was already a whole life that we had lived there—since Dos—who had always scoffed at Provincetown as a middle-class artist colony—had come up there to court Katy and had first moved into "Smooley Hall." All the parties, the days at the beach, the picnics, the flirtations, the drinking spells, the interims of work between trips, the moldy days of winter by stoves, the days of keeping going on a thin drip or trickle of income, stories and articles, bursts of prosperity, local property and cars, bibelots from Mexico or elsewhere, pictures and figures by local artists accumulated in P'Town front rooms walled in against the street—that was what our life had been when we had dedicated ourselves to the Cape, to the life of the silver harbor—and all the love and work that had gone with it, that we had come there to keep alive.[3]

Khaki was both a hard worker and a drunken womanizer but, above all, a deeply experienced fisherman with a keen interest in the science of fishing. He was hired by the U.S. Fish and Wildlife Service to work in Pascagoula, Mississippi, to advise on improving shrimp fishing in the Gulf. The cod were gone from Provincetown, and Dodie was eager to take the children away from Jack's domain.

Jack had learned to survive without alcohol but not without a woman, and he began in his own awkward but direct way to acquire a companion. He appears briefly as an angry solitary figure striding menacingly through the woods and swamps in Mary McCarthy's acid-bath semifictional portrait of Wellfleet and Truro, *A Charmed Life*, which she wrote in 1955 after marrying Bowden Broadwater, who worked as a fact-checker at *The New Yorker* and had been a favorite teacher of Reuel's at St. Bernard's School in New York. Of all places they could have chosen to live, they chose an old 1751 farmhouse and studio formerly owned by the painter Ann Sayre. The man she had left for Bowden, Edmund Wilson, lived less than half a mile away, and their unfinished relationship furnished the core of her novel.

Americans had witnessed the complete surrender of a civilized country to barbarism and were now to witness the rise of an almost parallel system in Russia, which was clearly violating the Allies' common pledge as set forth in FDR's "Four Freedoms" speech, establishing postwar democratic regimes in the former Nazi-controlled countries of Lithuania, Estonia, Latvia, East Germany, Poland, Hungary, Czechoslovakia, Romania, Bulgaria, Albania, and Yugoslavia. Each was swiftly and brutally absorbed into the new USSR, and by 1948 Soviet forces or fifth columns were threatening Allied-controlled Greece, Turkey, and Iran.

America's war had two important effects on the bohemian Left. The first was positive: the G.I. Bill and low-rate Veterans Administration mortgages permitted America to produce a new class of home-owning, educated working men and women from almost all ethnic and religious sectors, a democratic victory that the progressive socialists and communists alike had yearned for. The second, however, was that given the enormous wealth and power of postwar America, even the most dedicated on the Left realized that "revolutionary" change was now almost impossible.

In 1955, Dodie abruptly abandoned Pascagoula, Khaki, and her children. With nothing but her old small suitcase, she moved to the jazz harpist Daphne Hellman's house in Truro for the winter and then to New York City. Every year seemed to bring a new job, including a stint in VISTA on a Native American reservation in Oklahoma and then two years in the Philippines in the Peace Corps. There was a brief marriage to the man she had fallen in love with so many years earlier, while fellow counselors at Camp Treetops in the 1930s. In summers, she pitched a tent on one of Boston's Harbor Islands, where she camped on the beach and cut paths through the woods. She often returned to the Cape to stay with old friends, like Hutch Hapgood's daughter-in-law, Tam Hapgood, Tiny Worthington, Joan Colebrook, and Daphne Hellman. Her spirit was still unbroken at her death in 2011. She knew she would finally meet Mr. Emerson, the only man who had never failed her.

PART III

FALL

14.

TIGER CAT

After a year of anger over the divorce with Dodie and her gaining custody of their three children, Jack Hall began to search for a mate. While still dependent to a degree on a family trust, he was now earning a living as a builder and designer, working with Jack Phillips and Hayden Walling on semi-modernist buildings around Phillips's ponds or with a growing number of his own clients. He found himself somewhat constrained by his lack of an architectural license, but he had no wish to go back to school for three years, and his clients didn't care, plus any number of his architect friends were willing to stamp his drawings for the building inspector.

The Baker farm no longer interested him, containing too many ghosts of his failed marriages to Cammie and Dodie.

He tried romances with a number of local ladies beginning with Eben Given's reclusive sister, Thelma, who after a short, brilliant international career as a violinist had suddenly abandoned it to live with her mother in Provincetown; then with Phyllis Duganne's daughter from an earlier marriage, Jane Parker. Eventually, Jack found his way to his newly divorced neighbor on Bound Brook Island, Joan Clark, but her two young children quickly reminded him of his failures as a parent to his own three.

And so, in 1947 he married arguably the very worst mate possible, Jean Shay.

Jean, now thirty-two and tomboyishly pretty with a mop of blond curls, was provocative, angry, and a full-fledged alcoholic. Her anger was rightfully earned given her mother's abandonment of her when she was six, leaving her with her alcoholic father Frank, who loved her but was fully aware of his failures and attempted to farm her out to various friends, including Mary Heaton Vorse and Phyllis Duganne. But her wild rages and constant attempts to run away were too much for both, given their own parenting problems. Frank was what we now call a functioning alcoholic—still a tall, handsome, vigorous man who always had a new writing project in hand, whether it be a collection of sea chanteys or a history of the Cape, as well as a large vegetable garden, but he was almost always drunk by nightfall.

Frank and Edy Foley had married in 1930 and bought their house on Mill Hill Road in Wellfleet in 1938, where Jack always found a welcome amid their cluttered living room, hung with paintings by Dickinson, Charles Kaeselau, and other Provincetown painters and books that Edy had written with her closest friend, Katy Dos Passos, such as *Down the Cape* (1936) and *The Private Adventure of Captain Shaw* (1945). Jean led an independent life and became a skilled black-and-white photographer under the tutelage of Sid Grossman, the charismatic founder of the Photo League, later exposed as a radical communist front. Sid, whom everyone adored, ran the league's school in New York and in Provincetown in the summers. He was perhaps as close to a father figure as Jean had found.

She had managed to reestablish a relationship after a wild period with her father and with her stepmother, Edy Foley Shay, as well as her aunt Pat Foley, now married to the painter Edwin Dickinson.

Jean and Jack both had a deep love for the Cape's bohemian world and wide acquaintanceships within it and also a mutual love of the arts—she photography and now his serious progress as both a painter and a designer—and finally in very strong allegiances to the Left, even though Jack had become disillusioned with Stalin. Unfortunately, what they shared was outweighed by their depressive personalities, fueled by increasing drinking and Jean's abysmal parenting after Jack regained custody of his children.

Jean Shay and Jack Hall, modern house, Bound Brook Island, ca. 1950

Having lost interest in the farm and eager to build a truly modernist house on the island, Jack had teamed up with a young New York architect who summered in Provincetown, Warren Nardin, whose wife, Gloria Vinci, was a gifted photographer and fellow acolyte of Sid Grossman's. Nardin had redesigned one of Jack Phillips's pond houses and hired Jack as a designer in his New York office, thus beginning his New York career as a successful, albeit unlicensed, architect. They selected a plot on one of the high bluffs overlooking Duck Harbor adjacent to the Baker farm, which was now for sale. They erected a sprawling, clean-lined house with the first "butterfly," or double triangle, roof in North America.

As soon as the new house was roughly habitable, Jack and Jean began to rent the Baker farm to Francis and Katherine Biddle, Philadelphia aristocracy who had first come to the Cape to visit Francis's brother George, who had purchased an old farm in nearby Truro.

The Biddles were aristocratic. Francis's family dated back to Quaker settlers who made an earlier trading fortune and founded the largest bank in America, which President Andrew Jackson transformed into our first national bank in a series of highly partisan litigations with Nicholas Biddle, the head of the private bank. Katherine came from an equally prominent New York family, her full name being Katherine Garrison Chapin. Her family had founded two of America's leading girls' schools, Chapin in New York and Garrison Forest in Maryland. She was a respected and widely published poet whose poems had been turned into lyrics for songs sung by Marian Anderson and Paul Robeson. She had vigorously supported both artists when their public performances were banned by government officials who adhered to Jim Crow restrictions.

Jack finally sold the farm to them almost fully furnished, complete with his family rugs and furniture so he could start fresh with sleek blond Scandinavian modern furnishings in their new modern house.

When Jack regained custody of his children, the Biddles' home became a refuge for the children from Jean's drunken rages, because they knew they would find a warm welcome at their old home from Katherine and her two Irish maids.

As luck would have it, the Biddles were huge fans of amateur theatricals and of group readings of books and poems, which helped to form a bond with the much younger Halls. Jean had performed in many plays both at the Provincetown Players in New York and at her father's Provincetown Barnstormers' Theater as an adolescent, and Jack, while normally shy, had a suppressed thespian side.

Once settled on the farm, Katherine Biddle invited Saint-John Perse to stay with them. Perse had been exiled from Vichy, France, for his anti-Nazi politics during the war and had moved to Washington, D.C. The handsome beret-clad poet's romantic presence on the island had captured both Biddles' affection. During his stay he was photographed by Jean Shay and painted by Jack, whose own beret wearing might indeed have been inspired by Perse. Francis Biddle was to later help obtain Perse a position at the Library of Congress. Perse won the Nobel Prize in Literature in 1960.

Jack and Jean were hardly alone among their friends in allowing alcohol to erode professional promise and domestic happiness. The bohemians, much like the Greeks and Romans, worshipped many gods and muses, but among them Bacchus was the most frequently honored. Alcohol has always been known to lower inhibitions, and Freud, whom everyone was reading, had identified inhibition as the suspect guardian of the libido and sexual arousal. So alcohol became the favored fuel for the bohemians' pursuit of sexual adventures and creativity, while providing the added frisson of anti-authoritarianism during Prohibition.

Provincetown, like most seaports, had always been a drinking town and was conveniently a long way from Boston and the federal Prohibition enforcement agents. Rendezvous with Canadian rumrunners' speedboats at night off Provincetown were fairly easy. There was a town joke that if the fisherman one saw rowing out easily to the harbor's Long Point seemed to be struggling on his return even with an empty dory, he was probably dragging a full net of Canadian whiskey.

Jack and Dodie's friend Manuel "Manny" (born Nasciamento) Zora became a legendary Provincetown rumrunner during Prohibition. His boat, the *Mary Ellen*, was never captured by the coast guard, who gave him the mythical name the Sea Fox. Zora was born in Portugal and came to Provincetown at thirteen in 1908 and soon became known as the strongest dory rower in town. His Prohibition escapades later became the subject of a feature film and book (Scott Corbett's *Sea Fox* from 1956). Manny was catnip to women, and his huge hands, deeply tanned and carved features, and charisma ensured many liaisons with visiting bohemian ladies, finally ending with his marriage to the former *Masses* editor Berkeley Tobey's beautiful artist daughter, Judy. Judy had first come to Provincetown as an actress. A photograph of Manny in his role as a fisherman in Arthur Robinson's play *Fish for Friday* adorned the walls of all the popular bars and restaurants. It was not difficult to see why he became Khaki Captiva's role model.

In one famed Portuguese harbor story, Manny and his cousin Picana had taken the *Mary Ellen* beyond the twelve-nautical-mile U.S. jurisdiction for a dangerous rendezvous with a Canadian rumrunner off Race Point. They ran straight into an enormous storm whose waves topped their boat. His cousin sank to his knees and cried to the heavens, "It was not I, God. It is he, Manuelo, who did this bad thing!" For years these words were yelled to Picana from every Portuguese boat in Provincetown.

Manny was a devoted member of the Progressive Party and had campaigned for Henry Wallace, often introducing him at events. At a 1944 Wallace rally in Boston, after a man accused Wallace of having no working men in the party, Manny slowly rose and, displaying his huge, callused hands, said, "Look at these hands . . . and repeat: there are no laboring men in the Progressive Party!" Manny was one of the few Portuguese members of the Beachcombers' Club, and his friends included everyone from Burl Ives to Norman Mailer. Jack Hall painted his portrait cutting codfish.

The favored watering hole of 1930s bohemians, both during and after Prohibition, was the Flagship, a low-slung shingled building on its own pier extending into the harbor opposite the Art Association that was famed for its "Zombie" cocktails, and with Marvin Waldman, Jack's former gardener, at the piano. Its competitor, the Sixes and Sevens club, had reclaimed the old fish house on Mary Vorse's wharf, once used by the Provincetown Players. It was probably the first real nightclub in Provincetown and was jammed most evenings to hear a jazz band, which included two painters, Jerry Farnsworth and Courtney Allen, both club founders.

While not open to the public, the Beachcombers' clubhouse, the "Hulk" next to the Flagship, provided generous alcohol to its two hundred members every Saturday night starting at 6:00. Founded in 1916, it had an impressive list of members: Bill L'Engle, Eugene O'Neill, Charles Hawthorne, Philip Malicoat, Edwin Dickinson, John Dos Passos, and some of Dodie's new North Truro friends, John Kieran and Henry Morgan, then both celebrated radio and television commentators, along with the *New Yorker* cartoonist Jack Markow.

Almost every Provincetown diary of the period is filled with tales of parties built around the host's home-brewed alcohol. In addition to home stills, almost every couple either knew a bootlegger or had their own makeshift still. The favored Provincetown bootlegger named Clays was famous for his orange-peel alky (orange rind and pure alcohol); Edmund Wilson included him in his great critical work, *Axel's Castle*. At the Smooley, the shared house of Katy Dos Passos, her brother Bill Smith, and the Foley sisters, their still, named "the Boy," was a legend among the young.

Drinking, which had been primarily a male pastime, became a mixed sport, with women more than welcome in any speakeasy, and by 1933

America, still under Prohibition, was consuming more alcohol than any other country in the world. President Franklin Roosevelt both before and throughout his presidency quite openly enjoyed a scotch at lunch and later as many as four old-fashioneds during the cocktail hour while smoking packs of Camels in his jaunty cigarette holder.

Edmund Wilson was an admirer of Bubs and Chauncey Hackett's pure alcohol cocktails. He and everyone he knew sought invitations to Niles and Betty Spencer's house on Commercial Street to imbibe Betty's bottles of their lethal home-brewed "Tiger Cat" alcohol, with its hand-designed labels. Niles was a gifted painter and heir to Rhode Island's historic Slater Mill, the first American textile factory. He had gone to RISD and later studied with George Bellows and Robert Henri but seldom showed his work. Betty, also a painter, was attractive and sociable, often seen in Harlem jazz clubs escorted by Paul Robeson.

Wilson memorialized a cocktail party at the Spencers' in July 1930 to which he had brought his then wife, Margaret Canby, from their rented coast guard boathouse. Among the guests choking down Betty's Tiger Cat cocktails assembled on the Spencers' porch overlooking Provincetown Harbor were Susan Glaspell, Mary Heaton Vorse, and Katy Dos Passos. After dinner Betty began to criticize those bohemians who had abandoned Provincetown for Truro and Wellfleet, including the L'Engles; Katy was not a target because she had retained the Smooley as her and Dos's main residence. As the Tiger Cat began to take its toll, one by one the guests staggered home, including the Wilsons, with Edmund bellowing out "Cocktails for Two" for the town's benefit. He knew he would not be alone in recording the evenings' proceedings in his "Nocturnal Diaries."

Some bohemians drank for both social and professional reasons. Most writers and painters revered alcohol as a muse without whom they were often at a loss for inspiration. Drink was regarded as the bringer of both jollity and creativity. Reed, Jig Cook, Dos Passos, Wilson, Hemingway, Fitzgerald, Tennessee Williams, Mailer, and many others established a daily regimen they believed inspired their best work. Most often it required a table with a Remington typewriter and an ashtray and a pack of cigarettes on one side (Lucky Strikes were ten cents a pack) and a bottle and glass on the other. As they reached the bottom of a page or the end of a paragraph, they alternated a drag from the cigarette or a gulp from the glass as the other hand pushed the typewriter's carriage bar to the ringing left. This rhythm often became a ritual that led to serious writer's block when attempts at sobriety were made.

Indeed, alcohol was the ruin of many a young bohemian's promise, including that of Jack Hall's new father-in-law, Frank Shay, and his old Greenwich Village pal the poet Harry Kemp, now the Provincetown town crier, wandering through town dressed in a shabby Pilgrim costume and bumming drinks from tourists. A very few artists and writers, like O'Neill, could abstain while working. O'Neill believed nothing he wrote while drinking was worthy and held strong views on sobriety while writing: "The artist drinks, when he drinks at all, for relaxation, forgetfulness, excitement, for any purpose except for his art. . . . You've got to have all your critical and creative faculties about you when you're working. . . . I never try to write a line when I'm not strictly on the wagon. I don't think anything worth reading was ever written by anyone who was drunk or even half drunk when he wrote it!" Sadly, most deluded themselves that alcohol was their friend. Tennessee Williams lived in Provincetown for long periods from 1940 to 1947, where he wrote some of his greatest work, became a functioning alcoholic, and at last was comfortably gay, but his work did not improve over time.

Wilson, regardless of the prior evening's debauchery, would arise and go immediately to his desk, usually unshaven and in his bathrobe. He only broke for a sandwich at lunch and then, as evening approached, he would shave, brush his teeth with his washcloth (a habit inherited from his father), and don a white shirt, tie, and jacket or suit depending on the evening. He would then proceed to drink a bottle of whiskey through the evening, in addition to a bottle of wine with dinner, and would sustain the same routine seven days per week. While Wilson could maintain this pace through almost fifty years, other close friends like Scott Fitzgerald could not. Scotty's work diminished before his death at forty-four, and Wilson noted in his diary that during their friendship he might have written more for Scott's approval than his own. Wilson felt a similar sense of loss when Dos Passos left the Cape after Katy's death.

Wilson's regimen was chronicled by his longtime friend Adelaide Walker as his marriage to Mary McCarthy disintegrated: "Edmund certainly had an alcohol problem, which is no secret to anybody. But it's extraordinary in that he's the only person I've ever known who can drink and then turn out first-rate work. . . . He'd finish a piece of work and start drinking in a highly civilized way and then just go on and on. He'd drink everything in the house. That would last sometimes for several days and he'd go to bed and be sick, and then wouldn't drink for a fairly long time." Wilson's children observed with fear his "water glass" at the dinner table filled to the top with gin, but for him the day's work had been accomplished.

Robert Nathan (1894–1985)

Not far away from the Wilson's in Truro, a weekend guest was having his own battle with alcohol. Charles Jackson, already a raging alcoholic, was staying with the bestselling novelist Robert Nathan, author of *Portrait of Jennie*, on his estate near Truro Center. At the close of the visit, Nathan asked Harl Cook to drive Jackson to Provincetown to catch his train, but instead Harl took him bar crawling and put him hopelessly drunk on the last train. Later, during a brief period of sobriety, Jackson revisited that weekend in his final novel, *The Lost Weekend*. It became not only a bestseller but an equally famous film. In a rare, raw, and honest portrait of a drunk, Ray Milland played Jackson in a scene in which the bartender describes him as a man whom one drink made drunk and yet a hundred were not enough.

Charles Hawthorne had observed the effect of alcoholism on his students and on Provincetown itself. He watched as the Victorian Provincetown he came to in 1898 became a tourist-dependent town whose main attractions were no longer fishermen and artists but its access to rumrunners. By the time he turned his classes and studio over to Hans Hofmann in 1934, Provincetown had become a much rowdier and alcohol-drenched town. The painters who came to study with Hofmann were mainly funded by the WPA's Federal Art Project or later the G.I. Bill, so money for liquor was readily available. A bottle of beer was five cents and a quart of Kentucky straight whiskey $1.50. For painters like Jackson Pollock, Barnett Newman, Mark Rothko, Franz Kline, and Willem de Kooning, drinking was combined with work much the same as for writers, particularly those who chose to work at night. The bottle and ashtray stood on their palette table above a paint-splattered, cigarette-littered floor. It's a wonder that they weren't all incinerated, given the flammables in their crowded studios. If they weren't drinking in their studios, they were in the Flagship or the Atlantic House in Provincetown or the Cedar Tavern on West Eighth Street in the Village, all favored artists' "strutting ground."

These were, of course, the lucky ones who either were able to stop drinking or never used alcohol as a source of creativity.

Slater Brown, E. E. Cummings's old drinking pal from *The Enormous Room* and the 1920s Village, had pretty much destroyed his promise by age fifty, marrying and then abandoning wives and children—first running off with O'Neill's stage director Jimmy Light's wife, Susan Jenkins, then leaving her and their son. Edmund Wilson discovered Brown in bed with his actress wife, Mary Blair. Dos Passos included him as a seducer fleeing an angry husband in *Manhattan Transfer*. He married again to a photographer who took their daughter to Provincetown and opened a highly regarded nursery school. He would occasionally visit drunk, mainly to see his old Village pals, the Wilsons, Dos Passos, and Bubs and

Slater Brown, almost one hundred years old

Chauncey Hackett. Dodie Hall remembered him making a pass at her on one of those visits while in the Truro Post Office.

In his fiftieth year he met Henry James's deaf and very wealthy grand-niece Mary James, whose sister Louisa was married to Alexander Calder. He stopped drinking entirely and lived another fifty years, dying at one hundred.

As Jack Hall's marriage to Jean spiraled out of control, he swore to also stop drinking. Before he regained his sobriety, Mary McCarthy noted in a 1954 letter to her son, Reuel, while she was living in Wellfleet and married to Bowden Broadwater, "It seems there was a fairly wild beach picnic graced by the presence of Jack Hall who is drinking again after fifteen years since Jean Hall has left him and moved in with Mr. Loesser. Ruth [Jencks] is in a terrific state of alarm about this. The next day after the beach party . . . there was a cocktail party at Janet Aaron's [Daniel Aaron's wife]. . . . Ruth's eyes were bulging over Jack Hall's 'look,' she kept whispering 'he's helping himself to a drink.'" Jack began a painful journey through various "methods" from religion to quacks. He finally came to Bill W. and Alcoholics Anonymous in August 1954 after a horrendous monthlong bender in which he painted a frightening self-portrait that would have seemed familiar to Charles Jackson. He never, ever drank again.

Jean ran off with their married neighbor Bob Loesser, who had purchased Sonia Brown's harbormaster's house, and before she left, Jean took all the children's toys and clothes to the town dump in anger over Dodie's having re-won custody.

She soon left Loesser, obtained a Juárez, Mexico, divorce from Jack, and joined AA herself. She slowly repaired her relationship with both Jack and his children and began a successful career as a publicist in New York. Jean developed lung cancer from her years of chain-smoking and died alone in her apartment surrounded by the paintings she had inherited by Dickinson, the L'Engles, and Karl Knaths as well as the letters and books her father had written or published with O'Neill, St. Vincent Millay, and Dos Passos and the books her stepmother had co-written with Katy. All were looted from her apartment after her death and would often appear at auction with no family to claim them.

15.

THE ABSTRACTORS

Hans Hofmann (center), Friday critique, Provincetown, 1948

n 1934 the torch of explorative American painting, which had been lit
in Provincetown at Charles Hawthorne's 1899 Cape Cod School of
Art, was passed to Hans Hofmann. Hawthorne, the charismatic Yankee, had presided over America's adoption of European modernism after
the revelatory 1913 Armory Show. Hofmann, the equally charismatic
German Jew, was to preside instead over a uniquely American school of
painting: abstract expressionism, or, as Europeans were later to refer to
it, the New York school. All their students were among America's most

talented. Hofmann's students no longer painted in plein air on the rotting harbor wharves as Hawthorne's had, but now worked in Hawthorne's old Miller Hill studio.

The two teachers had observed World War I from opposite sides and then later assisted their students' struggle to recover from the trauma of both the war and then the Depression, which gave rise to the election of Roosevelt in America in 1932 and Hitler the next year in Germany.

Hofmann and his wife, Miz, also a painter, had established their successful Bavarian School of Painting in Germany in 1915. He had created a large circle of European artist friends while he lived in Paris, including Picasso, Matisse, Braque, and Kandinsky. In 1932, Hofmann was invited to teach at UC Berkeley and a year later received an urgent telegram from Miz warning him not to return because Hitler had been elected chancellor. He obeyed and went instead to New York, first to teach at the Art Students League, then to open his own school there and in Provincetown. Miz was finally able to join him in 1939 amid the huge transatlantic migration of Germany's Jewish intellectuals.

Hans and Miz soon became a centerpiece of the Provincetown landscape. As the school flourished, he bought the Miller Hill studio from Hawthorne and later acquired Waughville from the marine painter Frederick "Wizard" Waugh, which permitted Hofmann to give up the cramped hot Days Lumberyard studio Fritz Bultman had lent him. Fritz had initially studied with Hofmann in Bavaria and boarded with Miz and remained an intimate friend.

Hofmann was a beautiful, towering monster of a man, almost completely deaf and never appearing to teach or speak in English. Once he encountered a fellow European émigré painter, Boris Margo, on the street in Provincetown. Margo's studio was a dune shack on the Atlantic side. Boris proudly shouted to Hans that he had finally bought a Jeep to transport him and his paintings over the dunes. Hofmann, puzzled, responded, "A sheep? Better, a goat!"

The Hofmanns stayed in Provincetown from May to October and often longer. There Hans dominated his classes with his massive presence— gesturing wildly with his huge hands while totally concentrating on his students' work, be they gifted or not. He was possessed of enormous

Fritz Bultman in his studio, ca. 1947
(Maurice Berezov Photograph, © A.E. Artworks, LLC)

vitality, arising at 5:00 a.m. each day to paint for five hours before his grueling teaching day began. After teaching, he would often return to his studio to paint again until dinner.

His English never became fully coherent, and as he turned off his hearing aid during his classes, he depended almost entirely on gesture and imagining his students' responses to his questions. Joan Mitchell, the gifted second-generation abstract painter, had longed to study with Hans but fled terrified after one class because she couldn't understand a word. His enthusiasm for exploring color was immense, and his students soon treated him as an all-knowing god, even though he rarely showed or seemed to have interest in advancing his own reputation as a painter.

It is said that there was no major abstract painter (or critic) who had not, at some point, attended Hofmann's legendary Friday afternoon student critiques. Certainly, critics like Clement Greenberg and former students like Joseph Stella believed so.

Josef and Anni Albers aboard the S.S. Europa *to New York,
en route to Black Mountain College, November 25, 1933*

In 1933, Hofmann had given a seminal talk in New York on his theory of the "plasticity" between the paint and the surface. Hofmann insisted that painting should have a third dimension and be liberated from a flat surface. It was attended by a group of young painters now with some money to live on, thanks to George Biddle's WPA Federal Art Project—Arshile Gorky, Willem de Kooning, and Jackson Pollock—and the two leading rival critics of abstract painting, Clement Greenberg and Harold Rosenberg. The deep impression Hofmann made on the audience led to an annual summer pilgrimage of the most talented artists in America to study with him. Hans reached out to painters he most admired to staff his early courses. First came Josef Albers, who had fled Germany after the closing of the Bauhaus in 1933 to teach at the newly founded Black Mountain College in North Carolina. Hans then added Adolph Gottlieb, the American-born abstract expressionist. Others soon followed. In 1935, Lee Krasner brought her lover Jackson Pollock to join her in Hofmann's classes, and Arshile Gorky was brought by his lover at the time, who was also a painter. The two couples rented a cabin for seven dollars per week and did nothing but paint and swim in the nude.

Those interwar years were shaped by radical politics, poverty, and the Freudian or Jungian examination of self. Painting became both political and personal as artists abandoned the School of Paris in which images were still visible in the works of Picasso, Braque, and their colleagues for a new, unknown land in which there were no images, no galleries, no critics, no patrons, and certainly no accepted standards for their totally nonrepresentational work.

In 1935, George Biddle had approached FDR through Harry Hopkins and urged Roosevelt, playing on their Groton and Harvard friendship, to establish an adjunct program within the newly formed Works Progress Administration to fund artists to create paintings and murals to decorate the proposed New Deal's public building program, including libraries, post offices, schools, and federal buildings. Roosevelt had agreed and appointed Biddle the first director of the Federal Art Project, which at its height in 1942 employed more than five thousand artists, including Thomas Hart Benton and his young protégés Ben Shahn, Jackson Pollock, Gorky, Rothko, Jack Tworkov, Niles Spencer, and countless others.

George, like his brother Francis, had gone to Harvard Law School, but quickly realized that his true calling was art. He studied at the Académie Julian in Paris, with Bill and Brownie L'Engle, in Madrid (Velázquez), and in Munich (Rubens) but, like the L'Engles, departed Paris as the Germans invaded and upon his return home enlisted, seeing serious combat. World War I changed him, as it had his other Cape friends, Dos Passos and Dickinson. He wandered for a while, living in Tahiti and then Mexico with his third wife, Hélène. There they became close to Diego Rivera and the Mexican revolutionary muralists who influenced his later FAP decision to enlist other Left bohemian figurative painters, including Benton and Grant Wood, as muralists. During this period, Biddle moved further to the left and created his own murals: *The Tenement*, for the Justice Department in Washington, and a series based on DuBose Heyward and George Gershwin's *Porgy and Bess* (Biddle had become deeply affected by the plight of Black people in the Jim Crow South).

The FAP salary was $23.52 per week in return for, in most cases, a painting every four to six weeks. A department store clerk who worked a fifty-hour week was lucky to earn $20. With their new riches, the FAP artists in the 1930s had been able to rent real studio space and buy groceries, paints, and booze. Indeed, the reputation of the New York school as swaggering alcoholic womanizers began with the largesse of the FAP. Sadly, this cultural paradise ended in 1943 when right-wing members of Congress demanded FDR fire Biddle and disband the FAP as an alleged "front" for communists, deviants, and Jews. Fortunately for these young artists, the war economy was now easing the Depression and creating a massive industrial culture that would propel America into position as the richest country in the world.

The bohemians knew all too well about Hitler's conflation of "modern art" and "Jewish art," but not so much about Stalin's. Unlike Hitler's, the Soviet prejudice was less ethnic than class based—that is, the party under both Lenin and Stalin wanted pictures of "tractors" not abstraction, but they couldn't care less if a Jew painted the tractor.

Shortly after he came to power, Lenin chillingly expressed his views: "I'm no good at art. Art for me is just an appendage and when its use as propaganda—which we need at the moment—is over, we'll cut it out as useless: snip, snip!" Lenin's dogma set the stage for the demise of Soviet abstraction. On April 23, 1932, Stalin's Central Committee declared that art must rigidly serve the revolution by only being realistic, optimistic, and heroic. This meant either death, submission, or emigration for the most daring artists of the revolution. Kandinsky and Chagall fled; Malevich, who had proclaimed, "Objective representation . . . has nothing to do with art. Objectivity is meaningless," submitted; and most of the modernist abstract futurists and constructivists were either tortured, sent to the gulag, or starved.

Safe in New York and Provincetown, painters and critics could afford more unfettered arguments about Stalin's directives. What had once been a rather unified artists' community in Greenwich Village and Provincetown was now being pulled in opposite directions by the teachings of Marx and Freud.

In 1936, the critic Meyer Schapiro wrote in the *Marxist Quarterly* that the proper role of the artist should be asking questions about the impoverished masses and oppressed minorities and clearly implied that abstraction was "unconstrained egotism" and thus not worthy of a "Comrade."[1] The Stalinist school of painters, desperately wishing to be considered comrades, began criticizing the abstract painters' false struggles for "originality" and celebrated their Stalinist loyalty to "social realism." These comrades included FAP painters such as Thomas Benton, Grant Wood, Ben Shahn, the Soyer brothers, and indeed the FAP director himself, George Biddle.

Stuart Davis later bluntly summed up these culture wars: "In 1934 I became socially conscious, as everyone else was in those days . . . this meant meetings, articles, picket lines, internal squabbles. . . . Lots of work was done but little painting."[2] Davis had been impressed by Theodore Dreiser's 1935 American Writers Congress, which was dedicated to "the struggle against war, the preservation of civil liberties and the destruction of fascist tendencies everywhere." Attendees included many communist sympathizers: Waldo Frank; Erskine Caldwell, the author of *Tobacco Road*; Josephine Herbst; and Malcolm Cowley.

The artists decided to organize a similar conference, and a rowdy group of 360 led by Davis and Niles Spencer (both Stalinists) met in February at New York's Town Hall for what they titled the American Artists Congress. Other pro-communist artists from abroad attended, including George Grosz and the Mexican muralist David Alfaro Siqueiros. Among the American attendees were Milton Avery, Adolph Gottlieb, Karl Knaths, Ben Shahn, Max Weber, and Isamu Noguchi.

These Soviet-style "Congresses" soon became an embarrassment to many like Malcolm Cowley as the news of Stalin's NKVD assassinations of socialists and anarchists in the Spanish Civil War's International Brigades, the Moscow purge trials, and the Molotov-Ribbentrop Pact cooled the ardor of many pro-Stalin intellectuals. A few, like Jack Tworkov, were able to remain Stalinist while pursuing abstract expressionism. Others, influenced by the triad of abstract critics (Greenberg, Schapiro, and Rosenberg), adopted Trotsky's Marxist position that the artist should be influenced neither by the bourgeois monetized marketplace nor by political pressure. Others, like Rothko (the only one born in Russian territory) and Barnett Newman, remained anarchists subject to no one's rules but their own—and thus were often starving.

Without definition or champions, abstract expressionism could have been another short-lived phenomenon like pop art or field-of-color painting, but it was fortunate to have attracted three of the most daring critics of the time, who fearlessly and with supreme self-confidence set out to define and support this new artistic endeavor.

Of the three, Clement Greenberg, the tough Yiddish-speaking self-proclaimed art critic, was perhaps the most influential and certainly spent the most time in Provincetown with Hofmann and his students. Greenberg (1909–1994) was honest about his lack of formal art training; he once said, "I do not deny being one of those critics who educate themselves in public."

Helen Frankenthaler in her studio, Provincetown, July 1950

He loved the bohemian world of Provincetown and the Village, with their partisan politics and easy morals. Married and divorced young, he was constantly in search of romantic partners, having an open affair with Mary McCarthy while she was married to Edmund Wilson, perhaps made easier by his having joined the *Partisan Review* as its art critic in

1940. Among his other lovers was Helen Frankenthaler, nineteen years younger and just beginning her career. Greenberg could be overbearing, hurtful, and unfaithful, but he was deeply loyal too and remained her life-long champion through her subsequent marriage to Robert Motherwell and beyond.

Greenberg could critique himself too. In a 1940 letter to a former Syracuse classmate and friend, Harold Lazarus, he wrote, "Yes, the honors pile. But I want gossip, sexual intrigue, back-biting and hair undoing. I want women, confidences, confessions & broken hearts. Dissipation, indiscretions, glitter, dash, sparkle, sin."

Greenberg certainly deserves credit for recognizing the latent talent of Jackson Pollock. Pollock, never a gifted draftsman, had spent much of the early 1930s as a struggling realist working under Thomas Hart Benton on WPA murals and other public works projects. An alcoholic, bisexual, and very angry young man, he became absolutely dependent on both Greenberg's and Hofmann's emotional support as he moved dangerously into unknown territory in his new "drip and spatter" work.

Greenberg's rival in the new world of so-called gestural self-expression was another New York Jewish seeker who had tried various professions before that of self-proclaimed art critic. Harold Rosenberg was born in Brooklyn and grew into a tall, striking hulk of a man with heavily furred brows and a full scalp of dark hair. Leaning on his cane, the result of a childhood leg disease, he was every bit as influential as Greenberg. Where Greenberg championed Pollock, de Kooning, and Hofmann, Rosenberg, who had also begun writing for the *Partisan Review* and later *The New Yorker*, was closer to Gorky, Franz Kline, and Motherwell.

Both worked the sawdust floors of their subjects' favorite watering spots, on the lookout for artists' confessions or romantic liaisons. They did not approach abstraction from the same perspective. Greenberg, cynical about the positive influence of politics on artistic work, believed the artist should devote his whole emotional being to the work at hand, while Rosenberg took a more Marxist approach, proclaiming the canvas was an "arena" in which the artist brought the conflict of the outside world of politics and the artists' own personal conflicts into palette combat. Of course, this led to partisanship. Barnett Newman, a close adherent of Rosenberg's viewpoint and an ardent anarchist, became famous for his tirade filmed in his studio by the young documentarian Emile de Antonio. When Clement Greenberg's name was mentioned (and Barnett had been drinking), he angrily responded, "Fucking Clement Greenberg . . . do you know critics have the same relevance to painters that ornithologists have to birds!" Of course, Newman had stolen and reworked the quotation from his anarchist hero Kropotkin.

Edwin Dickinson, Ross Moffett, and Karl Knaths
in front of the Provincetown Art Association, June 22, 1967

Artists and critics do not an audience make, and in order for the creators of abstract expressionism to actually make a living, it took two young women willing to risk opening a gallery to show their work and introduce them to potential patrons. The first was Peggy Guggenheim, who had opened her Art of This Century gallery in Manhattan in 1942 after fleeing France. The gallery's name was inspired by Samuel Beckett, then a lover, who urged her to be involved in the "art of her times." Her main interests were still cubism and surrealism, and much of what she exhibited was from her own collection. From late 1941, now married to Max Ernst, she collected heavily for the Guggenheim Museum, which was not to open until 1959. But she also dared to give the young Jackson Pollock his first show, and suddenly abstract painting was more important than the surrealists! Peggy also gave Hans Hofmann his first show in America at her gallery in 1944, when Hofmann was sixty-four, and despite the war it received praise from Greenberg and many others. Her other abstract gamble was on Robert Motherwell, whom she championed from his earliest work. The gallery closed in 1947 when Peggy returned to her palazzo in Venice.

Jackson Pollock at work, Springs, New York, 1949

Contrary to the version told earlier of Max Ernst and Matta's arrest in Wellfleet during the war, Charles Jencks, the architectural historian whose family's former army barrack was nearby, held to his own more contemporary version: Peggy, Ernst, and Pollock were staying one summer in Jack Phillips's Paper Palace. One night in the midst of a drinking bout, Ernst suggested they fill the candelabra dangling above the kitchen table with paints instead of candles and then rotate it wildly above a fresh canvas on the table—thus the birth of Pollock's "splatter" painting, according to Jencks.

Betty Parsons, the thirteen-year-old schoolgirl whose life was changed forever by the Armory Show, did not start her artistic life like Peggy's, collecting or exhibiting the works of others. Parsons was a trained painter whose work was widely respected before the Depression wiped out her family's money and she was forced to return from Europe and find work in New York. She was soon hired by several galleries for her keen eye for new talent. Although shy, Betty had a great gift for connecting buyers with work. In 1944 she was offered her own space, and in 1946 it was relocated to 15 East Fifty-Seventh Street and named the Betty Parsons Gallery, opening as Peggy Guggenheim was closing her own gallery on the same block.

Parsons quickly assumed responsibility for Pollock's career and those of Robert Rauschenberg, Mark Rothko, and Barnett Newman. Rothko and Newman worked for her for many years, helping to hang her shows. Helen Frankenthaler recalled, "Betty and her gallery helped construct the center of the art world. She was one of the last of her breed." In fact, she was, because better-funded dealers like Sam Kootz and Sidney Janis, having observed her successful advancement of the artists whose work she had championed, began to lure them away. Parsons was justifiably angry at these raids by better-funded dealers and saddened by the lack of loyalty from her artists from Pollock to Hofmann and others whose careers she had carefully nurtured. Still, she bravely continued to recruit and present a new generation of abstract artists until her death in 1982.

Actually, the post–World War II years in Provincetown produced a greater mix of artistic styles than had existed before the war. There was much more money in America and a greater common interest in the ideas being presented by writers, sculptors, photographers, and painters about the future of American culture and politics, not unlike the pre–World War I period of *The Masses* and *The Dial*.

Many artists were neither students of Hofmann's nor practitioners of abstract expressionism but working in adjacent studios, socializing, and enjoying nonaesthetic bonds of friendship, be they political or social.

Among the major non-abstract-expressionist painters on the Outer Cape during that period were Edwin Dickinson (1891–1978) in Wellfleet and Edward Hopper in Truro. There were many others, of course—Milton Avery, Ben Shahn, and George Biddle—but none who so depended on its unique light and solitude.

Dickinson, like his close friends Hawthorne and Hofmann, was a master teacher but preferred small groups of students and eschewed their bravura class performances. Only financially secure later in his life, he taught in order to survive until his extraordinary draftsmanship and depiction of a former America slowly drew critical attention. While his style was much more original than Hawthorne's, he took two things from Hawthorne: his "premier coup" style of painting—that is, doing the entire work in just one sitting—and his deep interest in the lives of his subjects, often Portuguese fishing families.

Dick, as he was called by his friends, and his wife and fellow Hawthorne student Pat Foley first lived in Provincetown before moving to Wellfleet. There they lived near starvation with their two children in a knocked-together studio on Chipman's Cove, surviving by raising chickens and forgoing a car, traveling to Wellfleet or Truro by foot or bicycle. Dickinson finally gained national recognition in 1943 when he brought his large unfinished painting *Ruin at Daphne*, an architectural fantasy, to New York to complete while he taught classes at the Art Students League and Cooper Union and Pat taught at Miss Hewitt's. Dick kept working on the painting (he never considered it finished) when it caught the eye of his friends Bill and Elaine de Kooning. Elaine began filming Dick working on the painting, and the black-and-white film, *Edwin Dickinson Paints a Picture*, became a legend. In 1954, *Ruin at Daphne* was sold to the Metropolitan Museum of Art, where it can be viewed in all its majesty as one of America's great mid-century works.

While shy and reclusive, Dickinson was considered charming by all, a description that could never have applied to his Truro neighbor Edward Hopper. Hopper was also shy and reclusive but would never dream of teaching and disliked any human contact unless totally on his terms. His long marriage to his diminutive wife, Jo Nivison, also a painter, was at best a James Thurber nightmare of a union, with constant fighting,

Edward Hopper in his studio, Truro

abusive behavior, and long periods of angry silence. Dodie recalled Jo bursting into the Hoppers' neighbor Marie Stephens's house up the hill on Fisher Beach. Stephens, a niece of Scott Fitzgerald's, and Dodie tried to calm her because it was clear Jo had been severely battered. Finally soothed, Jo left, only to return with gifts of antique English plates to thank them for their comforting.

The Hoppers met as fellow painters do while painting and married on July 9, 1924, quite late in their lives. Jo was still a virgin at forty-one, and Ed's only contact with women had been an occasional prostitute. Neither drank alcohol, which severely reduced their social circle in bohemia, but both had already attained reputations as seriously dedicated artists. Jo was a foot and a half shorter than her towering six-foot-five beanpole of a husband and had grown up fierce, raised by her Irish immigrant mother. She quickly became one of the Village's "New Women," admiring Margaret Sanger and Marguerite Zorach. She was attuned to hard times and studied with those who examined them, including Reginald Marsh, John Sloan, and Robert Henri. Jo had contributed to *The Masses* and acted at the Liberal Club with Floyd Dell's Greenwich Village Players, so Provincetown was clearly meant for her. She had arrived alone in 1915 to work under the modernist landscape painter Ambrose Webster and kept returning, becoming friends with Jig Cook and Susan Glaspell, Mary Vorse and the Dos Passoses. She and Ed first worked together there in 1923 along with Charles Demuth, Marsden Hartley, and the Zorachs.

They returned again in 1930 to rent a cottage at the Cobb Farm in Truro. Truro then had only five hundred residents and no stores; you did your shopping in Wellfleet or Provincetown. Because Ed never learned to drive and neither had really learned to cook, they began a lifelong custom of buying canned goods to last the summer. They disliked renting, and in 1933, with Hopper's growing success, they were able to buy a steep slope fronting one thousand feet of bay shoreline at Fisher Beach and commissioned a house with a large studio for Ed but none for Jo. Their new house was near Jack Hall's farm on Bound Brook Island and the Dos Passoses' old farmhouse off Fisher Road. The L. D. Baker estate still owned much of this area, and it was his son who sold the land to the Hoppers.

The road to Hopper's property, Stephens Way, was steep and deeply rutted, and most strangers ended up needing a tow if they weren't careful. Other than the Stephenses and Dos Passoses, the Hoppers' neighbors included Leo and Ella Mielziner, a fascinating couple with two sons, Jo and Kenneth. Jo, who was already one of the most famous Broadway set designers of the century, and his brother, the actor Kenneth MacKenna, who had changed his name as so many Jewish actors did, were often in residence. Given Hopper's open anti-Semitism it was an odd friendship but became an intellectually important one, because Jo Mielziner's sets for Elmer Rice's *Street Scene*, a huge Broadway success in 1929, were the inspiration for Hopper's masterwork, *Early Sunday Morning*.

The Hoppers entertained infrequently and parsimoniously—usually with old-school Provincetown painters like the Ambrose Websters; Edwin Dickinson; Ross Moffett and his wife, Dorothy Lake Gregory; Henry Varnum Poor; and the Dos Passoses. Jo Hopper had a crush on Katy Dos Passos, as many women did, and admired her jaunty ways and style and most of all her Siamese cat, Perkins, named after Dos's editor at

Scribner, Maxwell Perkins. The cat became a frequent and welcome guest at the Hoppers'. Ed rarely spoke, but Dos often joked that he had a feeling, just as they were leaving, that he might. When he did, it was unfortunately usually to complain about his treatment by critics and museums.

In 1939, the actress Helen Hayes and her producer husband, Charles MacArthur, commissioned Hopper to paint a picture of the old house they just bought in Nyack on the Hudson near Hopper's mother. After their first meeting Hayes, the most beautiful and thoughtful of actresses, wrote, "I had never met a more misanthropic, grumpy, grouchy individual in my life."[3]

Hopper angrily opposed FDR, the New Deal, and the WPA, often vilifying both the president and the artists who supported him. He voted for Wendell Willkie in 1940 but did serve as an air warden in Truro during the war and became increasingly interested in an Allied victory, but when FDR died in 1945, Jo wrote, "Nobody grief stricken here."[4]

Hopper found solace in writers who celebrated the simple agrarian America he had discovered in Truro—Emerson, Van Wyck Brooks, Robert Frost, and E. B. White. Dos Passos, who had grown increasingly grumpy and conservative after the war, suddenly found Hopper good company. Hopper and Jo were devastated to learn of Dos and Katy's terrible car accident in 1947 and attended Katy's funeral, which Edmund Wilson recorded so vividly in his diary.

Hopper was stung by Clement Greenberg's 1946 critique, classifying him as a photojournalist of painting à la Walker Evans. Greenberg had concluded, "Hopper simply happens to be a bad painter. But if he were a better painter, he would, most likely, not be so superior an artist." The deep wound of Greenberg's review was somewhat healed by Hopper's hugely successful one-man show at the Whitney in 1950, which drew twenty-four thousand, including the great architectural critic Lewis Mumford, who predicted that in twenty-five or fifty years Hopper would be "as famous as Van Gogh." Interestingly, Andrew Wyeth was also in attendance. If only three of his works were to survive, *Cape Cod Evening* (1939), *Gas* (1940), and *Nighthawks* (1942), no painter will have captured American loneliness as Hopper did. Despite his success, he and Jo continued to live frugally and angrily, constantly feuding with the Australian writer Joan Colebrook, now the owner of the Dos Passos house, over her refusal to allow a phone line to be run across her landscape to their house until 1954.

In the summer of 1949, Jack Hall's friend Fritz Bultman and his wife, Jeanne (formerly his model, and a lanky, former Minsky's Burlesque stripper), called to say they were organizing a series of discussions called "Forum 49" in Provincetown at Weldon Kees's Gallery 200, admission sixty cents. Each forum was packed, whether it was "What Is an Artist?," "French Art v. American Art," or panels on architecture, psychology, poetry, and jazz. The gallery was also showing the work of panelists including Bultman, Karl Knaths, Hofmann, and Adolph Gottlieb.

The opening July 7 panel, "What Is an Artist?," featured George Biddle, Hans Hofmann, Adolph Gottlieb, and Serge Chermayeff. At the panel, Gottlieb defended abstract painting thus: "The artist must take the risk of creating work that will not be recognized as art." The panel on politics was moderated by Dwight Macdonald, then publisher of *Politics*, and that on architecture featured Marcel Breuer and György Kepes. "French Art v. American Art" included Robert Motherwell, Karl Knaths, and Adolph Gottlieb, yet again, because Gottlieb was a close friend of the brilliant impresario Weldon Kees. The panel on poetry was moderated by Howard Nemerov and that on psychoanalysis featured Dr. Leo Spiegel, then the owner of Jack Phillips's Paper Palace on the Truro ocean beach where Pollock and Ernst had played with their spatter-painting candelabra. Spiegel's daughter, the acclaimed playwright Wendy Kesselman, now owns the house.

The panelists' collective emotions were summed up by Hofmann, who reminded the audience of the destruction of German culture in just a few years by fascism and warned of the looming danger of the HUAC hearings on American culture.

"Let us not forget the tragic past of the cultural pioneers of Modern Artistic America. They have been badly neglected, misunderstood, ridiculed and maliciously prosecuted as charlatans or fools or as Communists to the extent of a final personal catastrophe to the artist for many of them and a near-cultural collapse for this country."

Motherwell had accompanied Bill and Elaine de Kooning to the forum, and Bill wrote a glowing review of the proceedings for *ARTnews*.

Jack Hall and Jean Shay attended every evening, and both had work in Kees's gallery. Jack was now painting seriously and studying with Hofmann, Dickinson, and Xavier Gonzalez, the Spanish painter who had purchased a house in Wellfleet Center. Jean was excited by the number of great photographers, including Walker Evans and Robert Frank, who were now in Provincetown. Jack's final wife, Mardi Hall (married to Rhodes Hall at the time), was also in attendance, and she and her best friend in Provincetown, the primitive painter Bubs Hackett, also had work in Kees's gallery.

This heady mix of the country's leading artists, star architects of the Bauhaus movement who were now beginning to erect their low-slung houses around Jack Phillips's ponds, and other intellectuals from the major ranks of poets, writers, and critics suddenly made Provincetown a Paris, where you might find Tennessee Williams, Walter Gropius, or John Ashbery sitting next to you at the bar.

The 1950s marked the culmination of Hofmann's teaching; his earliest students were now the established masters of the abstract movement— Gorky, de Kooning, Rothko, Gottlieb, and Pollock—and being joined by a second generation, including Motherwell, his new wife, Helen Frankenthaler, Franz Kline, Rauschenberg, and Larry Rivers.

Motherwell, the son of the president of the Wells Fargo bank, had grown up wealthy and extremely well educated. His sophistication and financial security aroused envy even among his closest friends like Rothko and de Kooning, but his charm, loyalty to fellow artists, and dedication to his craft always trumped envy. A social animal, he gave glamorous and memorable dinner parties with Frankenthaler, filled with fascinating company dancing to Frank Sinatra on the phonograph. Motherwell lived well in Provincetown for forty years, driving his classic MG convertible, maintaining a town house in New York, and traveling widely. With

Hofmann's encouragement he had begun his large collage canvas series, *Elegies for the Spanish Republic*, which were to secure his place in American painting.

Motherwell championed original thinking and work and always remained proud of his fellow explorers of abstract painting. It was he who invented the term "the New York school." He said of their daring collective voyage to an unknown shore, "If the abstraction, the violence, the humanity was valid in Abstract Expressionism, then it cut out the ground from every other kind of painting." Reflecting on that journey after his one-person eighty-seven-canvas show at the MoMA in 1965, he said, "I suppose most of us felt that our passionate allegiance was not to American art or to any national art, but there was such a thing as modern art; that it was essentially international in character; that it was the greatest painting adventure of our time, that we wished to plant it here, that it would blossom in its own way."[5]

In 1958, at seventy-eight, Hans Hofmann was finally tiring of teaching and increasingly interested in devoting his remaining time to his own work. The students still came, but many were no longer interested in abstraction as much as in Hofmann's sense of color and self-introspection. His teaching assistants were now young enough to be his grandchildren; the German-born painter Wolf Kahn and the seventeen-year-old Paul Resika were some of the last generation of young Turks who were to carve out careers quite separate from those of Hofmann's past assistants.

In that last summer of 1958, his famed Friday afternoon critique was still jammed with students who arrived early to obtain seats as near Hofmann as possible. The room still fell silent as he entered in his formal costume of paint-spattered blue shirt, tan pants, and sandals. And, as in the past, as each student's work was presented, he examined it carefully before commenting. Often he illustrated how it might be improved by superimposing a large variety of colored paper fragments he kept for the purpose.

When he did comment it was pure Hofmann Zen: "Too heavy in every way. There is no area which offers rest. It is the sound of a trumpet. It is too loud," or "You must remember the difference between flatness and flatness" (the class clearly bewildered, Hans laughs). "I mean flatness in an empty sense and flatness in an enriched sense."[6])

That fall, the doors to the studio classroom closed. School was over, but what a class it had produced. Hans and Miz continued their morning harbor swims, and he rarely left his studio until his death in February 1966, at the age of eighty-five.

16.

THE CRIMES OF STALIN

"The Victory of Socialism in Our Country Is Guaranteed": Stalin stars in a 1932 poster.

Joseph Stalin

The narrow, sandy roads from Provincetown through Truro to Wellfleet were dotted with houses occupied by bohemians who had joined and then abandoned the Communist Party over the more than forty years of its American existence.

In Provincetown, John Dos Passos had left after his experience in Spain observing Stalin's NKVD at work. Mary Heaton Vorse, once a true believer, now clinging to the Marxist theories of the rights of labor but not supporting Stalinism, still remained loyal but increasingly distant from the party after World War II. She had invited Granville Hicks, then an ardent party member, to speak in Provincetown in 1936, but he was barred from using the town hall by the selectmen as a "Communist." Hicks, a respected literary critic, left the party in 1939, appalled by Stalin's Nazi-Soviet nonaggression pact. He wrote an article for *The Nation* titled "The Blind Alley of Marxism" in 1940 and voluntarily testified in the 1950s before HUAC.

In adjacent Truro, the Bauhaus émigré György Kepes's neighbor Boris Kaufman, the cinematographer, had finally escaped the blacklist. The Russian-born Kaufman's two brothers had remained in the Soviet Union after the revolution and became famous filmmakers, while Boris moved to Paris and served in the French army in World War II. When he arrived in America after the war, his birthplace and close relationship with his brothers immediately attracted the attention of the FBI and HUAC. He had trouble finding work until Elia Kazan hired him in 1954 to film *On the Waterfront*, for which he won an Academy Award for cinematography. The government relented in its surveillance of Kaufman only because Kazan had cooperated with HUAC by naming many colleagues as present or former party members. Kaufman went on to film many great films, including *Baby Doll* (1956), *12 Angry Men* (1957), *The Fugitive Kind* (1960), and *The Pawnbroker* (1964). He and his family continued to summer in Truro and kept in touch with his brothers in Russia, but he scrupulously avoided politics after 1954.

On Fisher Road, in the Dos Passoses' old farmhouse, Joan Colebrook had left the party and become an ardent anti-Stalinist. Colebrook, an Australian-born journalist and *New Yorker* writer, had been an enthusiastic party member both in Australia and in England until the Molotov-Ribbentrop Pact. During World War II she and her children were evacuated from London and arrived on the Cape in 1940. In 1941 she began renting Jo Mielziner's house, just above the Hoppers' house. She wrote a series of books examining the West's failure to grasp the extent of Stalin's plan for Soviet domination.

Mielziner was perhaps the most famous set designer of the twentieth century, having apprenticed with Bobby Jones during his staging of O'Neill's plays. Jo was particularly close to his Truro neighbor Eero Saarinen, and he and Saarinen co-designed the Vivian Beaumont Theater in Lincoln Center. He worked most closely with Tennessee Williams on many of his greatest plays, designing the sets for *A Streetcar Named Desire* (1947) and *Cat on a Hot Tin Roof* (1955).

Joan, who was thrice married and famous for her erotic connection to men, found the home she had longed for when Dos Passos agreed to sell her their small farmhouse next door to the Mielziners after Katy's death in 1947. She transformed the house and its garden and orchard into a center for fellow intellectuals and fierce anticommunists.

Joan's next-door neighbors, Bert and Ella Wolfe, had made the same journey from party to antiparty. Bert had first come to Provincetown as a young supporter of John Reed's splinter Communist Labor Party in 1919, then had gone to Mexico to live with Diego Rivera. Next he attended the 1928 Comintern conference in Moscow, where he supported Bukharin as Lenin's rightful successor, causing Stalin to later banish him from Russia. Wolfe then left the party to support Norman Thomas, the Socialist presidential candidate. He returned to Provincetown in 1940, and it was Wolfe who introduced Alfred Kazin to Mary McCarthy. While teaching at Harvard in 1948, Wolfe wrote the classic and much criticized Marxist group biography, *Three Who Made a Revolution: A Biographical History*, about Lenin, Trotsky, and Stalin.

In Wellfleet, Dorothy and Philip Sterling (born Schatz) had finally left the party. Sterling had begun his career in the Federal Writers' Project and later rose up as a CBS radio writer and public relations expert, producing major programs about Rachel Carson and the NAACP among others. His wife, Dorothy, worked for *Time* and *Life* from 1939 to 1949. Like her husband, she became deeply involved in the protests against the treatment of southern Black people and wrote extensively and well about their plight. Her 1958 book about Black civil rights workers, *Tender Warriors*, with photography by the party member Myron "Mike" Ehrenberg, won praise, and she later collaborated with her neighbor Winifred Lubell, who drew illustrations for Sterling's book *The Outer Lands*, about the Outer Cape.

Winifred and her husband, Cecil, were longtime party members who had moved to Wellfleet from Croton. Cecil had been subpoenaed before a Senate committee investigating potential communists in April 1956, where he took the Fifth but admitted his friendship with Mike Ehrenberg and Mike's brother-in-law, the Soviet spy Samuel Krafsur. Winifred, a gifted artist, had contributed illustrations for the *New Masses* and worked in the WPA. But both had become disillusioned, although a few of their friends remained party members.

The year 1952 was a dangerous one for bohemians who were either still in the party or close to those who were. The House Un-American Activities Committee was in full cry, seeking subpoenas for those in the cultural world of publishing, film, and theater. The Rosenbergs had been sentenced to death for their role in passing atomic secrets to the Russians, and Whittaker Chambers's memoir of his years in the party, *Witness*, had just been published, further encouraging Joseph McCarthy in his investigation of Reds in the State Department. Earlier McCarthy had infamously appeared on black-and-white television clutching a piece of paper and ominously claiming, "I have here in my hands a list of 205 names known to the secretary of state [Dean Acheson] as being members of the Communist Party who nevertheless are still working and shaping the policy of the State Department!"

Loyalty oaths (swearing to having no communist affiliation) were now required by most universities and public schools and even large corporations like CBS. Ike had defeated Stevenson thirty-three million to twenty-seven million, and John Foster Dulles had replaced Dean Acheson as secretary of state. More than a million homes had TV and could follow the McCarthy hearings as well as Liberace and *Victory at Sea*. In the movie theaters, people were watching *Viva Zapata!*, depicting an abortive Mexican revolution, starring Marlon Brando and Anthony Quinn, directed by Elia Kazan, now hated by the Left for "naming names" before HUAC the year before. Stalin's death on March 5, 1953, of a cerebral hemorrhage had no seeming effect on the growing wave of communist hysteria.

On Broadway, Lillian Hellman's *Children's Hour*, starring Patricia Neal, was controversial, given Hellman's testimony before HUAC, in which, unlike Kazan, she refused to name names and told the committee, "I cannot and will not cut my conscience to fit this year's fashion."

In Betty Parsons's and Peggy Guggenheim's galleries, one could view Willem de Kooning's *Woman I*, Mark Rothko's *Black, Pink, and Yellow*, and Adolph Gottlieb's *Unstill Life.* The Boston Museum of Fine Arts was holding a major show of the Bauhaus founder Walter Gropius's work.

Bohemians were reading Ralph Ellison's *Invisible Man*, Mary McCarthy's *Groves of Academe*, Bernard Malamud's *The Natural*, and David Riesman and Nathan Glazer's *Faces in the Crowd*; Archibald MacLeish was to win the Pulitzer for his *Collected Poems, 1917–1952.* The polio epidemic had stricken more than fifty thousand Americans before Dr. Jonas Salk created his miracle vaccine in 1954.

Huddled around the dining table in Jack Hall's new modern house on Bound Brook Island were Jack's wife, Jean Shay; the medical writer Charles Flato, barely three feet tall with his humped back, fedora, and cape out of Grimms' fairy tales, as well as his ever-present cane; his Horseleech Pond neighbor and patron, Luke Wilson, and his wife; and Sid Grossman, Jean's photography teacher and founder of the Photo League, which had just been labeled a communist front by HUAC and its members blacklisted.

Over drinks and cigarettes, the group wrestled with strategies for combating the continued "witch hunts" of party members by both the House and the Senate. Party members like themselves who heeded the directives from the "Nineteenth Floor" of the CPUSA's offices off Union Square, despite Stalin's purge of the early heroes of the revolution, including Trotsky, his controversial destruction of the socialist and anarchist forces in the Spanish Civil War, and his cynical Molotov-Ribbentrop Pact with Germany, which allowed Russia to destroy and absorb Poland and the Baltics. They even forgave the Soviet Union's breach of its wartime (Four Freedoms) understanding with the Allies that democracy would be restored in the former German-occupied countries of Europe now occupied by Russian troops and finally the news that Russia had obtained our atomic secrets through American members of the party.

Against all that darkness, those around the table still believed that without Russia there would have been no victory against Hitler and that it was America that had broken faith with Russia by secretly developing atomic weapons and occupying or interfering with countries like Iran, Greece, Austria, and Yugoslavia, which were allegedly within the Russian sphere of influence. Above all, for them, America was still failing to fulfill its obligations to its own people: much of the nation's wealth was held by a small group of corporate owners, Jim Crow flourished even as Black soldiers returned to a hostile South, and labor unions were under increasing legal pressure by owners using communist-front allegations to destroy their legitimacy.

As Lenin had asked, referring to the Marxists' problem of working people's refusal to rise up against capitalism, "What is to be done?" Many of those around that table had done what they honestly felt the party required of them. Flato had joined the party in 1935, while working first at the WPA, and then under La Follette's Senate committee on labor, and later for Nelson Rockefeller's South American affairs committee during the war. Suspicions about his loyalty began in 1945 after a Soviet agent's list of U.S. spies was acquired by the government; although no full investigation occurred, he was dismissed from government service on "loyalty" grounds.

In 1954, both Flato and Luke Wilson were called before the Senate's Jenner Committee, which was investigating communist penetration of the government. Luke Wilson had served in the military on various senior assignments during the war. Each claimed their Fifth Amendment right against self-incrimination, although each acknowledged knowing the other. After their testimony, Flato lived quietly as Wilson's neighbor, on land Wilson owned, adjacent to Jack Phillips's beach. There Flato commissioned a house designed by Serge Chermayeff and later had an addition built by Hayden Walling that deeply offended Chermayeff, who never spoke to Flato again.

During perestroika in the 1980s, the NKVD files were briefly opened, and Flato's role in two of the most important Soviet spy rings was exposed. Flato's "Myrna" group of American spies reported directly to Stalin, just as the files also revealed that Alger Hiss had also directly reported to Stalin.

After his 1954 testimony it became clear to Luke Wilson and his wife, Ruth, that the government was not through with them, and they fled their Horseleech Pond house for Rome. Interestingly, Luke's father, a well-known Washington businessman and promoter of international relations, had been listed on J. Edgar Hoover's "Red Network" list. Luke's parents controlled the ownership of Woodward and Lothrop, Washing-

Alger Hiss under arrest, 1951

ton's largest and grandest department store, and had given their seventy-acre Bethesda estate Tree Tops for the new home of the National Institutes of Health and the National Cancer Institute.

Sid Grossman, the magnetic founder of the Photo League, was a beloved photography teacher in Provincetown and New York. Among his students were Jean Shay, Gloria Nardin, and other realist photographers like Vivian Cherry, whose classic 1950 photographs of Dorothy Day gained her fame. The FBI had planted an informant in his Provincetown classes who then accused him of being a party member. Grossman denied it before the committee but admitted to having once been a party member. His professional life ruined, he died in 1955.

The CPUSA was now led by Earl Browder, and on its governing committee sat Robert Minor, formerly married to Susan Glaspell, and Steve Nelson, the former Communist Party courier and commandant of the NKVD police in the Lincoln Brigade. Nelson had returned to his cabin in Truro, which he had built in 1955 after two federal trials failed to convict him of being a party member. Nelson had chosen Truro because many of his former "comrades" in the Lincoln Brigade and members of the party had moved to Provincetown, Truro, and Wellfleet—George Maas, a close friend of Jack Hall's, and Mike and Ann Ehrenberg (Ann's sister was married to the Soviet spy Samuel Krafsur). The Ehrenbergs were a charming couple whom everyone loved. Mike had been both a soldier and a photographer during the Spanish Civil War and afterward an active member of the Photo League with Sid Grossman.

Steve Nelson

Nelson had been a seminal figure in the lives of those who served in the Lincoln and International Brigades. A charismatic Croatian immigrant, formerly named Stephen Mesaros, he had immigrated with his family to Philadelphia after World War I and after only five years of school had become a skilled carpenter and in 1925 joined the Young Communist League.

Showing real organizing skills, he was sent to organize fellow Croat miners in the Pennsylvania coalfields. It was during this period he met his wife, Margaret Yaeger, also a party member, who helped him improve his English. They began working for the party as a team, first in Detroit on the auto assembly line, then in New York, where he attended the New York Workers School. Nelson rose rapidly as a valued field organizer and recruiter. In 1931, they were sent to Moscow, where they studied at the Lenin School and Steve served as a courier for the Comintern in Germany, Switzerland, and China. They returned in 1933 to again organize coal miners in Pennsylvania.

When the civil war in Spain began, he was sent by the CPUSA to fight, but as he disembarked from the *Queen Mary* in March 1937, he and his companions were arrested for attempting to enter Spain in violation of the neutrality treaty. Upon his release, he illegally crossed the border from France and joined the Lincoln Brigade as a commissar under his old party friend Oliver Law, the first African American brigade unit commander.

Law was mortally wounded at the Battle of Brunete, and Nelson assumed command of the Fifteenth Battalion, only to be wounded himself during a series of battles and recalled by the party leader Earl Browder to the United States. Nelson left behind a reputation as a loyal enforcer of Stalin's NKVD orders to eliminate anarchists and socialists who refused to follow party orders.

On his return, Nelson quickly climbed the party's ranks and was elected to its national board, where he served as a district secretary in Pennsylvania, where McCarthy's committee first took an interest in him. Using the testimony of a favorite FBI and McCarthy "witness," Matt Cvetic, Nelson and five others were convicted after several trials of violating the Smith Act and sentenced to five years. In 1956, three years after Stalin's death, *Pennsylvania v. Nelson* was heard on appeal before the Supreme Court, which reversed Nelson's conviction, finding Cvetic's testimony to be perjured and granting a new trial. Without Cvetic's testimony, the government decided the case was not worthy of retrial.

Now a free man, Nelson again became a member of the party's national committee and attended its historic Twentieth Congress in New York City in February 1956. The CPUSA was now under round-the-clock FBI surveillance, and most of those who attended did so at the peril of their jobs and freedom. The party chairman, William Z. Foster, requested for the first time that no attendees bring pen and paper to the meeting, and all note taking was prohibited. This alone aroused concern, and the suspense was finally broken by a "comrade" who, at the request of Foster, read a just-released translation of Secretary-General Nikita Khrushchev's February speech to his Soviet party conference titled "The Crimes of Stalin."

Khrushchev had taken one and a half hours to outline in chilling detail Stalin's crimes against the Soviet people. At its conclusion, he bestowed the most dreaded title in the Soviet Union upon Stalin: "enemy of the people." The speech confirmed all the anti-Stalinist accusations regarding his bloody purge trials and the serial murder of loyal Communist Party members, including the recent discovery of the bodies of 1,108 delegates from around the world to the 1934 Congress of the Soviets who had been secretly arrested and executed. Stalin ordered their bodies stacked and buried at night in rows in the banks of the Moscow River. Their bodies had only recently been exposed by historic flooding.

Of the stunned silence that followed, Nelson later wrote, "Tears streamed down the faces of men and women who had spent forty or more years, their whole adult lives, in the movement." For twenty years, the U.S. party had regularly denied all accusations of wrongdoing by Stalin. Now they learned that the "cream of the Bolsheviks, the men and women who made the revolution, were wiped out."

Nelson rose and said, "This was not why I joined the Party," and one by one, many sobbing, they slowly filed out of the hall in search of a lost life. One was Howard Fast, who had been an adamant Stalinist all his life, and the author of *Spartacus*, *Citizen Tom Paine*, and *Freedom Road*, now blacklisted and forced to write under pseudonyms.

Nelson later admitted that his role as a party enforcer in the International Brigades culling out anarchists and socialists whom they called "social fascists" had splintered an already shaky "popular front" of volunteer soldiers, and that these tactics had destroyed support and trust among Republican forces. Nelson devoted the remainder of his life to supporting the political and social goals of the Lincoln Brigade, whose members remained close. He served as national commander of the brigade and wrote his autobiography, *Steve Nelson, American Radical*. Until his death at ninety in 1993, Nelson continued to protest the Vietnam War and raise aid for the Sandinistas in Nicaragua.

Jack Hall became a friend of Nelson's and, like many others, chose not to believe the dark stories of his role as a Stalinist NKVD enforcer, even though he now knew of Stalin's continued use of the NKVD to assassinate those who appeared on Stalin's paranoid list of "enemies of the people," shooting them from behind even in the midst of battles like Stalingrad, where the "enemies" were fighting to save "the people." While Jack no longer found the party, as led by Stalin, something worth supporting, like so many he continued to believe that Soviet Russia's original revolutionary goals of equal opportunity for all and its espoused goal of world peace were sacred. This was also a period of nostalgia for some former party members who could at least celebrate the Soviet Union's honoring of Picasso and Paul Robeson with the Stalin Peace Prize. Picasso's famous dove paintings serve as a memento of that era. The party still brought back memories of those prewar beach parties under the stars where songs were sung, often by those who had fought in Spain, marched in Paterson and Lawrence, gone south to protest the Scottsboro Boys decision and Jim Crow, or helped produce the plays and songs on the HUAC list of honor. Jack in his beret accompanied Steve and his fellow survivors of the Lincoln Brigade on the bus to Washington to protest the Vietnam War, where he can be seen in the documentary *The Good Fight*, narrated by Studs Terkel.

In some ways, it made them feel stronger and proud to have been part of a band of "comrades" in the sense Jack Reed and his progressive companions once used the word, and in a new sense for those of them who were socialists, Trotskyites, communists, or just plain anticapitalists. Jack, like many in the 1950s, had adopted, or was soon to adopt, new gods, and not a few of his fellow bohemians joined him in embracing AA and the Society of Friends. (Interestingly, both Whittaker Chambers and Alger Hiss's wife, Priscilla, were Quakers.) He became first an "attender," then a member, of Yarmouth Friends Meeting and, when in New York, of the Fifteenth Street Meeting in the Village. Sitting in silence with the morning light streaming through the windows of the old meetinghouse brought him a peace he had never found elsewhere.

17.

THE LOST GENERATION'S CHILDREN

Few of the bohemians maintained close ties with their parents or siblings. They had become pilgrims on a solo journey for independence from everything in their past, including their upper-class, working-class, or immigrant parents, and more important the places they grew up: Bob Minor's Montana; Louise Bryant's Utah; Jack Reed's Portland, Oregon; the Midwest of Floyd Dell, Jig Cook, and Susan Glaspell; or the ethnic enclaves of Jewish New York. They sought a new life where they could not be placed by their parentage, accent, or religion. A place where both men and women were "comrades" striving to build a creative, politically active, and sexually free life.

But because they were human, with age came an inclination to mate, even if briefly, thus marriage, and often pregnancy—whether welcome or from failure to follow Margaret Sanger's advice. Children challenged bohemian couples' ability to subsist on sporadic incomes, their impulsive traveling and their goal of a new equality between man and woman. Creative men had rarely worried about the duties of child-rearing, and now creative women felt entitled not only to the vote but to a similar right to a professional life.

Many of the bohemian children's most vivid memories were of being raised in fairly careless marriages at one long, large, and rowdy cocktail party, with occasional sandwiches and diaper changes from a revolving roster of local babysitters while their parents relentlessly pursued their ambitions, travels, political battles, and affairs.

Edmund Wilson

Rosalind Wilson, Edmund's first child with the Provincetown Players actress Mary Blair, vividly recalled the kindness of strangers like Count George Chavchavadze, Paul's brother, who had rented a nearby house one summer and would religiously pick her up each morning to take her fishing at every pond in Wellfleet. Rosalind, like most of the second generation of Cape bohemians, grew up with parents mainly dedicated to their own lives, and when mixed with multiple divorces, the world they created for their children was both unsafe and enticing. She wrote this of growing up with her terrifying father: "My father loved his children and his animals but often forgot about them for long periods of time and when he looked around again, after skipping several chapters, was confused by the scenario. Anyone closely connected with him was likely to develop a helter-skelter way of life. He would want me around when it was convenient and turn me out when it wasn't." Her half brother, Reuel, from Edmund's later marriage to Mary McCarthy, remembers the occasional meal or a bit of attention paid him, but basically he was left with his posse of boys—Charlie Jencks, son of Gardner and Ruth, and Mike

Macdonald, son of Dwight and Nancy—to roam the woods and dine or sleep wherever they could. Reuel is captured on film by Henri Cartier-Bresson in one of the most poignant father-son photographs ever taken, with Reuel squirming away from his father as Edmund desperately attempts to clutch him in a faux parental embrace.

Of course, there were moments when the children were suddenly remembered: Rosalind and young Eben Given, son of the painter Eben Given and the writer Phyllis Duganne, recalled the magical tricks Edmund Wilson would perform and his wonderful marionette shows. Wilson knelt sometimes for days with young Eben at his side creating puppet scenes. Their shows enchanted the children but were painful to their parents because it turned out each puppet was designed to caricature a friend of Wilson's.

Edmund had acquired an "elephant" edition of Audubon's *Quadrupeds of North America* at some point in the 1930s, and he carefully had individual animals removed and framed as birthday or wedding presents for the children of his friends. Provincetown, Truro, and Wellfleet houses were filled with framed bears, skunks, and squirrels now treasured by an aging group of bohemian children.

Agnes, Shane, and Eugene O'Neill, Provincetown, 1922

From the beginning, bohemian parenting left a generation of battered but often gifted progeny. Eugene O'Neill and Agnes Boulton's two children never seemed to have had a childhood. Oona, New York's "Number

One Debutante of 1942," spent her early years in the midst of O'Neill's troubled marriage to Agnes, and married the fifty-four-year-old Charlie Chaplin just as she turned eighteen. Her brother Shane, a haunted Village addict, committed suicide in 1977. O'Neill's out-of-wedlock first child, Eugene junior, whom Gene met only when he was five, was a handsome and talented academic at Yale who committed suicide at age forty. O'Neill never spoke with Oona after her marriage to Chaplin, who had once been a close friend, nor did he ever make contact with Shane or Eugene after he moved with Carlotta to California.

Jig Cook's two children, Harl and Nilla, while clearly loved by their parents and their new stepmother, Susan Glaspell, grew up in a world of alcohol, which doomed Harl, for all his charm and potential, to a life of failed relationships. His only child with Leo Cook committed suicide at an early age. Nilla had a son, Topie, with her Greek husband but shipped him off at fourteen to New York to be picked up at the dock by Dodie and Harl and brought to live with Susan in Truro. She later left Greece to become a follower of Gandhi in India and later roamed the world, often in desperate trouble.

Mary Heaton Vorse wrote movingly of her inability to control her son and daughter from the Vorse marriage or her son with Joe O'Brien, due to her constant travel and writing deadlines. The children grew up in a world of their mothers' affairs and easily adopted the Jazz Age culture of roadhouse romances, taking to Prohibition's pure alcohol with abandon.

Bubs and Chauncey Hackett's children were raised in a household where their father, who had once clerked for Justice Holmes, mainly worked on his stamp collection whenever he and Bubs weren't entertaining their hard-drinking crowd. Bubs, with her red hair and eccentric charm, had little maternal instinct and would leave the children marooned in their cribs to bicycle off for assignations with Harl Cook and other admirers, only to return to find Chauncey had forgotten to feed them or change their diapers. Their gifted son Tom graduated from Harvard, only to spend a lonely single life driving a cab before dying in New York.

Jack Hall's wives had similar childhoods. Dodie's father too had abandoned her to lead the life of a professional bachelor painter on Staten Island, and she and her mother never bonded.

Jean Shay grew up in a haze of alcohol, often forgotten by her father and abandoned by her mother. Jack's last wife Mardi's father, divorced and an alcoholic but of extremely pleasant disposition, was deeply kind and charming and never worked, but spent his days praising her and playing whist.

Those of the early second generation often seemed destined to reproduce both the strengths and the weaknesses of their parents—continuing their dedication to creativity, self-indulgence, and total lack of parenting skills.

Max Eastman seemed to grow increasingly self-absorbed, serially unfaithful to wives and lovers alike, fascinated by his own good looks—marching through Paris streets after a beaux arts ball with his premature white hair and bronzed body clothed only in a jockstrap. He was furious with his first wife, Ida Rauh, when she became pregnant with their son, Daniel. When they divorced shortly after, he not only did not seek custody of his son but didn't see him again for twenty-three years. Daniel led a tragic life of divorces and alcohol without any of the accomplishments of his father. Eastman's beloved widowed sister, Crystal, died in 1928 leaving two small children, whom he immediately placed in a foster home and never visited.

Even for those children who had at least one parent who deeply loved them, the carousel of divorce brought rotating, often destabilizing new surrogates. Very few of the bohemians remained married to their first spouse, and those who did usually had numerous love affairs. Divorce was inexpensive, and because few bohemians had money, their only asset was the children, who almost always were assigned to the wife, leaving the ex-husband free to remarry quickly. Edmund Wilson's four marriages became the standard for many like Jack Hall but were trumped by Jack Phillips's five and Norman Mailer's six. Not that women were far behind; Joan Colebrook had four and Polly Boyden three, though two were to the same husband.

Jack Phillips's daughter Hayden remembers sitting on the small beach at Horseleech Pond with Noa Hall, two small girls discussing their fathers' current divorces. Both girls were the center of custody battles. Jack Hall was suing Dodie for the return of his children, now living in Truro with Khaki Captiva, and Jack Phillips was suing Libby to block her from taking Blair and Hayden to Mexico with her lover. (See Hayden's marvelous 2021 memoir of life as a child of parents who each married five times, *Upper Bohemia*). Their respective fathers had just sold or rented the houses the girls had grown up in, Jack Hall selling the Baker house to the Biddles and Jack Phillips having rented the big house he had built on the pond opposite Dr. Rollins's camp to the famed translator of Bertolt Brecht and of Hitler's *Mein Kampf*, Ralph Manheim. Manheim was in the middle of a torrid affair with Anna Matson, Hayden's beloved godmother. Manheim had caused other damage by seducing Mary McCarthy at a beach party in the summer of 1941. (Perhaps that's why Wilson hated beach parties.) Mary found herself pregnant, and the strangely tolerant Wilson assisted her in obtaining an abortion. Another summer Manheim left his wife for Christine Magriel, the first woman graduate of MIT's architectural school, who was then separated from her husband but living in one of Jack Phillips's renovated army barrack above Joan's Beach.

Interestingly, it was the Europeans who tended to remain married, with the traditional discreet affair; the Chavchavadzes would not have dreamed of divorce, nor would later émigrés like Hans Hofmann or the Bauhaus crowd—the Chermayeffs, Breuers, or Kepeses.

Divorces or affairs placed an extra burden on the "New Woman," who almost always ended up with the lion's share of the child-rearing. They included Mary Vorse, Margaret Sanger, and Mary McCarthy, who were increasingly vocal about it both in conversation and in their writing. Elizabeth Hardwick's essay on Mary McCarthy in *A View of My Own* describes the conundrum: "A career of candor and dissent is not an easy one for a woman; the license is jarring and the dare often forbidding. Such a person needs more than confidence and indignation. A great measure of personal attractiveness and a high degree of romantic singularity are necessary to step free of the mundane, the governessy, the threat of earnestness and dryness."

James Thurber, her male counterpart, advocated contrary misogynistic views in his *New Yorker* cartoons, and Edmund Wilson lived it as his close friend Dawn Powell observed in her diary: "In order for a genius to be a genius, he must have a selfless slave between him and the world so that he may select what tidbits he chooses from it and not have his brains swallowed up in chaff. For women this protection is impossible."[1]

Their children's early sexual experiences were often stimulated by their proximity to their parents' affairs. In addition, the narrow streets of Provincetown and the well-known ocean and pond trysting sites of Truro and Wellfleet were not made for keeping secrets. Also debatable was the almost universal adoption of the German *Natur* tradition of adult and family nude bathing.

For many children, their first encounter with adult nudity other than their parents' was both liberating and frightening. Penny Jencks, daughter of Ruth and Gardner, remembered both emotions on seeing other women's breasts and pubic mounds and various men's large or small penises at all-too-close range, but it clearly served as a fertile inspiration for her subsequent life as a noted sculptor of the human body.

Jack Phillips's beach was the early center of nude family bathing, often led by Dwight Macdonald, who was dedicated to insisting his friends disrobe. Some welcomed the chance to display pert breasts, as did Mary McCarthy and Jack Phillips's wife Libby Blair, about whom Dodie Hall said, "She would go to the beach in her swimsuit but disrobe as soon as she spotted a man approaching who may have not yet had the pleasure of examining her rather enticing body." Mary Garrison's daughter Prudence "Prudie" Grand had similar traumatic memories of her mother and friends in the nude.

Of course, many of the children inherited their parents' artistic, political, or creative gifts. Jack Phillips's children from his five wives serve as examples. His oldest daughter, Blair, became a sought-after singer in concerts and intimate performances and married first Malcolm Cowley's son, Rob, a publisher, and then the famed Provincetown and New York painter Paul Resika. Her sister Hayden married several times and had children but pursued her writing career to great success, publishing biographies of Frida Kahlo, Arshile Gorky, and Isamu Noguchi. Jack's children with Agnes "Mougouch" Magruder and her two daughters from her marriage with Gorky, whom he treated as his own, went on to creative lives. Natasha married a martial arts master, and her sister Maro, also a painter, married Stephen Spender's son, Matthew, and they raised a gifted family of their own in Tuscany. Of Jack's two daughters with Mougouch, Susanna became a recognized painter and married Chaim Tannenbaum, a Montreal academic who sang with Leonard Cohen and the McGarrigle sisters. Her sister Antonia married Martin Amis and raised their sons in London and at Jack's Horseleech Pond turkey houses before the marriage failed. Jack's last child, with Florence "Flossie" Hammond, Jonathan, inherited his mother's theatrical skills and became an actor in Los Angeles.

Perhaps the bohemians' children were in one respect similar to all children of gifted parents—either unable to escape the shadow of the famed parent or always seeking a completely different, more stable, and less demanding life.

The sons of the pioneering modern architect Serge Chermayeff and his wife, Barbara, Ivan and Peter, both became internationally respected designers, architects, and teachers and were two of the founders of the pioneering architecture firm CambridgeSeven. Ivan, in partnership with Tom Geismar, designed the Mobil logo and many other famous trademarks, while Peter became the world's recognized expert in the design of aquariums, with installations from Boston to Genoa.

Ruth and Gardner Jencks's children, Penny and Charles, went on to create unique careers in the arts. Penny became a sculptor whose work includes her highly acclaimed statues of Eleanor Roosevelt in Riverside Park off Seventy-Second Street in New York, Robert Frost on the Amherst College campus, and Aaron Copland and Leonard Bernstein at the Boston Symphony's summer home, Tanglewood, commissioned by the composer John Williams. Her younger brother, Charles, moved to England after architectural school where he became the controversial creator of the theory of postmodernism. Unlike Gropius and Breuer, his teachers at Harvard, and lifelong friends, Jencks was not content with conventional architecture and explored combinations of science and design in countless books and finally in enormous sculpted landforms, first with his wife, Maggie Keswick, at Portrack, her family's estate in Scotland, and then in Korea, Italy, and across the British Isles. He always credited the unspoiled landscape of his childhood on Bound Brook Island and his parents' circle of bohemian intellectuals as the inspiration for his work.

Many of bohemia's children followed creatively in the footsteps of their parents. Edmund Wilson's last child, Helen Miranda; Jack Hall's daughter Noa; Susanna Phillips; Ben Shahn's daughter Judith; and Robert Frank's daughter Mary all became recognized painters. Paul "Button" Magriel, the son of Christine Fairchild and her husband, Paul, a Latvian immigrant who became head of the Dance Collection at the MoMA, went on to become a math prodigy and ultimately the most feared backgammon and poker player in international gambling circles.

Gifted or not, they mainly carried on their parents' dedication to progressive politics and in many cases the preservation of their way of life on the Cape—maintaining their parents' simple old farmhouses or Bauhaus modern structures, increasingly anomalies in the post–National Seashore Cape, where the new model was a year-round suburban house complete with heat, a lawn, and a two-car garage.

18.

PROVINCETOWN EITHER WAY

For years, one of the most frequently stolen signs in America stood at the entrance to Provincetown, stating boldly PROVINCETOWN EITHER WAY, pointing left to the shore road to town, which passed the picturesque row of Days's one-room beach cottages, each with the name of a flower, and right to the state highway, which ran to the town's East End past Pilgrim Lake, ending at the ocean.

Indeed, from its earliest bohemian period, Provincetown's tolerance and general bonhomie attracted gay people, both single and in pairs.

The crowd of young artists drawn to Charles Hawthorne's harbor painting school included the open lovers Charles Demuth and Marsden Hartley and a number of gifted female couples, several of whom created a unique style of printmaking that had a major influence on the craft. Prior to the 1930s, the term "lesbian" was not used, but pairs of well-educated "maiden ladies" lived in open partnerships, or "Boston marriages," from 1915 on. Many of these liaisons had been formed in Paris in Gertrude Stein's circle, like the pair of Ethel Mars and Maud Squire, both white-line woodcut print artists. Hutch Hapgood likened Mars's unconventional appearance, with her dyed purple hair and orange lips, to a "Matisse portrait."[1]

Actually, the first painting school in Provincetown was established in 1896, several years before Hawthorne's. It was known as the Dewing Woodward School of Painting, artfully omitting the founder's first name, Martha. She and her female companion ran the school for some time, attracting mainly women students.

Like their Bloomsbury counterparts, bohemians were always suspicious of gender boundaries, and this, combined with the slim likelihood of legal prosecution and the erotic possibilities presented by bars full of young sailors, made Provincetown a potent attraction. But it was the deeply Catholic and conservative population of its Portuguese West End, not its Yankee East End residents, who first realized there was serious money to be made catering to gay visitors in bars, clubs, restaurants, and single-sex guesthouses. By the 1920s, there were many such guesthouses in the West End as well as Portuguese-owned single-sex clubs along Commercial Street bordering the harbor.

One of the first and most popular gay restaurants was the Cesco Bonga, established in 1916 by Mary Heaton Vorse's stepbrother, Fred Marvin. Marvin's lover and valet was also a skilled cook famous for his spaghetti. The restaurant was located next to the Beachcombers' and thus drew a convivial clientele, both straight and gay. The Moors, another popular Portuguese-owned predominantly gay bar and restaurant, was established in 1939 in the West End, as was the Seascape House on Commercial Street, frequently patronized by celebrities such as Leonard Bernstein and Louise Nevelson.

One of Provincetown's most famous gay clubs after the war, the Atlantic House (familiarly known as the A House), was owned by Reggie Cabral. It was a dance club frequented by gay and straight alike; its legendary Cabaret Room was the precursor of the many gay cabarets of the present. Here one could hear major talent—Billie Holiday, Eartha Kitt, and Ella Fitzgerald. Tennessee Williams met his lifelong partner, Frank Merlo, there in the summer of 1947. Another trailblazing club was the Ace of Spades at 193A Commercial Street, one of the first members-only lesbian clubs. That status protected it from increasing pressure by the all-male Provincetown police. The club remained rigid about requiring a membership card, and that policy resulted in the turning away of Jackie Kennedy when she was brought to the club by Gore Vidal, her stepbrother's stepson. Vidal was a frequent visitor to Provincetown after he and Norman Mailer patched up their broken friendship after the war.

During the second half of the century, there were really two ways for gay people to live—openly, which could be extremely dangerous for both their careers and sometimes their physical safety, or closeted, as most did. Closeted often meant being married, frequently with children, and only openly gay with their most trusted friends. As much as the bohemian Cape accepted homosexuality, the three towns that formed their community had, and in many ways still have, strong prejudices against openly gay life. The Provincetown of the late 1950s was like Greenwich Village, a relatively safe bubble outside of which lurked serious penalties for flaunting one's homosexuality.

George Tooker and Jared French, Provincetown, 1940s. Photographer believed to be Paul Cadmus (© 2021 Estate of Paul Cadmus / Artists Rights Society [ARS], NY. Photograph by PaJaMa, courtesy of Gitterman Gallery)

The true pioneers of bohemian open homosexuality made their appearance in the late 1930s. Paul Cadmus and a ménage of lovers began to come to Truro and Wellfleet, spending their nights closely studying sailors on shore leave in Provincetown's waterfront bars. Cadmus was a gifted draftsman who had been highly influenced by the *Masses* artist Reginald

Marsh's portrayal of the rough life in Greenwich Village. Cadmus had already offended the U.S. Navy's hierarchy with his display of his "shore leave" paintings and at the same time achieved the notoriety he craved. He traveled in sophisticated bohemian circles: his sister was married to Lincoln Kirstein, the wealthy founder of the New York City Ballet, and Cadmus's guests on the Cape in those years included George Platt Lynes and Carl Van Vechten, each of whom was a gifted photographer of the nude male physique.

While Cadmus found both inspiration and pleasure in the openly gay life, his work has not achieved the cultural status of another openly gay pioneer. Tennessee Williams was twenty-nine when he was introduced to Provincetown in 1940 by friends in the Village who were studying with Hans Hofmann. Williams had become increasingly interested in abstract painting and the painters who were exploring it, among them Lee Krasner and Jackson Pollock. Williams was not yet completely comfortable nude on the beaches with other gay men, nor totally secure in picking up strangers for one-night stands, but he was learning fast. His first summer he wrote to his friend the novelist Donald Windham in New York: "The most raffish and fantastic crew that I have ever met and even I—excessively broadminded as I am—felt somewhat shocked by the goings on." He returned for the summers of 1941, 1944, 1946, and 1947 and grew more assured in his open homosexuality, and became an even heavier drinker.

He and his bohemian playwright predecessor Eugene O'Neill had both found the Cape's beaches and pace of life conducive to creating their best work, and each had the special gift of separating himself from people and alcohol when he was working. In some way, the surrounding sea seemed to exorcise their demons, resulting in some of our greatest plays.

Williams found two friends who would provide him with the retreat he needed, first a fellow southerner, Fritz Bultman, the son of a wealthy New Orleans funeral director and superb painter, and Karl Knaths, another gifted painter. Knaths lived with his sister-in-law the woodblock engraver Agnes Weinrich. Both Bultman and Knaths not only had high regard for Williams's work but found him sexually attractive as well. Williams might bring back a sailor or other pickup to the Knaths one-room cabin he had rented, but once the encounter was over, he would throw them out, take a shower from a garden hose and punctured bucket he had rigged, and climb into bed, not to sleep, but to write all morning.

Tennessee Williams at his typewriter, 1940

On rough shelves that hang beside that bed are Williams's penciled inscriptions for the plays he wrote there; they include two early works, *The Parade* and *Orpheus Descending* (1940), which later became the basis for the film *The Fugitive Kind*, and *The Glass Menagerie* (1944), which was first performed in Provincetown at the renamed Provincetown Playhouse, where the young Katharine Hepburn and Bette Davis served as ushers. In 1947, his last summer, he completed *A Streetcar Named Desire*. The then-unknown Marlon Brando had ridden his motorcycle to Provincetown just to read for the Stanley Kowalski part. Williams was impressed and asked Brando if he could repair Williams's toilet but did not forget that reading. Nineteen forty-seven was a particularly productive summer for Williams, who completed the first drafts of both *Night of the Iguana* and *Suddenly Last Summer*.

Williams, like O'Neill, was a full participant in the intellectual ferment Provincetown could provide. He became close to Hans Hofmann, whom he greatly admired, not only because Hofmann often painted in the nude, but also because of Hofmann's theories regarding the role of space in painting. Hofmann wrote, "Space must be vital and active . . . with a life of its own."[2] This greatly encouraged Williams's own interest in using "plastic space" pacing in his plays.

Through Lee Krasner and Jackson Pollock, who had first introduced him to Provincetown, he met other Hofmann students, with several of whom he had affairs, including Robert De Niro Sr. (the actor's father), Larry Rivers, and probably Pollock himself. One of his Provincetown friends was Carson McCullers, and they shared rooms in the summer of 1946 while she was completing *The Member of the Wedding* and he *Summer and Smoke*. They remained close through their lives perhaps because McCullers was bisexual and, like Tennessee, a southerner who also found freedom in Provincetown.

Williams, like O'Neill, never returned to Provincetown after having done some of his finest work there, and perhaps Tennessee was summing up his time there in Blanche's line from *Streetcar*: "I have always depended on the kindness of strangers."

One last openly gay bohemian deserves mention, and that is the then newly graduated Harvard poet Frank O'Hara. Fleeing from a strict Massachusetts Catholic childhood, O'Hara first studied piano at the New England Conservatory but became fascinated by poetry and writing and transferred to Harvard after service in the navy during World War II. At Harvard, as he so aptly put it, he learned "to play the typewriter" rather than the piano and was deeply influenced by two undergraduate friends: John Ashbery, later to become a major postwar poet, and O'Hara's roommate, Edward Gorey, both gay.

Before his tragic death in 1966 at forty, O'Hara had a meteoric career. His immediate and highly personal poetry made readers feel almost as if they were overhearing him dictate his reactions to everything he did or saw. He shared Tennessee Williams's deep interest in the philosophy of painting but was a much closer observer, rising from a ticket collector at the Museum of Modern Art (in order to get into the Matisse show for free) to curating the MoMA's transformative 1959 show *The New American Painting*, which featured some of the emerging stars of abstract painting. The exhibition also enjoyed a highly praised European tour, contributing to abstract painting's succeeding the School of Paris.

O'Hara's charm and his ability to immediately bond with people made him a welcome comrade at the Cedar Tavern, whether its tables' occupants were gay like Jasper Johns, Larry Rivers, and Merce Cunningham or straight like de Kooning, Motherwell, Alex Katz, and Joan Mitchell. O'Hara joined them all in Provincetown for summers in the late 1940s. There, he and Tennessee participated in both naked beach frolics and serious conversations about the creative process. O'Hara was painted in the nude or clothed, with his broken nose, wiry body, and captivating smile at various times and places by Larry Rivers, de Kooning, Katz, and Alice Neel, among others. Many of his early poems celebrated Provincetown's special place in American gay culture.

While these early hedonist heroes led their lives openly and proudly, most gay bohemians did not, for fear of being outed or because of lingering Victorian values, or because they had elected to lead a closeted life complete with wife or husband and often children. For the latter, Provincetown was a Japanese "floating city" filled with forbidden pleasures like the Atlantic House that could be visited only clandestinely. The postwar era was still a time when many gay men frequented bars wearing a red necktie to signal their sexual orientation.

Some never admitted their orientation, like Fritz Bultman, who married his leggy and absolutely charming model, Jeanne, and raised two boys while becoming one of Hofmann's most brilliant students. His body of work continually grows in critical esteem. His Provincetown colleagues Karl Knaths and Myron Stout never married and lived without a seeming sex life as they produced equally fine work.

Robert Giroux of Farrar, Straus and Giroux was a frequent summer visitor to Wellfleet after editing Edmund Wilson's *To the Finland Station*. Bob was probably the most admired editor in publishing after Max Perkins, editing seven Nobel Prize winners. He was the first editor for works by Jack Kerouac, Hannah Arendt (in America), Flannery O'Connor, Bernard Malamud, John Berryman, and Robert Lowell, among dozens more. He presented as the quiet, gracious husband of an often-absent wife (the Cuban aristocrat the fifth Marquise de la Gratitud) while actually the lifelong companion of a man he had met in grammar school.

Much more flamboyant, but never openly gay, was the self-styled

Peter Hunt, born Frederick Lowe Schnitzler to immigrant parents in a New Jersey tenement. Bohemia's Baron Munchausen, he claimed to have been washed ashore from a yacht whose other occupants were Scott and Zelda Fitzgerald. In fact, after serving in World War I, he gravitated from Greenwich Village to Provincetown in the late 1920s, like so many other bohemians. Peter often sported a black cape and Parisian broad-brimmed hat, leading a pair of Afghan hounds, charming visitors whether aristocrats, painters, or tourists, and was both wildly funny and attractive to both sexes.

By 1930, he had managed to rent or buy a row of buildings running off Commercial Street that he renamed Peacock Alley. There, inspired by the English bohemians Roger Fry and Vanessa Bell, he established Peter Hunt's Peasant Village, modeled on their Bloomsbury design enterprise, the Omega Workshop. Hunt scoured the Cape for used furniture, which he, and later a band of young acolyte peasant painters, decorated with folk art motifs. Houses owned by descendants of the bohemians are almost sure to have a stool, chair, table, or toy decorated by Hunt and his companions.

So successful did he become that his catalogs circulated throughout Europe and America. In 1935, he designed the Cape Cod Room in Chicago's glamorous Drake Hotel, complete with faux-peasant decorations. His books on folk painting, including *Transformagic* (1945), can still be found in used bookstores. Hunt's camp but guarded sexuality made him a favorite with society ladies who were beginning to summer in Provincetown. Helena Rubinstein, the cosmetics queen, had purchased several large adjacent houses in town and became a major patron and friend.

The war changed Americans' tastes, and used furniture painted with faux-peasant designs gave way to sleek aluminum and plastic furniture designed by more recent bohemian arrivals (also off a boat): Marcel Breuer and the Cranbrook Academy graduates and designer couples Hans and Florence Knoll and Charles and Ray Eames. Hunt finally retired to a modern house in Orleans designed by his friend Nathaniel Saltonstall, whose Wellfleet Mayo Hill resort, the Colony, would permit only modern furnishings!

The bohemian Cape also seemed to serve as an antidote for those who had been closeted in marriage. In some ways, the self-proclaimed anarchist-pacifist social critic Paul Goodman was semi-closeted, always living behind the veil of two common-law marriages to women who worked to support his nomadic, academic life and raise the children he had with each of them. Born to a Jewish family in Greenwich Village that had been abandoned by his father, Goodman thrived in the public school system, developing a voracious appetite for studying America's cultural problems, whether the unplanned growth of its cities, the relationship citizens should have with their government, or the understanding of the new postwar burst of American poetry, novels, and plays. He always claimed he was bisexual but basically used his two marriages as a base from which to explore gay life, resulting in his dismissal from all three schools at which he taught, Manumit School, Black Mountain College, and the Art Institute of Chicago, for affairs with male students. He casually justified them as love affairs to which all humans are entitled, his anarchist approach to sex harking back to Emma Goldman and Margaret Sanger.

Goodman seems to have come to Wellfleet before the war as a contributor to the *Partisan Review* and friend of Dwight Macdonald, Philip Rahv, and Mary McCarthy. He had adopted their common belief that man should live in unspoiled natural surroundings, and he and Dwight became even closer when both were fired from the *Partisan Review* for their antiwar views. Goodman then began to contribute pieces to Dwight's new magazine, *Politics*, which lasted from 1944 to 1949 until Dwight's wealthy wife and fellow anarchist, Nancy Rodman, withdrew her funding as their marriage deteriorated.

The roly-poly, bespectacled Goodman found Wellfleet's intellectuals sympathetic to his ambitious thinking, but it was *Commentary*'s founder, Norman Podhoretz, a Truro resident, who made Goodman a household name. Goodman had submitted his book on the problems of America's seemingly alienated youth, titled *Growing Up Absurd*, to seventeen publishers, all of whom rejected it. Podhoretz had been seeking a piece on educational reform and ran installments of Goodman's manuscript. The enormous critical response motivated Random House to publish it in 1960, and it became an immediate bestseller.

This success combined with Goodman's growing fame as the co-founder of Gestalt therapy, then enormously fashionable among New York intellectuals, would seem to have led him to put down permanent roots in Wellfleet, but Goodman was never at rest either sexually or romantically, and he moved on, maintaining his last common-law marriage until his death.

If you were to be driving down Wellfleet's Pamet Point Road just before you reached Mary McCarthy's house on the right, you might have slowed down to listen to an English-accented voice singing songs from Brecht's *Threepenny Opera*. The singer and pianist would have been the theater critic for *The New Republic* and *The Nation*, Eric Bentley. Bentley had arrived in Wellfleet just after the war after being rejected by the U.S. Army for being gay. Now living in Wellfleet with his wife and two sons, Bentley at that point might have been as eminent a critic of theater as Edmund Wilson was of literature. He had come down from Oxford in 1938 and moved to America to complete graduate degrees at Yale before moving to UCLA, where he met Bertolt Brecht shortly after Brecht had escaped Nazi Germany. As difficult as Brecht was to get on with (his co-creators Kurt Weill and Lotte Lenya loathed him), he and Bentley managed to collaborate to great effect, and Bentley's translations became the authoritative English versions of all of Brecht's plays and songs.

Bentley first presented as a tall, rather academic Englishman with a quiet charm, but underneath breathed a fiery intellect who took no prisoners in his theater reviews, gaining the distinction of being sued for defamation by both Tennessee Williams and Arthur Miller. He later cogently summed up his criticism of their work: "Psychological conflict is not drama, the proper stuff of drama is not neurosis, but immortality."[3] Readers of his still widely used classics, *The Modern Theatre* (1948) and *In Search of Theater* (1953), will note his rather low enthusiasm for America's playwrights, including O'Neill.

Bentley spent many years as a distinguished professor at Yale, Columbia, and Harvard, but his true love seems to have been cabaret, as both a gifted singer and a pianist, and he might have been happiest starring in one of Berlin's many prewar Weimar Republic nightclubs. He gave several explanations of his closeted Wellfleet years. In a 1991 interview with *The Advocate* he was quoted as saying, "It's not that you went into a marriage certain you are gay and knowingly deceiving your wife. You went into a marriage, typically, not being certain and thinking that because you like or love a woman, you will very likely end up straight, and you had every reason to be straight in those days."

In an earlier and even more poignant self-examination he said:

I generally avoid the word *bisexual*. People who call themselves bisexual are being evasive. They don't want to be regarded as homosexual—or they want to be regarded as supermen, who like to sleep with everything and everybody. Nevertheless, if one can avoid these connotations, the word would be applicable to me, because I have been married twice and neither of the marriages was fake, neither of them was a cover for something else, they were both a genuine relationship to a woman—a genuine and erotic relationship to a woman, one of whom became the mother of my two sons.[4]

There were a number of attractions that the Cape offered Bentley—neighbors who were co-contributors to *The New Republic* and *The Nation*, such as Wilson and Dos Passos, assorted fellow left-wing Marxists under siege from the revived postwar HUAC committee, and, of course, Provincetown.

Bentley's second mother-in-law was Hallie Flanagan, and that alone connected all the dots in the bohemian Cape, because Flanagan had headed the New Deal's Federal Theatre Project from 1935 to 1939. Most of the live theater world was on the dole in 1935, devastated by the Depression and the more glamorous and feel-good movies that cost only twenty-five cents, as opposed to several dollars for a live play. Harry Hopkins, Roosevelt's most trusted adviser, persuaded FDR to create the project and urged that his former Grinnell College crush, Hallie, be appointed its first director.

One of Hallie's first appointments had been to make Bentley's Truro neighbor Susan Glaspell the head of the Midwest office of the FTP. This came at a good time for Susan, because she had just been abandoned by her lover, Norman Matson. In addition, Hallie's friend George Biddle had been appointed the director of the Federal Art Project by FDR and was summering in Truro as well.

The FTP reinvigorated American theater, employing fifteen thousand actors, playwrights, and set designers. Its Negro Unit in New York was a huge theatrical success, presenting Orson Welles's *Voodoo Macbeth*, based on the nineteenth-century Haitian Black ruler Henri Christophe. However, the party had indeed infiltrated the FTP under the guise of the Popular Front that bound most of the bohemian Left to Russia, and HUAC had discovered its favorite communist formula in the FTP's productions: plays with left-wing labor and economic themes combined with interracial casts and unsegregated audiences. In fairness, Hallie had been dazzled by her 1926 stay in Moscow and by Stanislavsky. The fear of the Black person was even greater than the threat of communism to the southern congressmen who chaired and dominated HUAC. When Flanagan came to defend the FTP before the committee, its chairman, Martin Dies of Texas, removed his cigar for a moment to challenge her standard defense of mixed-race casts and audiences, proclaiming, "[Racial] equality forms a vital part of the communist dictatorship and practice."

Eric and his mother-in-law shared a common disdain for HUAC's persecution of the creative Left, and one of Bentley's more provocative plays was titled *Are You Now or Have You Ever Been*, HUAC's lead question to every citizen they suspected of being a member of the Communist Party.

After his Cape years, Bentley stepped out of the closet in 1969 at fifty-three and announced his homosexuality and began an active role in gay culture and politics.

Just up the road from the Bentley house, next door to Mary McCarthy, was a small, secluded house originally owned by the American film and stage actor Osgood Perkins. Perkins was a *Mayflower* descendant and Harvard graduate and one of the first silent film stars to make the successful transition to talkies, including the hit film *Gold Diggers of 1937*. He was widely respected for both his film and his stage work (*The Front*

Page of 1928). His fellow star Louise Brooks said of him, "You know what makes an actor great to work with? Timing, you don't have to feel anything. It's like dancers with a perfect dancing partner."

Perkins died at forty-five in 1937, leaving a five-year-old son, Anthony, who inherited the Wellfleet cottage. Anthony, or Tony, as he preferred, elected to pursue his father's career and to create space from his clinging mother. Tall, dark, and troubled, he won a series of lead roles opposite some of the screen's most glamorous leading ladies of the 1950s and 1960s. Like his neighbor Eric Bentley, he also led a much different life in Wellfleet. Perkins confessed that he had never been with a woman until he was thirty-nine. Both before and after that, there were a series of lovers, including Tab Hunter, Rudolf Nureyev, and Stephen Sondheim. Jack Hall's daughter Noa treasured a signed picture of Tony, Tab, and their dog, with whom she played on Bound Brook beach, and later became his neighbor after she and her husband acquired Mary McCarthy's former house.

When Perkins was forty-one, he met the twenty-five-year-old Berry Berenson, Bernard Berenson's great-niece, at a party in New York. They acted together in several films and married when she was three months pregnant with the first of their two sons.

The world changed for Perkins after he starred as the terrifying Norman Bates in the 1960 blockbuster *Psycho.* After that, privacy for him, Berry, and the various male lovers whom he continued to pursue was almost impossible except in Wellfleet. His film career included a number of Cape attachments, including starring in Eugene O'Neill's *Desire Under the Elms* (1958) and co-starring with Tuesday Weld in *Pretty Poison* (1968). Weld had deep Cape connections as a fellow *Mayflower* descendant and was, like Perkins, despite their photogenic looks, a very private and intellectual person (among her husbands were Dudley Moore and Pinchas Zukerman).

In a sad landmark in a new era in gay life, Tony Perkins died of AIDS in Los Angeles in 1992 surrounded by Berry and his two sons. Berry remained in their Wellfleet house until her equally tragic death—on one of the 9/11 planes en route to visit her sons.

A different, openly lesbian life was being led by Tony Perkins's neighbor Mary Meigs, who owned the house between his and Mary McCarthy's. Meigs was a tall, extremely handsome but elusive figure who purchased the house in 1954, when Mary McCarthy and her husband, Bowden Broadwater, bought the adjacent one. Meigs came from a wealthy and very Victorian Philadelphia family. She realized she was gay at Bryn Mawr and from then on led an open but discreet lesbian life, joining the WAVES during the war and then teaching before pursuing a life as a painter and later a writer with her partner, Barbara Deming.

Deming, a respected and dedicated prisoners' and women's rights activist, also came from a distinguished family. Together they created a social circle that included painters like Mark Rothko and the ceramics artists Henry Varnum Poor and his stepdaughter Anne, in addition to Edmund and Elena Wilson. Edmund was smitten by Mary from his first meeting and always believed he would persuade her to love him, much to the amusement of both his wife, Elena, and Mary's partner, Barbara.

Mary McCarthy's brother, the actor Kevin McCarthy, while married, was also bisexual and tried unsuccessfully to seduce Meigs while also entertaining Montgomery Clift at his sister's house next door. Somehow Meigs, without any effort on her part, seemed to attract both sexes, but ultimately she and Mary McCarthy parted over the latter's acerb portrait of Meigs as Dolly Lamb, an untalented painter and do-gooder in *A Charmed Life*.

All were pioneers in the creation of a Cape that increasingly accepted anyone with talent or charisma. Many were contemporaries of Cole Porter, and some undoubtedly pals, and could have been particularly appreciative of his lyric line in "Let's Do It" (1928): "Cold Cape Cod clams 'gainst their wish do it . . . let's do it, let's fall in love."

PART IV

WINTER

19.

MARDI

Martha "Mardi" Hall, ca. 1939

M artha Ellicott Tyson Manley Parker, known to her friends and family as Mardi, was a Baltimore girl. Born in 1917, she was a southern aristocrat gifted with old Maryland's charming manners, style, and innate sophistication. Her mother's families—the Manleys and Tysons—had once been prominent Tidewater landholders, but the real money had come from the Quaker textile-factory-owning Ellicotts, whose mills so dominated their river community that it named itself Ellicott City. But then the Civil War's blockade of cotton, the Depression, and weaker generations left her mother and aunts living in small apartments in Washington surrounded by artifacts from the great estates that were now gone with the wind.

Mardi and her sister, Harriett, were the progeny of their mother's marriage to a fellow survivor of the Reconstruction era whose father, a

Vermonter, had been a prominent Civil War general and later a Washington bank president whose fortune had evaporated soon after sending his son, Myron Parker, to Princeton. Myron, or Colonel Parker as he was known to his friends, was a convivial alcoholic whose inability to maintain a job finally led to a divorce, but throughout his life he remained a devoted, beloved father to Mardi and her sister and spent the last years of his life living with Mardi and Jack (his fellow Princetonian) in their East Eightieth Street New York apartment.

Mardi matured early; she was lithe and full figured, and men were attracted to her and she to them. Her mother scraped together enough money to present her to Baltimore society and provide a few years of education at the Bryn Mawr School, where she was fortunate enough to have Edith Hamilton, the author of *The Greek Way*, as a teacher.

With no funds for college, she became a model in Baltimore and Washington, including modeling at Luke Wilson's department store, Woodward and Lothrop. She married early to Edward Gemmell, who had found a job in the admissions department at Andover before the war separated them. When it was over, like so many young couples, they found they were now quite different people and divorced. Mardi remained friends with Ed, as she did with every man she married or slept with.

Rhody Hall and Mardi, New York City

Her second marriage was to a man named Hall, but Monroe Bostwick Hall was a far different Hall from Jack Hall, who was to be her final husband. "Rhody" was tall, dark, and handsome; the many photographs of him by Carl Van Vechten depict him at his 1930s cinematic best with thick, slicked-back hair, a strong chin, and a football player's body clothed in a bespoke, dark blue double-breasted suit.

His father, Benjamin Elihu Hall, had made an early fortune in the railroads and possessed a large estate in the Adirondacks before his bankruptcy in 1929. Rhody and his sister, Alice, had lived in Peking with their parents in the 1920s, and Rhody had an air of mystery that made people overlook his towering temper and ugly drinking bouts. His sister, Alice, later renamed Amanda by her new husband, had, much to her father's shock, met and fallen deeply in love with a short, Jewish intellectual named Gilbert Seldes. They were wed in Paris in 1924, with Picasso and Scott Fitzgerald in attendance. Seldes was already, together with Edmund Wilson and Malcolm Cowley, transforming American journalism at *The New Republic*. Wilson described a visit to the Seldeses at Amanda's father's twenty-five-hundred-acre Lake Saranac estate in his diary *The Twenties*.

Gilbert Seldes, 1932. Photograph by Carl Van Vechten

Amanda, like her brother, was tall and good-looking, and she was madly in love with Gilbert for all thirty years of their marriage. However, she had little interest in being a parent to their two children, Marian and Tim. Enter Aunt Mardi, who had discovered she could not have children, and while she had no interest in babies—once a child could read and converse, she was a boon companion—she filled her life with young people who fell under her spell. Both of Amanda's children and the three that Rhody brought from a prior marriage remained close to Mardi throughout their lives.

After Amanda's death, Gilbert spent many of his summers in Truro where his annual joint end-of-season party with Wendy Day, the daughter of Clarence Day, attracted the local bohemian gentry. Amanda and Gilbert's actress daughter, Marian Seldes, and her second husband, Garson Kanin, were one of the great couples of the American theater, and Mardi attended about every one of Marian's opening nights. Marian's brother, Tim, became an editor at Doubleday and then a literary agent, the eventual owner of one of the great early agencies, Russell & Volkening.

As tolerant of heavy drinking and carousing as she was (there was no jazz club in Manhattan where she was not warmly welcomed at the door), Mardi finally realized that Rhody was bound and determined to destroy his great promise, and they parted as friends, and she remained a beloved honorary family member to the Seldes children.

Before they parted, Rhody and Mardi spent most of 1949–1950 in Provincetown, while Rhody attempted to organize a fishermen's cooperative. The Portuguese captains were a conservative bunch, however, and cooperatives smelled of socialism or even communism, and this tall aristocrat did not gain their confidence. Oddly, Dodie had clear recollections of seeing Mardi (in her sweater and pearls) and Rhody drinking in Provincetown's harbor bars favored by Dodie's second husband, Khaki Captiva, and Manny Zora. During that interlude, Mardi resumed her girlhood friendship with Bubs Hackett, whom she had known in Washington, D.C., when Bubs and Chauncey lived there. It was Bubs who encouraged Mardi to paint.

Despite all their Provincetown connections, Mardi and Jack had never met until they were introduced at a cocktail party in New York.

Mary "Bubs" Hackett, ca. 1950

They married on April 20, 1957, after Mardi got a one-day divorce in Montgomery, Alabama. Thus began the happiest years of Jack's life.

They eventually settled into a large apartment on East Eightieth Street with Mardi's father and Jack's two daughters, who were now working in New York. Still, they spent long summers at Jack's newly redesigned Atwood House on Bound Brook Island. He had purchased the long-abandoned house from its absentee owner and slowly began gutting its interior, which had already been stripped of its original floorboards and paneling. What emerged was a trim 1734 traditional Cape but with a clean modern interior complete with a wall of plate glass in the back and an impressive collection of modern furniture.

Four times lucky for Jack, and three for Mardi—each had now found the partner they were meant for. Jack, being shy and easily taking offense, was not comfortable in his skin, whereas Mardi was totally confident and a born hostess.

Indeed, they appeared an odd match at first blush—Jack now in AA and, devout Quaker, a longtime political supporter of the Communist Party, and Mardi frequently in trouble with her drinking, an agnostic,

Mardi Hall, ca. 1965

and a true liberal, suspicious of all isms. Yet they found common ground in their total acceptance of any and all eccentricities in their bohemian friends, their deep creativity, and their fascination with the cultural life of America. Perhaps most important, they developed an intense and passionate sex life made possible by Mardi's deep sensuality, spontaneity, and general joie de vivre, all qualities Jack had buried under layers of Protestant guilt and Victorian schoolboy cold showers.

Jack generally rose early and prepared breakfast, while Mardi rose late. By lunch she was turned out in a costume that would have thrilled any movie star of the 1930s. She read widely, both poetry and prose, spent hours working on her paintings or collages, and dined with as eclectic a crowd as bohemia could offer.

Together they became like Mary Vorse and Joe O'Brien, Brownie and Bill L'Engle, and John and Katy Dos Passos: social magnets in both New York City and Provincetown for the bohemians of their time. At parties with their Bauhaus friends, whom she knew intimately as individuals whereas Jack knew them mainly as fellow designers, Mardi would often sit next to Connie Breuer, a gifted jazz pianist, and sing Gershwin, Porter, or Big Mama Thornton lyrics in her smoky, Maryland voice, often until sunrise. She formed a deep friendship with the Russian émigré architect Serge Chermayeff's wife, Barbara, and her English mother, and Juliet

MARDI [241]

Kepes, the Bauhaus survivor György's English wife and fellow artist. She arranged a marriage between her sister, Harriett, and Bobby Zion, the highly respected landscape architect. Zion joked that he became a landscape architect because he had machine-gunned a hedge at the Battle of the Bulge and then had to spend the rest of his life trying to restore it. He was particularly famed for his creation of the "vest pocket" parks in New York, including Paley Park and the sculpture garden at the Museum of Modern Art.

She and Jack were also close to John "Jo" Johansen and his second wife, Mary Ellen. Jack had worked with Johansen on the design of Rikers Island in New York City. Johansen was a member of the so-called Harvard Five, all former Gropius students that included Breuer and Philip Johnson. The Johansens spent many weekends at Jack and Mardi's, only to have Jo leave Mary Ellen for Gropius's beautiful daughter, Ati, who had designed her own house in Wellfleet, where she had spent many summers.

Always part of this architects' mix was Jack's fellow amateur design building cohort, Jack Phillips and Hayden Walling. Phillips's final wife, Flossie Hammond, a charming actress and scholar, was the daughter of the Harvard classics professor Mason Hammond. She became a translator for Bernard Berenson, music tutor to David Rockefeller's daughters, and a gifted actress. Young enough to be Phillips's daughter, she formed an intimate and lifelong friendship with Mardi that bound the two Jacks even closer. Hayden Walling was now married to Odette Bonnat, a chain-smoking, heavily accented, former heroine of the Maquis. During the war she had been betrayed, imprisoned by the Gestapo, and lined up for execution when the commanding officer balked at executing a woman. Odette and Hayden were living in a lovely camp he had built on Jack Phillips's Horseleech Pond, but it was not a happy marriage, because Hayden was a magnet for almost any woman.

Architecture did part Jack and Mardi for three months in 1959 when Jack was invited to join one of the young leaders of American design, George Nelson, and his team in the design of the American National Exhibition in Moscow. Among the assembled team were Buckminster Fuller and Charles and Ray Eames. The exhibit was designed to flaunt the "American way," displaying sleekly designed vacuums, washing machines, and plastic furnishings that average Russians could only dream of. This was the height of the Cold War, and Khrushchev was not encouraging American visitors. Mardi tried to get every Russian-born bohemian to help her get a visa, but even Serge Chermayeff couldn't help. It later turned out that it was Jack's FBI file that blocked her visa. Meanwhile, Jack, the longtime "fellow traveler," was staying in comparative luxury at the Hotel Metropol, probably carefully watched by both sides.

Mardi was a natural interior decorator and had worked as one in New York and for many Christmas seasons ran the holiday suggestion table at the Metropolitan Museum's gift store. Any excuse for a party brought out her talents. She always managed to create a festive avant-garde atmosphere using nothing but colored paper and flowers. As a Baltimore girl, the Preakness, the second race of the Triple Crown run in Baltimore in May, always meant for Mardi a time for the singing of "Maryland, My Maryland" and the drinking of mint juleps at a large gathering. If the weather failed to cooperate, Mardi would always admonish her guests to come into the living room and live!

Mardi's cocktail parties were both brilliant and basic: start with one gallon of vodka, one gallon of gin, one bottle of Noilly Prat vermouth, add one old silver platter covered with fern leaves from the garden, with one baked ham thereon accompanied by a bottle of Grey Poupon mustard, black bread, and one large brie cheese, and *laissez les bon temps rouler*.

The 1950s were a time of jazz and psychiatry, and when the bohemian literati's conversation grew too psychiatric, Mardi would cry out, "Paging Dr. Freud!"

At her Preakness or Easter-egg-rolling party on the lawn might be found Philip Hamburger and his wife, Anna Matson, and their *New Yorker* colleagues, all of whom summered in Wellfleet or Truro: Bill Maxwell (J. D. Salinger's editor); Jack Kahn and his wife, Eleanor Munro; Arturo and Nancy Vivante; Edmund Wilson and his final wife, Elena; and Whitney Balliett, *The New Yorker*'s jazz critic, and his new wife, Nancy, a fellow *New Yorker* colleague.

Another party might mix Norman Mailer (always "Norman darling" to Mardi) and his current wife, Dwight and Nancy Macdonald, Joan

Colebrook, Bill and Nancy Webb (he the founder of Noonday Press and she a gifted sculptor), Harry and Elena Levin (the hosts of the Nabokovs during their many summers in Wellfleet), and Annie Dillard (the author of *Pilgrim at Tinker Creek*), who had just bought a house in Wellfleet.

Mardi and Jack were serious about their painting, although Mardi moved from painting to collage, including what she called "vitrage" sculpture made of pieces of broken, heavy colored glass, which she showed at Betty Parsons's gallery in New York. Jack had torn down the garage at the Atwood House and had erected a double studio on its concrete slab, one for him and one for Mardi, with separate entrance doors and no connecting doors inside.

Their artist friends ranged from those who had been early influences on Jack—Edwin Dickinson, Myron Stout, Xavier Gonzalez, and his first in-laws, Bill and Brownie L'Engle, and, for Mardi, Bubs Hackett, Fritz Bultman, and Serge Chermayeff. Jack had maintained his friendship with Chaim Gross and Bill Zorach, who had rented the Delight studio in the 1930s on the Baker farm, and he and Mardi formed many new friendships with artists who were later arrivals in Provincetown and environs— Jack and Wally Tworkov and their friends Shelby and Richard Cox, and the photographer Rachel Brown, the daughter of Slater Brown. Mardi took great pleasure in having introduced the painter Peter Watts to Gloria, the widow of Warren Nardin, Jack's co-designer of the modern house on Bound Brook.

Bound Brook had once more become like its pre-Depression self, with all its houses inhabited and several new ones added. As one entered the island, on the left stood the Atwood-Higgins House, now transformed by Mr. Higgins into a private museum. If you turned right onto the Upper Road, you came to Ruth and Gardner Jencks's house, now occupying the old town picnic ground. And at the road's end, overlooking the view to Provincetown, the marvelous, new, ethereal cottage Jack had built for Bob and Ruth Hatch. Continuing on the Lower Road were the father-and-son Atwood houses, the father's on the right, now gutted and modernized by Jack, with its new studio for Mardi. Opposite stood the Atwood son's seventeenth-century house, now occupied by the painter Judith Rothschild and her husband, the novelist Tony Myrer (*The Last*

Convertible). Judith was the first woman elected to membership in Provincetown's premier gallery, the Long Point, whose members included Robert Motherwell, Sidney Simon, Tony Vevers (now living in Rothko's old house), and Paul Resika. Judith, like almost everyone else, had first come to study with Hans Hofmann. Jack had designed an addition to her house to display her important art collection, which included Picasso, Braque, and Kandinsky.

Continuing down the narrow sand Lower Road to the silted Duck Harbor, on the left was the former harbormaster's house, now marooned half a mile from the sea, which had been owned for years by the Russian-born sculptor Sonia Brown. Sonia had sold the house to Bob Loesser, the town's leading realtor, who had run off with Jean Shay. Loesser's wife had promptly sold it to Harry and Elena Levin, who had met as students at Harvard. There Nabokov and Vera spent many summers speaking Russian with Elena and improving their English with Harry, now a professor of Joyce and Shakespeare at Harvard.

Across the road was Jack's modern house, which he had sold to Judge Lawrence Walsh, the New York prosecutor for the Knapp Commission's investigation of mob control of the docks, which was the basis for Elia Kazan's film *On the Waterfront*. Walsh proved too busy, and his wife found Bound Brook too remote, and the judge donated it to his alma mater, Columbia, as a summer residence for its president.

And finally, where it all began, there was the Captain David Baker farm, which Jack had sold to Judge Francis Biddle and his poet wife, Katherine. Jack and Mardi became close to the Biddles, although they were of another generation. Katherine's half sister, Marguerite Chapin, had moved to Italy as a young woman, where she married the composer Prince Roffredo Caetani, the seventeenth Duke of Sermoneta; their famous garden, Ninfa, remains enchanting. She and Katherine exchanged poetry, and Marguerite and Iris Origo co-published one of Italy's most respected literary journals, *Botteghe Oscure*.

Jack and Jean had begun acting or reading plays with the Biddles when they first started renting in Wellfleet, and this custom continued with Mardi. In his autobiography, *In Brief Authority*, Francis Biddle describes the Baker farm on Bound Brook thus: "Where we live the land is untamed, with sandy roads that for the most part do not lead anywhere. Our walks bring us through tangled locust and scrub oak and swamp alder between the little dunes down to the bay. We own an old house, with Indian shutters inside the window frames; and arrowheads on rare occasions turn up in the beds of September lilies. . . . Around the house, quail, fat and unhurried, call to us from their cover; now and then a red fox lopes across the island road."

Mardi might have become the uncrowned queen of bohemia, but as the chill of winter approached, she, like certain migratory species, felt a deep need to return to the irresistible charm of Manhattan. (They had sold their apartment as their funds dwindled and were living mainly on Bound Brook.) There she could sip cocktails and listen to jazz at the Oak Room or at their friend Daphne Hellman's famous Five Spot jazz club. She always managed to find an apartment in which to hang her frocks until the people she most loved reopened their houses from Province-town to Wellfleet, drawing her back again.

20.

THE NEW, NEW BAUHAUS

The Bauhaus, Dessau, by Walter Gropius

Their story began far from Cape Cod in Germany during the waning days of the decadent but culturally fertile Weimar Republic.

Walter Gropius had founded the Bauhaus (literally "building house") in a failed Berlin art school. Like many of its original faculty, he had served and been wounded in World War I. The old Prussian Germany was dying, and the young architects, painters, and craftsmen he had gathered around him were committed to creating a new utopian world: an aesthetic life combining all the arts in search of a unified design for living that was both functional and free from the influence of religion and the formal divisions that had separated the arts in the past. This search for an accessible, economical blend of simplified building, in which the arts could be combined with furnishings incorporating the new and still

dangerous thrills of abstraction and playfulness, held enormous appeal in
dreary postwar Europe.

Charleston on the Bauhaus roof, 1927.
Xanti Schawinsky (left) and Clemens Röseler

Amid street battles between the Brownshirts of the rising National
Socialists and their communist opponents, and crowds of desperate Ber-
liners clutching armfuls of increasingly worthless deutschmarks, the Bauhaus created its own world filled with Dada-esque costume parties, plays,
and films.

The Bauhaus faculty, ca. 1926. Walter Gropius is center,
with hand in pocket; Wassily Kandinsky is fourth from right.

By 1928 the Bauhaus had become a pilgrimage destination for young
artists and architects throughout Europe and even the United States.
It outgrew its facilities in Weimar and built a new complex in Dessau,
an industrial city north of Weimar where Gropius designed its famous

headquarters building. Unfortunately, that move and its final move to
Berlin brought it directly into the maelstrom of Hitler's National Socialists' attack on Jews and "degenerate" art, which Hitler associated with
the evils of modernism as interpreted by Jewish artists. And indeed, the
Bauhaus had attracted some of the most gifted young Jewish artists and
architects in Europe, including Paul Klee, Marcel Breuer, Herbert Bayer,
and László Moholy-Nagy.

As the anti-Semitic attack grew, Gropius believed it might be best
for the school if he withdrew as director, and he returned to a private
architectural practice in Berlin with Moholy-Nagy, enlisting Mies van
der Rohe to replace him. Mies, like Gropius, was not Jewish and was
something of a hero in Germany as the designer of its celebrated German
pavilion at the 1929 Barcelona World's Fair, a floating white rectangular
pavilion that had immediately become an international icon of the new
modernism.

Walter Gropius, Berlin, 1928, with his proposed design for Chicago's Tribune Tower

But the Nazis were not impressed. On April 11, 1933, shortly after Hitler was elected Reich chancellor, his new Berlin district attorney ordered the Bauhaus searched and arrested 32 of its 168 students.
Mies held an emergency meeting of the faculty, which voted to close the
school. This was but one motivating incident behind one of the greatest
diasporas of intellectual talent in the modern world as artists, architects,
composers, scientists, filmmakers, and intellectuals, many of them Jewish
or married to Jews, made their way, often perilously, to England, America,
and any country that would grant them entry. For the early and lucky
ones, London became a welcoming place even on the eve of Hitler's rise
and the Depression. There Gropius and Moholy-Nagy found admiration
but little work. Breuer had fled to Switzerland to work with Herbert
Bayer, but there was again little work and he arranged through friends
to fly to London. Concerned about being searched at the airport, being
a Jew with a German passport, he bought a copy of *Mein Kampf* and
placed his remaining currency in it and shipped it ahead to his friends.
Upon opening his package, his friends were shocked to find nothing but
Hitler's manifesto and immediately put it in the trash. When Breuer arrived, he immediately inquired whether they had the package with his
only money and they said they had placed it in the "tip." Breuer rushed to
the basement and discovered with relief that the trash had not yet been
collected.

Gropius was finally offered a splendid job at Harvard and a haven in
America for his wife, Ise Frank, and their daughter, Ati, to begin a new
life in yet another country. His first wife had been the legendary siren
Alma Mahler, the widow of Gustav. While she soon abandoned Gropius
for Franz Werfel, she always left memories.

Jack Hall, Hayden Walling, and Jack Phillips were already devoted
fans of modernism and the Bauhaus, but equally influenced by American modernism as practiced earlier by the Chicago skyscraper architect
Louis Sullivan and his disciples Frank Lloyd Wright and Philip Johnson.
Gropius, too, was a great admirer of Sullivan's and his mantra, "Form
follows function." (It was Gropius's fellow Bauhausian Marcel Breuer
who added "but not always" after Sullivan's famous line.) Both Wright
and Johnson had visited the Bauhaus and had helped promote the first

exhibition of its work in 1938 at the new Museum of Modern Art in New York.

But at this point in the late 1930s, Phillips and Hall were still mainly redesigning existing structures except for Jack Phillips's 1938 innovative Paper Palace beach studio. It was Phillips who decided to add formal architectural training to the skills he, Hall, and Walling were learning from their amateur building projects. In the fall of 1939 he left his camp on Horseleech Pond and enrolled in Gropius's Basic Design course at Harvard, the same introductory architecture course that Gropius had created for the Bauhaus. Jack Phillips was then a twenty-five-year-old charming and sophisticated New England aristocrat who after Harvard had studied painting with Fernand Léger and Pierre Lhote in Paris, where his first of five marriages was to a fellow painter. He was completely open about his admiration of Gropius and this opportunity to learn from the master.

Walter Gropius was now fifty-six, seemingly always clad in a suit and bow tie and formal in manner in a way only European intellectuals born in the nineteenth century could be (unless he knew you). This false view of Gropius as remote and humorless was encouraged by Evelyn Waugh's caricature of him in *Decline and Fall* (1928) as Professor Otto Silenus, an architect who liked to design "something clean and square." Waugh had met Gropius while in exile in London and took a dislike to him perhaps because of his extremely poor English.

Gropius required all his students to begin by creating a model of a house they hoped to build. Unlike the others, Phillips proudly displayed his model of the Paper Palace he had just completed, overlooking his vast Atlantic beach. Phillips had ingeniously constructed a large vertical shed with long windows facing the sea, using painted Homasote paperboard for its interior and attaching multilevel balconies halfway up the building. Holding Phillips's model upside down, Gropius commented on its unsupported balconies. "Does it leak here?" he asked. Phillips smiled and responded, "It does!" After a year, Phillips decided he was not meant to be an architect and left Harvard, although his friendship with Gropius would continue.

The late 1930s found a large group of European exiles gathered around Gropius in New York and finally in Cambridge, desperately seeking his help in finding work and housing for their families in the Depression. Gropius had always been uniquely gifted in his ability to discover academic appointments or jobs in design or architecture for an amazing number of his friends. Fortunately, his former architecture partner in Berlin, László Moholy-Nagy, was equally gifted in placement, having swiftly become the director of the Institute of Design in Chicago, where he packed the faculty with so many former colleagues that it soon became internationally known as the New Bauhaus.

Nevertheless, there was little money in architecture or part-time teaching during the Depression, and few architects, except Gropius, even built their own houses, because the future looked increasingly grim. Hitler's troops had conquered Holland, Belgium, and France in a mere six weeks in May and June 1940, and over the next four years Gropius, Breuer, and Moholy-Nagy received chilling news, on an almost weekly basis, of the death or disappearance of one former Bauhaus comrade after another. The only hope was that the vanished colleague might have managed to escape to Switzerland, Sweden, Portugal, or South America. The chances of finding refuge in America now were growing slim, particularly for those who were German and Jewish.

Despite the darkness, the Bauhaus exiles never abandoned their Weimar Dada desire for play in the face of evil, and through Phillips's continuing friendship with Gropius his cabins and the Paper Palace slowly became affordable vacation refuges for Gropius's circle as well as other European artists. In the serenity of the Cape's green woods, clear ponds, and vast ocean, they were able to renew their cultural bonds in their native tongue, whether German, Czech, Hungarian, or French (many had worked with Le Corbusier at the Bauhaus or in Paris). Here they could sing old songs at beach parties while bathing in the nude along Phillips's semi-abandoned beach or ponds. (One of the causes of the Bauhaus's move to Dessau was outrage over its faculty's and students' tradition of bathing nude in Weimar's local parks.) Around the beach fire, they could continue their endless questioning of how fascism could have triumphed over socialism and communism.

One of them was undeterred by these hard times from seeking a permanent home in this paradise. Serge Chermayeff (né Sergei Ivanovich

Issakovich) was born in czarist Chechnya. His father, a Sephardic Jew, had made a fortune in oil before the revolution took all. Sent to England at ten, Sergei somehow survived cultural isolation at Harrow School to emerge a towering, imperially handsome young man-about-town in bespoke suits during the day and in white tie and tails at night as one of the best ballroom dancers in London.

At twenty-four, Issakovich changed his name to Chermayeff, adopting a variation of the surname of his czarist cavalry officer "milk brother" (they had shared the same wet nurse). Anti-Semitism was rising in England, too, and it could affect employment, but the question was, what employment? Serge had led a wandering life since Harrow, but he had always had a flair for creating beauty and design in addition to conveying his ideas with immense charm and confidence regardless of his lack of formal training.

Serge married Barbara May, the daughter of a successful English builder, and began to design serious buildings and interiors in an England on the verge of Chamberlain's Munich Agreement with Hitler granting Germany part of Czechoslovakia. Soon, overcome by debt and denied entry to the United States, he departed for Canada with Barbara and their two young sons, Ivan and Peter. In England he had designed two buildings that are still considered among the best of the period: the sleek seaside De La Warr Pavilion (1935) at Bexhill-on-Sea with his émigré German partner, Erich Mendelsohn; and Chermayeff's own quite grand country house, Bentley Wood, on the South Downs in Low Weald, Sussex. *The Architects' Journal* in 1938 described it as "a regular Rolls-Royce of a house." During those years, he had also come to know the Bauhaus community in London exile, including Gropius, Breuer, and Moholy-Nagy.

They would meet again. In 1940 the Chermayeff family was finally permitted entry to the United States and came to stay with the Gropiuses at their newly built house in Lincoln, Massachusetts, outside Boston. With Gropius's help, Chermayeff found work as the new chair of the architecture department at Brooklyn College. Eager to see their new country, he and his family accepted an invitation to stay with Peter Harnden, a young, Yale-educated architect who was renting Jack Phillips's Paper

Palace studio. The Paper Palace had now become a legendary romantic party spot for both Jack's American bohemian friends and a growing circle of foreign artists who had begun to stay or work in Provincetown with Hans Hofmann. Among his illustrious guests were Roberto Matta, Arshile Gorky, Jackson Pollock, Max Ernst, and a host of young, attractive women.

Serge was smitten by the beauty of the long, unspoiled Atlantic beach and the green ponds amid the dappled oak and locust woods behind the great dune, and he basked in the warm welcome he received from Phillips.

Phillips, sensing a new comrade, took the Chermayeffs to see the only structure then on Slough Pond, a small building Hayden Walling had designed. The two Chermayeff boys (each to become a famous architect and designer in his own right) saw a pond brimming with frogs, pickerel, bass, and a large snapping turtle. Their father saw a site for a grand Bauhaus statement. Phillips immediately offered it to him, the cabin and twelve acres, for two thousand dollars, and Chermayeff accepted, buoyed by the proceeds he had just earned from his first exhibition at the Museum of Modern Art. And so the first of the Bauhaus circle came to own a home in the land of the Pilgrims.

The exiles had a better sense than most that no one could flee the war, and Pearl Harbor soon changed everything, requiring them to once again abandon their plans for a new life. Both the youngest and the oldest of the great Nazi-fleeing diaspora were swept up in the defense of their new country. Nevertheless, they had discovered a place to return to.

When the war was over, many of the young architects and designers, émigrés as well as Americans who had been guests of Phillips or Serge and Barbara Chermayeff in their still half-reconstructed cabin, had not forgotten the secluded ponds and vast empty ocean beaches that now remained embedded in their memories. Perhaps they could finally seek a more permanent relationship with that mythical landscape.

Phillips's chain of glacial kettle ponds seemed particularly magnetic. If you were to have flown above them in a helicopter, you could view the chain of ponds as they began in Wellfleet just across the newly tarred state road to Provincetown and then crossing the highway along Phillips's rutted sand road, which ran through pine, locust, and oak forest to the great Truro dunes towering above his Atlantic beach. The first pond in the chain had borne many names since the eighteenth century, including Snow's, Aunt Mary's, and Ryder. Early settlers used the pond mainly to cut ice for their summer icehouses to preserve food. At one end of the pond stood a good-sized abandoned icehouse that could be rented from the pond's owner. It had no toilet, stove, or electricity, but the surrounding forest offered complete privacy and quiet with a special deep-woods scent no visitor could forget, and the bathing was idyllic. It had been rented for some years by Stan Thayer, a young painter who used it mainly to lure pretty, young female painters, folksingers, and other guests, among whom was Xanti Schawinsky, Gropius's close friend from their Bauhaus days in Germany. Schawinsky had been the Bauhaus court jester, the organizer of entertaining films, live theatricals, and dances in which he played major roles. Handsome and fearless, Xanti attracted many of the most beautiful young bohemian Berlin girls to these events. Soon he began renting the Thayer icehouse for his wife and attractive "assistant," and Walter and Ise Gropius became frequent visitors when they were not staying with the Chermayeffs.

(from left) Irene Schawinsky, Ise Gropius, unidentified, Xanti Schawinsky, and son Ben at Ryder Pond, Wellfleet, ca. 1945. Photograph by Walter Gropius

Across the highway, the glacial ponds continued on either side of Jack's road running to the great dunes. The largest, Slough and Horseleech, were deemed "Great Ponds" by law dating back to the Puritans' Massachusetts Bay Colony, and while they could be privately owned (as they were by Jack Phillips), they were by law open to all to "fish or fowl" and later swim. This rule was perhaps a remnant of the Puritans' early contact with the Indigenous people, who believed that nature's assets belonged to everyone and could not be owned.

The first Great Pond on the left was Slough, where Serge Chermayeff had now replaced Hayden Walling's simple cabin, which he bought in 1949, with several long, raised rectangular buildings with flat roofs and eight-foot bay windows separated by colorfully painted exterior panels, all connected by decks. These had become international guesthouses for the Chermayeffs' Bauhaus friends, whose first exposure to the Phillips woods was often from a deck above Serge's pond.

(back row, from left) Eero Saarinen, Lily Swann Saarinen, Florence Schust Knoll; (front row, from left) Eliel and Loja Saarinen, Hans Knoll; (foreground) Eric Saarinen, ca. 1949

Before you reached the Chermayeffs' house on the other side of the road, there was a slope overlooking shallow, lily-pad-covered Herring Pond. There, in 1964, the Finnish architect Olav Hammarstrom, a traumatized veteran of Finland's wars with both Germany and Russia, had been hired to design a house for his fellow Finn Eero Saarinen and his American sculptor wife, Lily Swann. Their Finnish bond had begun with Eero's famous father, Eliel, who had left Finland before the war to run the Cranbrook Academy of Art in Michigan. In 1949 the father-and-son Saarinen teams designed the Christ Church Lutheran in Minneapolis, and in 1956 Eero designed the award-winning General Motors Design Auditorium in Warren, Michigan. Hammarstrom had worked as a valued draftsman for both father and son in Finland and now in America. The Saarinen house was actually built by Hayden Walling, using Hammarstrom's drawings, becoming one of the early joint ventures between foreigner and Yankee in Jack Phillips's woods.

The Saarinens' house (which many still think was designed by him) quickly became another social center for architects and designers whom both Hammarstrom and the Saarinens had known at Cranbrook. Hans and Florence Knoll and Charles and Ray Eames, both world-famous husband-and-wife furniture-design teams, began to rent along the road in summers and join their esteemed colleague "Lajko" Breuer, as he was called by his Hungarian friends, on his deck for drinks and arguments about design. It was Charles Eames who best described the Bauhaus approach to furniture design: "the best for the least for the most."

The next house visible on the same side of the road was Breuer's. He and Chermayeff had each bought land from Jack in 1944. Phillips left Harvard before Breuer had joined Gropius to co-teach the Bauhaus method and form their own architectural firm, the Architects Collaborative, which designed the Harvard Graduate Center in 1950. Breuer was considered a far better teacher than Gropius, at least by the next wave of America's leading architects, including I. M. Pei, Paul Rudolph, and Philip Johnson. Unlike Serge, Breuer had worked and taught through the war and did not build on his land until 1949. It was no ordinary site Breuer had purchased from Phillips. It overlooked not one but three pristine small ponds—Higgins, Williams, and Gull. It was in an old oyster-

Charles Eames and Eero Saarinen at drawing board, Cranbrook, 1941

man's house on Williams Pond that Henry Thoreau wrote in his *Journals* of taking shelter on one of his trips to Cape Cod.

Breuer had initially designed a simple summerhouse prototype for a contemplated cluster of five houses to be erected on the site, hoping to lure some of his Hungarian compatriots, including György Kepes (perhaps his closest friend), Stephen Borsody, a former Hungarian diplomat, and his old Bauhaus pal Xanti Schawinsky. But it was Kepes who built first, but on another beautiful Truro pond, using Breuer's house drawings.

A long orange sand rectangle had been scraped from the bed of brown oak leaves and pine needles on the hill overlooking Long Pond, where Ernie Rose, the grizzled descendant of an early Portuguese Cape family and the favorite builder among the local architects, was now studying those Breuer drawings on the rusty bed of his truck. Satisfied, Rose directed his men to dig holes for the concrete pilings in the now-cleared land on which they would lay the uninsulated floor to bear the house's floating form. The flat tar-papered roof was supported by two-by-four studs clad with plywood, except where large plate glass windows were set between the studs in the grooved frame so they could be opened from either side. Breuer's design called for bedrooms that were small and closets that were smaller, leaving the living sections as open as possible.

Rose found the job congenial. It was the same simple approach he used to replicate the eighteenth-century Cape houses he normally built using the cheapest materials available, except that these were double-clad and fenestrated for year-round occupancy. He observed that Mr. Breuer had purposefully conceived his only for summer use. Clearly, it was the view, not permanence, that interested Breuer.

The job completed, Rose presented his bill for $5,000 to Kepes and his English artist wife, Juliet. It was exactly the same bill he would later present to Mr. and Mrs. Breuer for their house. (In 1950 a conventional two-bedroom, two-bathroom ranch house cost $12,900.) Each had two children's bedrooms, and on the bare wood floors lay woven rugs designed by Anni Albers, wife of the German-born painter Josef Albers, later to be famed for his painting series of gradually receding colored squares. Albers, a much-admired teacher at the Bauhaus, had married Anni, who was Jewish and thus forced to join the diaspora to America. Anni had headed the textile section at the Bauhaus and later at Black Mountain College, where the Alberses had found refuge when they first came to the States.

The two houses differed slightly in size, decking, and cantilevered, screened porches (for as pleasant as their pond views were, the evenings brought mosquitoes). The furniture was sparse and designed to visually float above the floor so as not to interfere with the view through the glass walls. There were tubular metal chairs with woven seats designed by Breuer, the curved aluminum inspired by the handles on his bicycle at the Weimar Bauhaus; three-legged stools designed by the Scandinavian designer Alvar Aalto; and a sofa on thin metal legs designed by Florence Knoll. A collection of the best work by the postwar architects and designers now summering in Wellfleet and Truro.

The Bauhaus eschewed clutter, and Americans were going to have to forgo bookcases, huge closets, and unnecessary belongings if they were to claim modernity. Poor Connie Breuer, a gifted pianist, had her hopes for a piano quickly dashed by Lajko.

Kepes's new Long Pond house quickly drew other neighbors. Bernard Rudofsky, the Austro-Hungarian architect who had fled Nazi Germany for Brazil, built a small house on Kepes's sand road, where he, Breuer, and Chermayeff held an annual summer beard-growing contest. There, Rudofsky completed one of the most influential books in modern architectural theory—*Architecture Without Architects*. He and Breuer urged Josef Albers to join them, and soon thereafter Hans Hofmann hired Josef and Anni to teach in his Provincetown school, and thus another Bauhaus circle was rejoined.

György Kepes (left) and Marcel Breuer playing chess at the Breuer house

It was not all work. Kepes, Breuer, and their pond neighbors developed a mysterious passion for the Victorian English game of Ping-Pong, then popular only in Mao's China. Soon, every modern house had a table stored under its raised floor. But golf and even sailing or tennis were strictly viewed as sport for the suburbanites, not for them.

At the very end of Phillips's road on the left lay Horseleech Pond, the location of Jack Phillips's uncle's original duck-hunting camp and now the hub of Jack's landholdings. He and Hayden Walling had enlarged his uncle's primitive camp and during World War II built a series of small structures to hold turkeys along its shore. These redesigned turkey houses were now used to house children from Jack's five marriages during the summer. Jack had also built a number of adjacent buildings, the first being the Paper Palace in 1938, and over the years several others, both large and small, were located around the pond or higher up on the great dune overlooking his beach.

The largest of these Horseleech Pond houses had been built for a new wife, but after her departure Jack sold it to Luke Wilson, who had fled to Rome when the McCarthy hearings accused him of being a communist, leaving the house to his children.

On Jack Phillips's dune, above Horseleech, Olav Hammarstrom and his Finnish wife, Marianne Strengell, who had chaired Cranbrook's textile department, built a stunningly simple wood-and-stone-floored house, which had so impressed Eero and Lily Saarinen that they requested Hammarstrom build a similar one for them.

Perhaps archaeologists hundreds of years from now exploring the ruins of these houses might assume they represented a second "pond culture" based on earlier Native Americans' ephemeral structures.

There were two modernist outliers from the Bauhaus's Eurocentric pond culture. Jack Hall had built two on remote Bound Brook Island, and Nathaniel Saltonstall created another group of modern structures at his Mayo Hill Colony overlooking Wellfleet Harbor.

Saltonstall came from one of Boston's oldest families. His cousin Leverett Saltonstall, called Salty, had been Massachusetts's governor from 1939 to 1945 and gained wide popularity, particularly among Boston's Irish, who invited him to march annually with them at the front of their rowdy South Boston St. Patrick's Day Parade. He became a U.S. senator in 1945 and remained so until 1967. It was Salty who first began to lobby for the passage of legislation to create a national seashore park to protect the pristine coastline from Provincetown to the Cape Cod Canal.

Nathaniel Saltonstall was openly gay and a popular figure in Boston's social and intellectual life, having been a co-founder of its Institute of Contemporary Art, which had begun as a branch of the Museum of Modern Art in New York. He was the only formally trained architect of the original Cape's Bauhaus WASPs. With his Brahmin mien and coat and tie, he rarely mixed with the Phillipsville bohemians, although he was much admired for his buildings and the Wellfleet Contemporary Art Gallery he established. Saltonstall's major contribution to the Cape's modern architecture was his tastefully designed complex of rental cottages at the Colony, as it became known. Each cottage was carefully sited for a specific view of Wellfleet Harbor and for privacy from its adjacent house.

The grouping attracted an upper-crust clientele, from Lionel and Diana Trilling to Jackie Kennedy and Elizabeth Taylor. Saltonstall personally decorated each cottage with works of art from some of the Outer Cape's best artists, whom he also exhibited at his art gallery, first located at the Colony from 1949 to 1955 and later moved to Route 6 in Wellfleet. Among those he exhibited were Xavier Gonzalez, Jack Hall's first painting teacher; Gonzalez's wife, Ethel Edwards; and Dodie Hall's lover the sculptor Sidney Simon. It would have been hard to find any other building complex this sophisticated in the United States in 1949.

On Bound Brook Island, Jack Hall would never feel as comfortable with his patrician roots as Saltonstall did. Having spent his life since college as a wealthy radical bohemian, and having worked through two troubled marriages and alcoholism, he had finally developed his gift as a painter and building designer.

After the war, Hall had worked with some of America's leading architects, beginning with his Wellfleet summer neighbor Warren Nardin, who had redesigned the Horseleech Pond house Jack Phillips had sold to Luke Wilson. Together, they had co-designed and built Hall's modern house, and Jack then joined Nardin's firm in New York part-time and after his divorce from Jean in 1954 began working almost full-time in New York City.

After Nardin's death, Jack began an intense period of design work with the already famous George Nelson, whose firm was designing leading department store interiors, including their lighting and furnishings. Nelson was a friend of Peter Harnden, who had first brought Chermayeff to the Cape and was now an adviser on the Marshall Plan in Europe. Harnden invited Nelson to design and build the vast American National

Exhibition in Moscow in 1959. The exhibit attracted more than three million curious Russians eager to view America's postwar boom of leisure, plastic, and automobiles with fins.

Even before his work with Nelson, Hall had begun to design and build his own projects on the Cape, rather than merely redesigning existing dwellings. The first was Peters Hill Restaurant in Truro, located as advertised on a rise on the highway overlooking Provincetown Harbor. In essence this building was a long shed with Bauhaus clerestory windows under the roofline above sliding Japanese-style screen doors. Peter Brown, the Peter of Peters Hill, was the son of Jack Hall's Bound Brook neighbor Sonia Brown, the Russian sculptor who had exhibited in the 1913 Armory Show. The cook at Peters Hill was the much-married Joan Colebrook, the Australian-born journalist who now owned the Dos Passoses' Truro farmhouse. Her eldest son worked as a waiter. In the evening, music was provided by the harpist Daphne Hellman and her jazz trio. Daphne was the former wife of the *New Yorker* writer Geoffrey Hellman and also owned the legendary Greenwich Village jazz club the Five Spot. She had been a friend of Jack's since her debutante days at St. James, Long Island. Peters Hill was short-lived but a deeply beloved spot for Cape bohemians and a "must" stop on their way to and from Provincetown.

Hall's most outstanding Cape achievement was built closer to home. The Jenckses had bought land after the war to build a house on the former town picnic ground upon the highest point of Bound Brook Island. Their close friends Bob and Ruth Hatch had been longtime summer renters from mutual friends like Anna Matson and Edwin Dickinson in Provincetown and Wellfleet and had just bought a plot from the Jenckses in a lovely dell with a clear view straight across the bay to Provincetown. Bob, like Jack, was a Princeton graduate who had become a well-regarded editor at *Horizon* and was now the book critic for *The Nation*. Bob and his wife, Ruth, a painter, both held strong left-wing political views similar to Jack's, but they had never become friends.

The Hatches approached Jack about designing a summer cottage on their new property. On a very limited budget, Jack designed a house that combined everything he had learned or believed in about modern design:

simplicity; siting for the maximum exposure to natural beauty and the least impact on that beauty. His major innovation was the division of living spaces to emphasize the large communal space—living room and kitchen—over the freestanding and smaller bedrooms and bathroom. The shutters on the main structure protected the Plexiglas windows or screen panels facing the bay and could be raised in the summer and closed in winter.

Peter McMahon, in his definitive book on this period of Cape modern architecture, wrote,

> Of all the Cape Cod modern houses that have opened their doors to the public, Hall's Hatch House evokes the most visceral, astonished response, even from veteran architects. With soft fir cladding, a separate building for each of its three living spaces, and a spectacular sloping site overlooking Cape Cod Bay, the house is at once a sculpture on a pedestal and a piece of weathering driftwood, blending slowly into the landscape.[1]

Rarely in cultural history has such a disparate group of creators—designers, craftsmen, and architects, many from diverse countries, languages, and aesthetics—found a common refuge in one remote and unspoiled

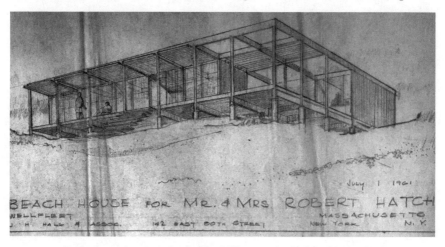

Preparatory drawings for the Hatch House, 1951, by John Hooker Hall

place. Perhaps like Periclean Athens it transpires that *Homo ludens* (man at play) can be even more creative than *Homo labor*—or, perhaps, the Bauhaus had merely moved once more!

Jack Hall's Hatch House's deck, facing Provincetown

21.

JOAN'S BEACH

Joan's beach" was named both for Long Island's Jones Beach, blessed to the memory of many Jewish bohemians who grew up in the Bronx and Brooklyn, and for Joan Sinkler, now the owner of one of Jack Phillips's redesigned military barrack overlooking New-comb Hollow Beach. Joan was a popular and attractive woman whose second and older husband, Wharton Sinkler, had been institutionalized after a foxhunting accident outside Philadelphia, the Sinklers' seat. She was a generous hostess and surrounded herself with a coterie of young men, the most notorious of whom were her alternate summer lovers, known as "White Peter" and "Black Peter." The first, Peter Watts, had arrived as a young painter in 1954 when he agreed to drive his painting professor at the University of Illinois, LaForce Bailey, to Provincetown. There he met Joan, who at her death left him the barrack and ten acres, a legacy that ultimately enabled him to establish himself as a leading Cape landscape painter. Peter only learned at her death that Joan's given name was Haddassah Goldenberg.

Peter was a Dionysian young man with a head of golden curls, and Joan was hardly the only woman interested in his attention. One summer he worked as a caretaker for the Chavchavadzes' house, which was being rented by Mary Grand. Mary telephoned him complaining of a balky screen door. Peter arrived and, examining the door hinges, declared, "It just needs two long screws." Mary swiftly responded, "So do I."

Peter was also a regular in the O'Connor-Macdonald Sunday softball game, officially known as the Co-operative Community Softball Game. It began at 10:00 a.m. on Wellfleet Harbor's Mayo Beach playground and ended as the noon siren sounded at town hall. Each team was fairly divided by height, and every batter under eight swung until he or she made contact. The game had been organized by Edwin O'Connor, then a rising novelist, and Dwight Macdonald just after the war when Ed, then thirty, began coming to Wellfleet to spend the summers in "the Woods" (which Jack Hall always referred to as "Phillipsville") near Jack Phillips's Horseleech Pond. In the 1950s, the Sunday lineup might feature Arthur Schlesinger Jr. at first base, Bernie Rosenberg, the editor of *Dissent*, at second, Norman Mailer at third, his cousin and sometime literary agent Cy Rembar at shortstop, Ed O'Connor in left field, and Dwight Macdonald in right, complete with his jaunty cigarette holder, which was no impediment, because he declined to pick up any ball hit in his direction. Edmund Wilson, in ballooning British shorts, occasionally batted but refused to run. Norman, attempting to impress the ladies present, once slid into third base and broke his leg. None of the players were much good, except Rembar and O'Connor, who almost always hit home runs.

Each Sunday a group began to form on Joan's Beach above the sandbank high-tide line, some in just swimsuits and towels, others, like Bunny Wilson, in a rumpled white shirt, Panama hat, and British shorts, leaning on his gold-topped walking stick. Several had brought *The New York Times* to read; others carried books, often ones that might hopefully impress their fellow beachgoers.

It was a different group from that which had populated Jack Phillips's adjacent beach in the prewar years, which was more of a painter and WASP crowd. Joan's Beach was more about writing and politics, and many were neither artists nor WASPs. Not a few had studied at Brooklyn College, which had become New York's new School of Athens. There sons and daughters of the Pale had learned the art of disputation in its classrooms and on the tough streets of Brooklyn, often speaking Yiddish and English interchangeably.

Nothing excited them as much as a worthy debate fought at maximum ferocity; it was the one contact sport in which most WASPs were often ill-equipped to compete. Whether the subject was politics, art, or culture, all the very best of Brooklyn excelled at argument, and they carried it to the Cape, whether on Joan's Beach or among sneaker-clad crowds at porch cocktail parties, tennis courts, or softball fields.

The leader of Joan's Beach conversation was usually Edwin O'Connor, a Boston, not Brooklyn, man, a Catholic, not a Jew, always dressed in his battered hat and terry-cloth robe, who would arrive on his bicycle from the Sunday softball game, where the selected discussion might have originated on the field itself. O'Connor had grown up in a Rhode Island mill town and, after serving in the coast guard, attended Notre Dame and then pursued a career as a journalist, first for the old *Boston Post*, where his storytelling skills won him an editor's job at *The Atlantic Monthly*.

Big Ed, as Daniel Aaron called him, was well over six feet tall and never owned a car, riding his bicycle wherever he needed to go, as Aaron did, both in Boston and in Wellfleet. O'Connor was magic with young children, perhaps because he never had any of his own. Rosalind Wilson and Arthur Schlesinger's children followed him devotedly to the beach, or anywhere else, whenever they could.

He was disciplined about his writing, usually up early to write for five hours in the morning, and in 1956, at age thirty-eight, he found huge success with his iconic novel of Boston's rowdy Irish political life, *The Last Hurrah*. Choosing to celebrate its publication in Wellfleet, he borrowed Arthur Schlesinger's Slough Pond army barrack/cabin, which the Schlesingers shared with their co-owners Gustav "Peter" and Vita Petersen. Peter was a Norwegian businessman who had married Vita after she had fled the Nazis from Berlin to paint again in New York. She was a founder of the New York Studio School. Their daughter, Andrea, later married across the pond to Peter Chermayeff. Ed purchased fifty steaks, which he proceeded to broil on every available grill and stove.

With the proceeds of *The Last Hurrah*, he was now able to buy twelve acres in the woods overlooking Joan's Beach. He hired Iris Origo's cousin Heyward Cutting, a young architect who had studied with Moholy-Nagy at the Institute of Design in Chicago and was now a partner of Chermayeff's. Cutting built another house for himself nearby. In order to site the O'Connor house, he and O'Connor had to stand above the pine trees on twelve-foot ladders. (O'Connor later shared ownership of the new house with his friend Aileen Ward, whose biography of John Keats had won both the National Book Award and the Duff Cooper Prize. Aileen was also a friend and fellow faculty member of Vladimir Nabokov's at Wellesley College.)

Jack Hall had a lifelong dispute with Heyward Cutting, but it wasn't based on design competition or that Cutting was a licensed architect, nor on Cutting's patrician good looks and Anglo-American pedigree (like Jack, he had gone to St. Bernard's and then returned to England to live with Iris Origo and their common grandparents and attend Eton). It wasn't even because Cutting had left Harvard to join the King's Rifles and serve with Montgomery's Desert Rats at El Alamein, where he was severely wounded. No, it was all because of Jack's beloved childhood English nanny who had been dismissed by Jack's mother because she felt Nanny and Jackie had become too close. His mother forbade Nanny ever to correspond or contact Jack under pain of losing her pension. Jack, still inconsolable at this loss, was horrified to learn that her next charge had been none other than Heyward. This was more than Jack could bear, particularly because Heyward enjoyed claiming that Nanny had loved him the most. As Jack's wife Mardi would often say in such circumstances, "Paging Dr. Freud!"

For some reason, Ed O'Connor totally charmed Bunny Wilson and brought out Wilson's best as a storyteller and man of immense cultural reach. They had a common love of magic and together created a mythical magician they titled the Great Baldini. Both also adored puppets and used them to mimic friends—Wilson in an often-cruel way but Ed just to have fun. (O'Connor was so good at mimicking Mary McCarthy's husband Bowden Broadwater's voice and manner that when Bowden called people, they immediately thought it was Ed putting them on.)

The O'Connor-Wilson beach conversations began to attract a new group of writers and scholars who were exploring America's postwar culture. The Joan's Beach Club Sunday discussions became an attraction that drew a larger and larger crowd of writers and their spouses: Dwight and

Nancy Rodman Macdonald; Mary McCarthy, Nancy's classmate at Vassar; Bowden Broadwater; Kevin McCarthy (Mary's brother the actor); Gardner and Ruth Jencks (who now owned the army cabin next to Joan Sinkler); Harry and Elena Levin; Alfred Kazin and his wife, Ann; Jason Epstein and his wife, Barbara (later co-founders of *The New York Review of Books*); and often Irving Howe, like Aaron and Dwight Macdonald an ardent Trotskyite; Philip Rahv; Norman Podhoretz; Dan Aaron; Richard Hofstadter; Stanley Kunitz; and Arthur Schlesinger, and his wife, Marian.

Always lurking in this highly charged bohemian circle was an underlying tension based on either dangerous liaisons or unsettled intellectual battles. Mary McCarthy's *Charmed Life* had targeted many sitting on that very beach, particularly Wilson and Ruth and Gardner Jencks, both of whom had seemingly forgiven her, but the scars remained. The Jenckses' son, Charles, later summed up that hurt: "I guess she thought her duty was to her art and not to her friends. It was the reverse of [E. M.] Forster, who said, 'I'd rather betray my country than my friend.'"[1]

Mary's book might have also been a response to Wilson's play *The Little Blue Light*, first performed in 1951 in Cambridge at the Brattle Theatre, with Jessica Tandy playing the much younger and dissatisfied wife (Mary) of a valiant liberal journalist (Edmund) and his wife's younger lover, the liberal journalist's young assistant (Bowden Broadwater). It was later performed in New York with Arlene Francis playing Mary, but it was not a success, and after the performance Rosalind Wilson found her father sitting alone at a bar, muttering, "There's a double Manhattan here that will be my friend."

Even though his kindness and his great skills as a raconteur made him the admired center of attention, O'Connor was extremely shy with women. However, one summer he fell under the spell of Ati, the tall, elegant daughter of Walter Gropius. Ati was newly married to the painter Charles Forberg and had attended Black Mountain College, which had been staffed partly by Bauhaus refugees, giving her a large circle of Bauhaus friends scattered around the ponds of Truro and Wellfleet, including the Breuers, Kepeses, Chermayeffs, and Schawinskys. Julie Kepes, György's daughter and a friend of Jack Hall's daughter Noa, recalled Ati and Charles swimming nude in Gull Pond next to their house and how beautiful they were. Her parents often stayed with Ati, but "Grop" never bought a house on the Outer Cape despite all the houses he had inspired. Ati was a gifted artist, and O'Connor persuaded her to illustrate his only children's book, *Benjy: A Ferocious Fairy Tale*, which at first glance appeared to be a story about a dog but was actually a veiled attack on Senator Joseph McCarthy, whom O'Connor loathed.

When Ati became pregnant with her first child, strangely O'Connor felt betrayed and never spoke to her again. Happily, Edmund Wilson introduced him to a beautiful young divorcée with a child who worked for the Democratic National Committee and the Carnegie Foundation. Veniette Weil was a willowy blonde with a Grace Kelly aura. They married in 1962 when O'Connor was forty-three and lived happily together until his early death in 1968. Edmund Wilson wrote of O'Connor, "He neither smoked nor drank, he was considerate and incorruptible. [He] was one of the few educated friends I have who struck me as sincerely attempting to lead the life of a Christian."

Arthur Schlesinger Jr.

Although Wilson found the Joan's Beach conversations exhilarating at times and enjoyed being the center of attention of new acolytes like

Dan Aaron, Arthur Schlesinger, Stuart Hughes, Alfred Kazin, Saul Bellow, and Philip Roth, he nostalgically longed for the gatherings on Jack
Phillips's and the Provincetown coast guard beaches of his youth. He
later wrote about this sea change: "The technocrats make a striking contrast with the old Jig Cook Provincetown. . . . They were all writers and
painters who were working and freely exchanging ideas; but these people
are mostly attached to the government or some university. . . . They are
accountable to some institution."

In fact, Aaron taught at Smith and then Harvard, Kazin and Bellow had positions at Black Mountain and Bennington, and Arthur
Schlesinger, Stuart Hughes, and Hofstadter were at Harvard, so Wilson's
charges were on the mark.

Alfred Kazin also described the Joan's Beach atmosphere: "The great
beach was replaced every afternoon by the great society. Every year Joan's
weathered old beach hut sank more abjectly into the sand while around
it rose the mercilessly stylized avant-garde house of a wealthy Leninist
from Philadelphia." Kazin was referring here to Jack Phillips's nearby
house, which he had converted for Luke Wilson, now fled to Rome.

*(back row, from left) Bowden Broadwater, Lionel Abel, Elizabeth Hardwick,
Miriam Chiaromonte, Nicola Chiaromonte, Mary McCarthy, John Berryman;
(front row, from left) Dwight Macdonald, Kevin McCarthy, 1947*

The new society on Joan's Beach analyzed postwar American literature in discussions often led by Bunny Wilson or Kazin. They debated
whether their generation's work measured up to the output that had
followed World War I—Hemingway, Fitzgerald, Dos Passos, and E. E.
Cummings, among many others. Certainly, the novel had again become,
like the movies, an American specialty.

Mailer was introduced to Provincetown in 1942 by his first wife, Bea
Silverman, while they were young lovers, he at Harvard and she at Boston University, then colloquially known by WASP Harvard students as
Jew U. He was already determined to pursue a career as a writer on the
left, and Dos Passos's *U.S.A.* was his model! Unlike Robert Nathan, he
was elected to *The Harvard Advocate*, the most prestigious of the school's
literary magazines. Bowden Broadwater was a classmate and also on the
Advocate, but they never became friends, although Broadwater admired
his writing. Mailer described himself at Harvard as "a poor Jewish boy
from Brooklyn."

Norman Mailer, September 1948. Photograph by Carl Van Vechten

He had begun his first novel while at Harvard. Originally based on his
experiences as an assistant in the mental wards at Boston State Hospital,

it gradually became a war story after he joined the service, and all that remained was his original working title, *The Naked and the Dead*. Returning from the Philippines, he completed it in Provincetown with Bea, and Little, Brown offered him an advance of only $300 because they worried about its vulgar army language. He accepted a higher offer of $1,250 from Rinehart, and their first royalty check to him was $40,000 (about $500,000 in today's money), enough to take Norman and Bea to Paris in 1946. There he and James Jones (*From Here to Eternity*, 1951) became close friends. It was Jones, after a long night spent talking and drinking at the White Horse Tavern, who threw his arms around his fellow veterans William Styron and Mailer and exclaimed, "Here we are, the three best young writers in America!"[2] *The Naked and the Dead*'s enormous success turned out to haunt Mailer because he never again achieved such critical acclaim for any of his subsequent novels. But his journalism and nonfiction would earn continued praise and two Pulitzer Prizes, for *The Armies of the Night* (1968) and *The Executioner's Song* (1979).

After the war, Mailer once again returned to Provincetown, and unlike O'Neill, Dos Passos, and Tennessee Williams he never left. His long writing association with Provincetown began again in 1950 with his Marxist-Trotskyite-inspired novel *Barbary Shore*. He and Bea had rented from Hazel Hawthorne on Miller Hill Road but amid too much booze and fights their marriage deteriorated.

Mailer met his second wife, Adele Morales, in New York, where she had been a student of Hans Hofmann's. In Provincetown, Adele introduced Norman to her painting crowd—Hofmann, Franz Kline, Fritz Bultman, and Larry Rivers. Mailer had not mixed with painters before, having mainly hung out with writers like Dwight Macdonald and his wife, Nancy, who played tennis with Mailer; Mary McCarthy and her brother Kevin; Tennessee Williams, who had just completed *Streetcar*; and Kurt Vonnegut, who had just finished his first novel, *Player Piano*.

Norman also formed close friendships with other Cape intellectuals who shared his anti-Stalinist views or had supported Wallace's Progressive Party presidential campaign. While campaigning for Wallace in California, Mailer had an affair with the actress Shelley Winters, who later admitted it was Mailer's Paul Newman–like blue eyes that had won her over.

Iowa Writers' Conference, 1959. (standing) Arnold Gingrich; (seated, from left) Paul Engle, Ralph Ellison, Mark Harris, Dwight Macdonald, Norman Mailer

Adele and Norman were serious drinkers and early marijuana users, partying hard in Provincetown's bars with Robert and Mary Frank and others. But the writing was not going well, and he began to turn to politics, co-founding *The Village Voice* in 1955 but soon falling out with his co-founders.

The 1950s for Mailer and many of his bohemian friends was a chaotic period of love affairs, alcohol, and politics. Civil rights, as in the 1930s, were again on the front burner, and Norman wrote *The White Negro* (1957) as a rebuttal to James Baldwin's *The Fire Next Time* in an effort to show that whites could also be cool and hip. Despite this, Baldwin and Mailer became friends, and Jimmy would spend parts of many summers staying with Norman in Provincetown.

In many ways, Mailer was more akin to the early bohemians like Jack Reed and Max Eastman, totally involved with the radical culture of their time and almost manic in their attempt to sleep with every beautiful woman, chronicle every social upheaval, and always be at the center of public attention.

As Joan's Beach summer days glimmered into dusk, Dwight Macdonald would usually entreat everyone to join him in one last nude swim, which many did, but oddly Norman Mailer always kept his suit on.

Alfred Kazin recalled, "Our happiest times were here, at the edge of the land, the ocean, the dunes. The beach was a great body, and on this beach we were bodies again. . . . [S]till stretched the outermost Cape, forever beating in your ears from the ocean, the emptiness of that long wild ocean beach where you could still contentedly walk, make love, and skinny-dip."

22.

NEW YORK JEW

Mardi always said her only disappointment after meeting Jack Hall was to learn that he was not Jewish, as many on first meeting thought him to be. This easygoing romantic partnering between Christian and Jew was a hallmark of the bohemians, who had little interest in organized religion beyond marrying and burying. Religion was, nevertheless, of deep interest to some, including Edmund Wilson, whose scholarly inquiry into the transition from Judaism to Christianity led to a number of books, including *The Dead Sea Scrolls*, and Alfred Kazin, whose book *New York Jew*, published in 1978, was one of a spate of similar explorations by his contemporaries. Howe, Saul Bellow, Bernard Malamud, Philip Roth, and Lionel Trilling, while they had no wish to return to the temples of their parents, were fascinated by the special role their Jewish heritage continued to play in their lives and work amid postwar bohemian assimilation.

Most eastern European Jews came from the czarist Russian Pale of Settlement stretching from the Baltic shores in Lithuania and Latvia through the grain and wheat fields of Ukraine and ending at Odessa and the Black Sea. Despite the czar's harsh restrictions on travel, the limited professions open to them, and sporadic pogroms by Cossack cavalry,

Irving Howe, Stanford University, 1932

in 1900 the Pale held almost five million Jewish residents. Theirs was a deeply religious, Yiddish-speaking, Orthodox culture, very unlike that of the middle-class German Jews, many of whom had already assimilated before coming to America.

Between 1881 and 1917, New York City became a magnet for Jewish families fleeing Russia, Poland, and Lithuania. Two million Jews emigrated from the Pale to America, roughly 10 percent of European immigrants during that period (two hundred thousand young Jewish men served in World War I). The neighborhoods where many found shelter bordered the Village. Jewish children flourished in the city's excellent public school system, and the most gifted found entry into the bordering colleges, starting with City College, Cooper Union, Brooklyn College, New York University, and finally Columbia or the city's many music schools and art night classes, such as at the Art Students League.

Unlike their parents, this generation acclimatized quickly, learning English and adopting American social customs. Many came from highly politicized families who had proudly brought from Europe their beliefs in socialism, Marxism, and the role of labor unions, and while their children rarely practiced orthodoxy or attended temple school, they maintained their parents' belief in social reform. Their daughters also found a huge, new world open for professional young women unknown to their mothers in the Pale.

Of course, they often encountered intense anti-Semitism in finding places to rent or later buy or entering professions that had been banned in the Pale, such as law, medicine, and education. An example of that virulent anti-Semitism was Henry Ford's newspaper, *The Dearborn Independent*, which republished the fabricated anti-Semitic *Protocols of the Elders of Zion* and called Jews "the conscious enemies of all that angels of Eden and Saxons mean by civilization." Ford blamed Jews for short skirts and jazz as well.

Nevertheless, the early immigrants found refuge in the International Ladies' Garment Workers' Union, the Horace Mann School, the New York Public Library, and Eugene Debs's Socialist Party and "comrades" among the young bohemians in the Village who were seeking not marriage or religious ties but only companions, lovers, and fellow intellectuals with charm and ability.

The pre–World War I period provided common ground for politically active young Jews and their Christian counterparts. The anticolonial and antiwar movements, socialism, *The Masses*, the 1913 Armory Show and its call to modernism, all freed them to explore America unencumbered by the prejudices of their parents.

The first wave of Jewish bohemians to reach Provincetown were often women born in the Pale like Emma Goldman with strong ties to the labor reform movement and their sisters in the Heterodoxy Club. Others, like Mike Gold, Jack and Biala Tworkov, Chaim Gross, Bill Zorach, and Mark Rothko, were lured by fellow painters or playwrights or non-Jewish lovers or spouses. None seemed to bring along orthodox religious practice, and if they did, the nearest synagogue was a long day's drive to Hyannis.

Even though the 1920s saw no great rise in Jewish bohemians settling in the three towns, the social atmosphere of the period was strongly affected by Jewish contributions to American culture. Tin Pan Alley continued to crank out songs by Irving Berlin, George and Ira Gershwin, Jerome Kern, and musicals by the young trio of Richard Rodgers, Lorenz

Hart, and Oscar Hammerstein II. Rodgers, when asked later to reflect on the period, said, "I'm trying to think if there was anybody not Jewish."[1]

In Provincetown, many of the early pioneers were in mixed couples like Ida Rauh, Crystal Eastman's law school friend, and Crystal's brother Max. Ida was not only a women's labor organizer and member of the Heterodoxy Club but a fine actress. She performed in the Provincetown Players the summers of 1915 and 1916 and later acted in and directed O'Neill's plays in their Village playhouse. She was close to Mabel Dodge and encouraged her short-lived marriage to Maurice Sterne, a Latvian-born Jewish painter. Rauh always used her maiden name, which made her a hero to her fellow suffragettes.

The population changed in the 1930s, when Roosevelt's WPA theater and arts programs attracted a new group of young Jewish bohemian artists, many the children of pre-1917 immigrants. They came to study with Hans Hofmann after he opened his Provincetown school in 1934.

One early Jewish Truro bohemian was the writer and labor organizer Waldo Frank, who had bought an old farmhouse near the Pamet River, where he lived for the remainder of his life. Frank, unlike most Jewish bohemians, came from a German family that was able to send him to boarding school and Yale. Frank was a gifted writer and early contributor to *The New Yorker* and *The New Republic*, as well as one of the original editors at *Seven Arts*, a short-lived but extremely influential prewar magazine. His first wife, Margaret Naumburg, was one of John Dewey's prized students and a pioneer in the field we now call art therapy. In Wellfleet and Provincetown, they became social and political friends of Charles and Adelaide Walker's (they had all visited Trotsky together in Mexico City in 1937). Edmund Wilson and Mary Heaton Vorse and John Dos Passos embraced Frank, who had been an active supporter of Stalin until the purge trials. In 1932, the Walkers had organized a group of pro-labor writers to bring material aid and report on the plight of striking coal miners in blood-soaked Harlan County, Kentucky. Those who joined their investigative trip included Wilson, Malcolm Cowley, Theodore Dreiser, Mary Vorse, and two Jews, Frank and their left-wing labor lawyer, Allan Taub.

In Kentucky, the mine owners controlled both the police and a paid group of strikebreakers, all of whom had been primed to oppose this un-invited visit by a group of "communists and Jews." Immediately harassed, arrested, bailed, and escorted by sheriffs' deputies at night from Harlan County, they were met by a group of vigilantes just across the county line. They were ordered out of their cars and threatened with death, but, because of the presence of Adelaide Walker and Mary Vorse, were finally allowed to proceed—all but Frank and Taub, who were brutally beaten. *Time* magazine covered the incident in its February 22, 1932, edition in an article titled "Free Food, Fracas, and Frank," a snarky piece that suggested these do-gooding lefties (and Jews) had it coming to them. Frank's career as an author plateaued in the 1930s, although he was still recognized as an expert on South American politics (he was an early supporter of Fidel Castro). His house now belongs to the writer Sebastian Junger.

Frank's neighbor Robert Nathan came from a wealthy Sephardic family related to Emma Lazarus and Benjamin Cardozo. Nathan was a descendant of Rabbi Gershom Seixas, who arrived in America in 1710 and was an incorporator of King's College, now Columbia University. Nathan entered Harvard in 1912 with such classmates as John Dos Passos and E. E. Cummings and turned out to be a gifted student, light-weight boxer, and fencer but dropped out his junior year to marry. Nathan and his wife moved to New York City, where he soon left advertising to write novels. Of the fifty he wrote, five were made into feature films, the most successful of which were *The Bishop's Wife* (1947), starring Cary Grant, Loretta Young, and David Niven, and *Portrait of Jennie* (1948), with Jennifer Jones and Joseph Cotten.

In the 1920s, Nathan moved to Truro, where he constructed a gentle-man's farm. There he entertained lavishly, including hosting Charles Jackson on his "lost weekend." Nathan remained the bohemian Cape's serial matrimonial champion having married seven times, besting even Norman Mailer. His last wife was the British actress Anna Lee, who had come to America to star in John Ford's *How Green Was My Valley* (1941).

Some of Nathan's neighbors, like Edmund Wilson and John Dos Passos, looked down on his fiction for its lack of political and cultural impact, but Wilson's Princeton pal Scott Fitzgerald became a great admirer of Nathan's work. In 1935, *Time* magazine reviewed his *Road of Ages* and cruelly focused on his Jewishness. It wrote, "But as a Jew, Robert Nathan found things difficult at Exeter and at Harvard. His ancestry supposedly kept him from being president of the Harvard Monthly. . . . Once called by his friends 'the Jewish Hamlet,' because of his lean, ascetic face . . ."[2]

Frank and Nathan were part of a large number of Jewish intellectuals who bought properties in the three towns of bohemia; many chose them, like their WASP counterparts, for their preindustrial simplicity, much as Thoreau had admired the Cape's nineteenth-century landscape.

David Scherman, not long out of Dartmouth and already a rising magazine photographer, bought five acres with two crumbling cabins on a Truro pond for two thousand dollars in 1939. The seller, Charles "Snowy" Snow, came from one of the Cape's oldest families and owned the only garage in town. Snow's garage and its bathroom became famous when Jo Hopper painted its elk skull over the door and presented it to Snowy on his wedding day. Scherman was not an imposing young man, but somehow was extremely attractive to women and equally popular with men. His rise to fame began on a voyage to Europe before the United States had entered the war. His ship was suddenly boarded by a Nazi U-boat crew and its passengers lined up; the man next to him said, "If you're Jewish, hide your passport." Scherman did so, but held on to his Brownie camera. Once the boarders' inspection was through, Scherman began to surreptitiously photograph the boarding crew, and upon reaching port, he wired the pictures to *Life* magazine. This launched his career as one of America's most gifted photojournalists, not only of the war, but of postwar America as well, with hundreds of *Life* black-and-white covers to his credit.

Never forgetting the ladies and now an army photographer, Scherman, who had met Lee Miller, the beautiful American photographer, in Paris, where she was living with Man Ray, offered to get her an appointment as a fellow army photographer. She became one of the first women admitted. Miller bade goodbye to Man Ray, and with her new lover, Scherman, recorded the bloody war from fierce combat to the Nazi death camps. One of Scherman's most famous *Life* portraits was of Miller nude in Hitler's Berchtesgaden bathtub, her muddy boots sitting beside the tub on Hitler's bath towel.

The couple remained together until Miller married the English art critic Roland Penrose. After the war, Scherman returned to *Life*, where he became an editor until its closure in 1972. He continued to summer or live in Truro, often renting one of his cottages to friends like the gallery owner Julien Levy, whose sophisticated European gallery assistant, Elena Mumm Thornton, married Edmund Wilson in 1946. Elena had studied in Germany with Hans Hofmann when she was seventeen. Levy's artists included Arshile Gorky, whose neck had been broken in a car accident while Levy was driving. Levy had been attempting to comfort Gorky, who had called Levy after reading his wife Mougouch's diary and discovering she was having an affair with Matta, his best friend and another client of Levy's.

Victor Wolfson, the son of Russian Jewish socialists who had fled to America in 1894, purchased twenty-eight acres and an abandoned house on Wellfleet's Lieutenant Island for three hundred dollars in 1931. Wolfson had gone to the University of Wisconsin and became a journalist and playwright. He worked with Charles and Adelaide Walker in founding the leftist Theater Union and also worked with them on plays using striking miners as actors in West Virginia. In 1937, his comedy *Excursion* had a successful Broadway run, attended by many of his Wellfleet friends, including Jo and Edward Hopper, and his closest neighbors, Paul and Nina Chavchavadze. Wolfson was one of the first Jews to be elected to the Beachcombers' Club and recalled the tragicomedy of his first meal as cook, a task required of all members. He had prepared matzo ball soup, but by the date of his dinner they had fermented and, when heated on the club's stove, exploded, covering the ceiling in matzo!

Wolfson was a flamboyantly difficult man, both charming and cruel at times. Oddly, he became extremely close to his czarist neighbors, the Chavchavadzes, where he was always welcomed in Russian by Nina. He wrote a piece about their friendship in *The New Yorker*, "Down in the Dust with the Prince and the Peer."

He married a Boston Brahmin, had three boys, each of whom he baptized at high tide in what was called the "Deep Hole" on Blackfish Creek near his house, having himself converted to Catholicism. Wolfson continued to write plays and worked for *Harper's Magazine* from 1948 to 1960, causing trouble and stomping around on his wooden leg, which he often removed and left standing on the Chavchavadzes' porch when visiting.

Wolfson was a friend of Elia Kazan's and remained so even after Kazan "named names" before HUAC. He had a final success as the writer and producer of ABC's twenty-six-part series *The Valiant Years* (1960–1961), based on Winston Churchill's wartime career. Wolfson spent two years in England with Churchill working on the series and recalled a luncheon at Chartwell during which Churchill reprimanded his son, "Randolph! Do not interrupt me when I'm interrupting!" Wolfson died in a fire at his Wellfleet home in 1990.

Mark Rothko's journey was not unlike that of many of his fellow writers and artists. Born Marcus Rothkowitz in the Latvian Pale, he came to join his parents in Portland, Oregon (the birthplace of Jack Reed as well), as a young boy speaking no English. He grew tall and robust and did so well in school that he obtained a scholarship to Yale in 1921. There he encountered entrenched anti-Semitism amid the university's fear of the rising tide of all-too-qualified Russian Jewish students. Yale had no Jewish faculty until 1943, no Jewish tenured faculty until 1947, and no Jewish trustees until 1965.[3] Rothko found both peace and success studying with Hofmann in Provincetown, where he bought a house and lived for many summers before selling it to friends, the husband-and-wife painters Tony and Elspeth Vevers.

After the war, almost every Jewish writer or painter seemed to have a non-Jewish lover or spouse and vice versa: Jack and Wally Tworkov; Harry and Elena Levin, his Russian wife; Robert Motherwell and Helen Frankenthaler; Gilbert Seldes and Amanda Hall; Lajko and Connie Breuer; Norman Mailer and the majority of his wives; Serge and Barbara Chermayeff; Biala Tworkov and Ford Madox Ford; Dan and Janet Aaron; Vita Mendelson and Pete Petersen; Sidney and Renee Simon; Sideo Fromboluti and Nora Speyer; Arturo and Nancy Vivante; the list could go on for pages.

The most vivid chroniclers of New York Jews' journey into the heart
and soul of postwar Cape bohemia were Alfred Kazin and Daniel Aaron,
each of whom lived in Truro or Wellfleet most summers and often longer.
Both were highly influenced by Lionel Trilling's meditations on Jewishness and its transformation by the American character as personified by
Emerson, Melville, Walt Whitman, and Henry James. Waldo Frank had
once referred to this experience as "being a Jew in America without losing Jewishness."[4]

Alfred Kazin, Smith College, 1954

Kazin attended City College of New York at the height of the Depression, when the entire student body fiercely swung between socialism
and communism. A gifted intellectual, he was elated to obtain his first
journalistic job at *The New Republic* in 1934 alongside his hero, Edmund

Wilson. Malcolm Cowley was then very much in charge of the magazine and fascinated Kazin, the son of poor Jewish immigrants who lived in the Brownsville section of Brooklyn, where his seamstress mother carried the family by sewing piecework. Kazin described him thusly: "I had an image of Malcolm Cowley as a passenger in the great, polished coach that was forever taking young Harvard poets to war, to the Left Bank, to the Village, to Connecticut,"[5] but it was Wilson who impressed him the most with, as Kazin described him, "the red face of an overfed foxhunting squire." Throughout his life it was Wilson's literary criticism that set the standard for Kazin's aspirations and had drawn him to the Cape.

After a short stint teaching at Black Mountain, where he had replaced Eric Bentley, Kazin was drafted and stationed in Europe ("still the greatest thing in North America," his friend Delmore Schwartz once joked), while he mainly worked as a writing instructor and became impressed by the military's huge effort to teach reading and writing to illiterate enlisted men, including Black soldiers. In 1942, he had already begun to spend time in Provincetown and Wellfleet with friends he had met at *The New Republic*, like Edmund Wilson, and Dwight Macdonald at *Fortune*. He first won the praise of both Wilson and Cowley in 1942 at the young age of twenty-seven for his first book of criticism, *On Native Grounds*. Tragically for Kazin, there could never be enough praise in his life; he was, by his own admission, bitter and restless. The bitterness, he again admitted, was from feeling he was always viewed with suspicion and never quite accepted, particularly as a Jew specializing in "American" literature in the WASP-dominated academy. His restlessness was to take him through many academic appointments, mistresses, and wives.

The Cape became a major part of Kazin's world after the war when he joined the *Partisan Review*, which had already attracted many of his closest friends, including Richard Hofstadter, a brilliant examiner of America's literary culture. The postwar *Partisan Review* (or, as Edmund Wilson called it, *The Partisansky Review*) had moved away from its socialist-Trotskyite roots and become increasingly anti-Stalinist and liberal. Its contributors were now predominantly New York Jewish intellectuals and academics (Trilling had finally been awarded tenure at Columbia because President Nicolas Murray Butler decided there was now room for at least "one Jew"). Some, like Hofstadter, Saul Bellow, Delmore Schwartz, and Daniel Bell, once Kazin's brother-in-law, were friends and political allies; others, like Sidney Hook, Irving Howe, and Trilling, became enemies, but political battles were a major pastime of these intellectuals, and many friendships were broken over the smallest cultural dispute.

When Dwight Macdonald, Mary McCarthy, and William Phillips moved to Wellfleet in the late 1930s, much of the *Partisan Review* crowd had followed suit and brought their interminable battles with them. As Kazin described it, "To be a Jew and yet not Jewish; to be of course a liberal, yet to see everything that was wrong with the 'imagination of liberalism'; to be Freudian and a master of propriety; academic and yet intellectually avant-garde—this produced the tension, the necessary intellectual ordeal, that was soon to make Trilling the particular voice of intellectuals superior to liberalism."[6]

The postwar era brought more funded teaching appointments and more opportunities for romantic liaisons, at Bennington, Vassar, Sarah Lawrence, and Columbia. You might find Saul Bellow, Philip Roth, Bernard Malamud, Clement Greenberg, or Kazin gathered in a bar of a September reviewing the women's freshman register and making bets on who would bed the prettiest blondes. Kazin, unfaithful through four marriages, always resented those of his peers who were more successful with women, calling Norman Mailer "the Talmudist of fucking, the only writer in years who has managed to be so serious about sex as to make it grim."[7]

Like many of his fellows, Kazin was a believer in psychiatry and often saw his shrink three times a week, while religiously recording his most difficult and intimate thoughts and feelings in his journals. By the 1950s, he had made Wellfleet a center of his life, playing in the O'Connor Sunday softball game with his young son and spending as much time as possible with his hero, Edmund Wilson. Kazin thought Wilson the last of the great capable WASPs—in the pantheon with lawyers (Justice Holmes), ministers (Wendell Phillips), diplomats (George Kennan), moralists (Emerson), writers (Melville, Stowe, Thoreau, Dickinson), and statesmen (Abraham Lincoln), men and women with deep moral cores that led them to be totally uninterested in the new capitalist America.

Kazin particularly admired Wilson's library housed in a separate building and his way of using conversation to establish social contact, always writing and responding in writing, never using a typewriter. Kazin described Wilson's style: "The formality of sentence structure even on the beach, like the aloofness of his manner when you were drinking and gossiping with him in his own house, was like nothing any of us would ever see again. Ponderously shy, abrupt, exact, and exacting, he was matter-of-fact in a style of old-fashioned American hardness."[8]

*Daniel Aaron, Smith College, ca. late 1960s
or early 1970s*

His contemporary in American studies and fellow Wilson admirer was Daniel Aaron. Aaron's father was a furrier whose business was destroyed by the Depression. He attended the University of Michigan at the recommendation of Howard Mumford Jones and then went to Harvard for graduate school, where, despite being told like Kazin that American studies was not for Jews, he made it his lifework. Unlike many of his peers, he combined a dedication to the Left and to anticapitalism with an early allegiance to Roosevelt and youthful support of what was nastily called "the Jew Deal." He also remained a supporter of Stalin until the Ribbentrop Pact, and even afterward retained a strongly pro-Russian bias, influenced by his Harvard contemporary Granville Hicks, then a well-known communist whom Harvard president James Conant nevertheless appointed to the faculty in 1938. Aaron was always a popular figure and an ardent partygoer, attending some wild ones Hicks threw at his New York farm complete with nude bathing. It was Hicks who helped Aaron obtain his first faculty position at Smith in 1939, where he became close to Newton Arvin, the great Hawthorne and Melville scholar and longtime partner of F. O. Matthiessen, and through Arvin was introduced to Edmund Wilson, who much admired Arvin.

Having fallen under Wilson's spell, like Kazin, Aaron began renting in Wellfleet and Truro in 1943 so he might enter the charmed circle of Wilson, Mary McCarthy, and Dwight Macdonald. Later, Aaron and his wife bought a house in Wellfleet that she sold later to William McFeely, the biographer of Ulysses Grant.

Aaron was also sympathetic with the new liberalism being espoused by Richard Hofstadter, and so moved from initially supporting Wallace in the 1948 election to Truman and then on to Adlai Stevenson in 1952. Aaron had taught JFK at Harvard and, unlike his fellow Cape bohemians Arthur Schlesinger, Edwin O'Connor, and Norman Mailer, was only lukewarm about Kennedy, feeling he was ruthlessly ambitious. Mailer conversely, having previously been a Wallace supporter, wrote a glowing piece on Kennedy for *Esquire*'s November 1960 issue titled "Superman Comes to the Supermarket." While the article did not impress Aaron, Kazin believed it to be the best American journalism of the time.

Aaron was handsome and charming and, like Kazin, a poor husband but a favorite of every woman, from the breathless girls of Smith to the wives of his friends. His book *Writers on the Left* (1961) is perhaps the best group biography of the political writers who influenced bohemia from 1910 to 1960, including marvelous interviews with Joe Freeman, Earl Browder, Max Eastman, Whittaker Chambers, Mike Gold, Upton Sinclair, and Donald Ogden Stewart.

Like Kazin's, Aaron's heroes were the WASP generation of an older America—Wilson and Van Wyck Brooks—not the new, tough intellectuals like Sidney Hook, Irving Kristol, and Norman Podhoretz, whom Aaron described as "tough debaters and fast-talkers, confident and competitive and often rude, they could make you feel thick-witted and wither you with a look."[9]

While these cocky postwar intellectuals often circled each other like strange dogs determining whether they might encounter prejudice, hostility, or friendship, or more, the bohemians of the postwar were a far more tolerant lot than the first generation. Only read the journals or letters of Wilson, Dos Passos, Cummings, or Macdonald, and you will come upon some astonishing anti-Semitic references, yet they were the first generation of American intellectuals to establish strong friendships and express open admiration for the lives and works of this first generation of America's Jewish writers and thinkers.

Oddly, the acronym WASP (white Anglo-Saxon Protestant), used throughout this work, came into the parlance only in the 1960s through the work of Digby Baltzell, a handsome, bow-tied, square-jawed blond WASP sociology professor at the University of Pennsylvania. Baltzell examined the WASP world in his work *The Protestant Establishment: Aristocracy and Caste in America* (1964), in which he introduced the term. He spent his summers in Wellfleet with his first wife, Jane Piper, a painter, and second wife, Jocelyn Carlson, whose family was one of the oldest in Wellfleet. Baltzell was an admirer and friend of Richard Hofstadter, with whom he shared the view that the current generation of the WASP ascendancy had betrayed their traditional duty of public service after World War II and were now concentrating their power to block the rise of more qualified leaders from the Jewish and Black ranks, as well as supporting stronger and more racist immigration statutes.

It was Kazin who assisted the dying Edmund Wilson in his wish to have a Hebrew epitaph on his tombstone. Kazin suggested one based on the Orthodox Jewish prayer for the year's end, which pleased Wilson:

Chazak Chazak Vinithazak
(Be strong, be strong, and let us strengthen one another)

23.

EDEN'S END

By the end of the 1950s, world wars and the Depression were fading into black-and-white history for a Technicolor America that had become the richest and most powerful country in the world. Americans now preferred standard-issue houses in groomed suburban developments to ramshackle farmhouses in remote rural areas. The old bohemian Cape began to vanish like Camelot, as did the original world of fishing and farming that had provided the beloved context for bohemian creativity.

Remnants of their lives, loves, and work were still to be found in the old farmhouses and "new" modern ones they inhabited—their bookcases filled with the sun-bleached volumes they or their friends had written and that now turn up at the town dump "swap shops" or library book sales. Political protests against an even stronger "capitalist democracy" were still carried on by a few newcomers, like Howard Zinn, Robert Jay Lifton, Barbara Deming, and Noam Chomsky. Gifted painters still worked, if they could find cheap space, but the schools of Hawthorne and Hofmann were not replaced.

Summers always seem longer in our youth and winters in our later years. The days of shooting canvasback and old-squaw from duck blinds on the remote ponds enjoyed by Jack Phillips and his uncle Dr. Rollins had come to an end. The icehouses at Ryder Pond that had once housed Bauhaus émigrés like György Kepes, Xanti Schawinsky, and Gropius all those summers ago had been torn down. Sonia Brown's icehouse at the end of Bound Brook Road had been converted by Jack Hall into a studio for its new owners, Harry and Elena Levin. The long ice-cutting saws and the nailed ice shoes of the horses who hauled the ice blocks off the ponds from Provincetown to Wellfleet were now found only in antiques stores.

A few descendants of the old Portuguese and Yankee families still hunted deer, pheasant, and rabbit on Bound Brook, but the National Seashore would soon limit their access, and the high-pitched hysteria of the Portuguese lurchers, medieval hunting dogs, a cross between shepherds and greyhounds or whippets, was now rarely heard.

A few still cut their Christmas trees in the fast-growing pitch pine groves and gathered garlands of Prince Rupert's ground pine to decorate their mantels, but most now shopped in the new nurseries springing up along the highway favored by suburban summer couples in the newly built ranch houses they intended to retire to. Old bohemian year-rounders still pulled their carrots, potatoes, and Eastham turnips with the purple base and white top and buried them deep in the sandpit of their brick root cellars under their old farmhouses, but most houses now had placed a furnace in that space. Some would still visit a neighbor's cranberry bog to wield a wooden-handled scoop to comb the crimson berries from the shallow water and make their own sauce for Thanksgiving and Christmas, but now there was a new First National supermarket—or "Primo Nazionale," as Rosalind Wilson and Count George Chavchavadze referred to it—on Route 6 at the corner of Cove Road where Dickinson's lonely camp on Chipman's Cove was now surrounded by rows of new houses on paved roads with names like Pilgrim's Way. Now the cranberry jelly was available in shiny cans and the bogs more valuable as house plots.

Through all their political partisanship, artistic creation, lovemaking, and drinking, a generation that cared so deeply about the bohemian ethos was evaporating. Congress's creation of the Cape Cod National Seashore in 1961 instantly attracted thousands of suburban homeowners. A new

America was replacing bohemia, one that embraced the Cold War with Russia and virulent anticommunism and placed a much greater emphasis on monetary success as a definition of worthiness, even if they identified themselves as painters, writers, or architects.

An unusual pair of senators from Massachusetts, the Irish Catholic champion of labor and health care Edward "Ted" Kennedy and Edward Brooke, the Senate's first Black member since Reconstruction, now became the champions for the Cape Cod National Seashore legislation and the movement started by Senator Leverett Saltonstall in the 1940s. Each had summer homes on the Cape—Kennedy in the once great colonial seaport of Hyannis and Brooke in the formerly independent Wampanoag Native American village of Mashpee. Both were concerned that the Cape's shores, both bay and ocean, were swiftly being overdeveloped and its long, glacial beaches posted with PRIVATE PROPERTY signs.

Cape land was still inexpensive when the Cape Cod National Seashore Act was passed in 1961 with the goal of protecting the Cape's coastline from Provincetown to the Cape Cod Canal. But the senators knew little time remained before what was rural would be suburban, while others viewed it as a folly, given that no national park had ever been created on land on which so many (read: white people) already dwelled. And opponents like FDR's former attorney general Francis Biddle, now ensconced in Jack's farm on Bound Brook Island, fought its passage for years as a "left-wing" taking of others' land without appropriate compensation and an unconstitutional challenge to private stewardship.

Their opposition stalled the bill in Congress for years, allowing developers time to buy the land that the park had intended to take and drive up the price of acquisition so that when the legislation was finally approved by Congress, there was only enough allocated money to protect the coastline from Provincetown to Dennis, roughly the midpoint, or "elbow," of the Cape. There would be no funding to protect Kennedy's Hyannis from becoming a town awash with bars, clam shacks, and cheap cottages for student beach rentals nor Brooke's Mashpee from being covered with sprawling golf courses and condos.

As fate would have it, Wellfleet, being close to Provincetown, the first town on the park's eminent domain list, and still having cheap undeveloped land, ended up with almost 70 percent of its land in the park, including most of Jack Hall's beloved Bound Brook Island and Jack Phillips's ponds. This last gesture of liberal politics ironically marked the end of bohemia as the park became a huge tourist attraction and quickly every buildable lot in Provincetown, Truro, and Wellfleet was under construction. Many of these new houses were often used by their owners for only two months in the summer.

Those who knew Jack Hall well understood his deep love of the island and his emotional attachment as he made his constant circling of its boundaries. In 1959 he and Mardi had been mostly living in Manhattan, where he was working at George Nelson's design firm, attempting to improve his finances, which, due to his poor management of both their inheritances, were no longer sufficient to permit him to fulfill his desire to devote full time to painting. They could probably imagine his New Year's Eve final walk around the island in honor of a decade's end.

Clad in his heavy parka and beret, he was meditating on all the dogs that had accompanied him on these walks and how he longed to again return to living full-time on Bound Brook with one.

The island was peaceful in the early evening glow, which the Provincetown painters referred to as the "golden hour." Its lightly snow-covered hills were not as easily discerned as they had been when he first came with Cammie, the pitch pines increasingly obscured their sensual curves and hollows since their seed had managed to blow across the canal onto the Outer Cape after the war. He would have had trouble riding his old horse Dapple over them now as the pines grew taller and mixed with the returning oak.

On the way to the beach, he passed the Levins' driveway and had a sudden notion to see the old house again. Back when Duck Harbor was almost as active as Wellfleet's main harbor, the Levin house had been the harbormaster's. It stood on a level bank, beneath which were the harbor's rope walks and salt pans, all powered by the two windmills located on small hills on either side. Jack had used Dapple to haul one half of a windmill's broken millstone to the Baker house to serve as its front doorstep. Beneath it is a kind of time capsule; he and Dodie had buried the cache of Dutch and English pipe stems, coins, arrowheads, and other early trade trinkets they had dug up while planting out the gardens.

The Levin house and its adjacent buildings now fronted a silted harbor transformed into a field of high bush blueberries and crisscrossed by 1930s public works' mosquito ditches. It was closed up for the winter with its storm windows mounted over its screens, preserving its many memories.

When Jack first moved to Bound Brook, the Russian sculptor Sonia Brown lived there with her husband and children. She had work in the 1913 Armory Show, and even as her reputation grew, she remained a warm and welcoming neighbor to him and Cammie. As her health began to fail, the Browns sold the place to Bob Loesser and his dog-raising wife. Loesser had become a successful real estate developer in Wellfleet after the war and formed a shady partnership with Wellfleet's legendary all-powerful town counsel, Charlie Frazier. Together, they somehow ended up with every tax foreclosure property in Wellfleet and Truro (including the land Jack had given Dodie on Duck Harbor). Charlie was universally feared for his skill as a lawyer and his powerful political influence, thus allowing his partner to be known as the "Loesser of two evils." After he ran off with Jean Shay, his wife sold the property to Harry and Elena Levin.

Jack was particularly fond of the Levins. Harry, a renowned Harvard professor and expert on Joyce and Shakespeare, had met Elena as a young Radcliffe undergraduate from the new Soviet Russia. Harry was shy and extremely private, while Elena was girlish and magically sympathetic to all who came her way. Elena's mother had been elected a socialist member of the postrevolutionary Kerensky government, but when Lenin seized power, she and other socialist deputies were executed as "enemies of the people." Elena and her three sisters and engineer father escaped to Manchuria. By chance, Wilson's first U.S. diplomatic representative to the new Soviet government was the plumbing heir Charles Richard Crane, a sophisticated and generous man. While visiting Harbin, Manchuria, he met Elena and her family, became fascinated with their plight, and volunteered to bring all four girls to America for their education.

It was Elena who hosted the Nabokovs when they began to visit Well-fleet and where they became close to Edmund and Elena Wilson. Elena and Nina Chavchavadze had been assisting Wilson with his Russian and his attempt, perhaps unwise, to translate Pushkin into English. Unfortunately, Nabokov, equally unwisely, determined to translate Pushkin into English, which led to an epic end to their friendship when Wilson criticized Nabokov's translation in *The New York Review of Books*. Perhaps Wilson was also driven by envy of Nabokov's critical and monetary success with *Lolita*, which Wilson believed plagiarized his early novel, *I Thought of Daisy*, which also depicted the infatuation of an older man for a pubescent girl.

There was still something of old Russia about the place; much like the Chavchavadzes, Elena had attracted a following of fellow émigrés who came in the fall to gather mushrooms and in the summer to pick blackberries and raspberries. Some were introduced by the Chavchavadzes and some by Elena Wilson, herself half-Russian, her grandfather having been the Russian ambassador to the United States. Others simply arrived unbidden, having heard of the warm welcome they'd receive.

Back on the road, Jack chose not to climb the hill to the modern house, because it still held too many dark memories of Jean's rage and his own failures as a parent, even though it had inspired Bob and Ruth Hatch to commission him to design their house on the other side of the island.

As he walked, memories of important moments and consuming passions floated up. He mused again about his long-held belief that the United States was not fulfilling its original role as a democracy and that Marxism might have been the answer. He recalled the war, the revelation of Stalin's brutal regime, and finally his involvement in Quakerism, AA, and the civil rights struggle, being beaten and jailed in Selma while marching with Dr. King.

Jack made his way up the now neatly shelled driveway to the Baker farm. The Biddles were now tucked up in their winter house in Washington, D.C. Francis had spent the last several years fighting the enactment of the National Seashore, and his prestige and reputation as Roosevelt's attorney general and a Nuremberg trial judge had made him a formidable advocate. Like Dos Passos, Max Eastman, Wilson, and other white males of their generation, Biddle had moved further to the right as he aged and now found America's raucous civil rights movement and other reforms not to his liking. These onetime lions of the Left, who had celebrated the Civil War's ending of slavery, were not yet ready to accept Black Americans as equals.

The farm was remarkably unchanged. The moon and stars, carved deeply into the front door lintel pilasters, still rose and set with the sun. The main house was now painted red, as were the two converted studio barns, one of which was now used by Francis as a study and the other to house their two maids.

Memories returned of Cammie and his early primitive carpentry and Dodie and their transformation of the swamp-like swale beneath their front door into lush vegetable gardens that were now thick with volunteer locust and pine trees and marching almost up the hill to the row of lilacs at the edge of the lawn. The Delight cottage, which had housed so many friends—Chaim Gross and his wife, Marvin Waldman, Dodie and her Croton best friend, Meg Barden—was unlocked, and its tiny kitchen, bathroom, and bedroom took him back almost thirty years.

He did not regret selling it to Biddle. It held too many memories of failures but nevertheless was the house that had given his life meaning and purpose. It would always be a place sacred to all he had learned of nature, women, politics, and art.

He returned to Duck Harbor Road now haunted by so many memories he decided to complete the "loop" home. He stiffly climbed the barrier dune and descended onto the beach. The Provincetown monument was still visible across the bay to his right as he strode through the winter beach wrack of dried eelgrass, crushed sea clams, oysters, and horseshoe crab shells toward Charlie Driver's house on the Truro line where the Bound Brook emptied into the bay.

He knew by heart the exact angle to capture a view of Bob and Ruth Hatch's deck between the scrub pine and beach plum before ascending the dune to the Upper Road.

There it stood like a Zen monument, the one perfect thing he had created in a lifetime of exploring design, beginning with his and Jack Phillips's amateur attempts to create modernist dwellings from old army barracks. The angular deck with its shutters lowered to protect the windows from winter's sandblast fronted a building that he truly believed would become his testament.

Then up the hill, past the closed-up Jencks house on the old town picnic ground, and down the Upper Road to turn off onto the "Nemo Trail" and Mardi. The trail had been made by the Jenckses' black poodle, Nemo, on her many visits to play with Jack's dog. As he approached the house, he could hear that Mardi had Charlie Parker on the record player, and he caught the scent of the locust wood fire he had kindled before he left. As the evening light faded to dark, he finally understood that no one could ever really own Bound Brook Island . . . not the first Native people, nor the European cod fishermen, Yankee whalers and farmers, and not even the bohemians on its shores.

Jack died in January 2003. While he suffered from dementia at the end, his love for Mardi, his sobriety, and his Quaker faith had brought him peace. His memorial service was held on a misty morning in Wellfleet's old white Congregational church complete with a piper in full kit playing his beloved bagpipe funereal tunes, beginning with "Flowers of the Forest." Filled with the progeny of the friends of his youth—Phillipses, Chavchavadzes, Chermayeffs, Breuers, and Dickinsons—it concluded with his favorite song of the Left: "Joe Hill."

Mardi died in March 2009, and her service was held in the Provincetown Art Association and Museum, where she and Jack had both shown their work. There was a jazz band consisting of her lifelong Cape friend the *New Yorker* jazz critic Whitney Balliett on drums, Doctor Peter Ecklund on trumpet, and the Brooklyn College English professor Dick Miller, who had played with Woody Allen, on piano. Of course, they played "Didn't She Ramble."

Unlike at Jack's service, alcohol flowed and the speakers grew more candid. Norman Mailer suggested that he and Mardi should have been lovers, and his last wife, the statuesque beauty Norris Church, in tears, suggested that Norman was, as usual, engaging in wishful thinking.

They have all left us, those flawed, rowdy, careless bohemians who sought unreachable utopias where all men and all women were equals and where governments were constructed to provide equal access to education, health, and a rich cultured life. Like Jig Cook, they envisioned an Athenian America where its citizens engaged in intense public discourse, be it in writing, painting, or architecture. Where its heroes were those who served as public intellectuals disputing theories of what was best in full view of its citizens. They would not have comprehended Fox News.

They were appalled by America's use of military power for any purpose but defense. They opposed the toxin of "big money," as John Dos Passos called it, which was transforming elections and legislation into battles to benefit either the rich or the even richer. Imagine *Masses* editorials on the 2020 election! John Reed and Emma Goldman would once again be labeled "terrorists."

For them, the rights of workers were paramount regardless of whether that support branded them Marxists. They would be shocked that corporations now totally control the workplace and organized labor is unable to influence working conditions, wages, or benefits. That loyal workers no longer can expect retirement payments while executives garner enormous bonuses even during bad years and that our allocation of wealth is now the most extreme in America's history with 5 percent of the population having more wealth than the bottom 95 percent.

For them capitalism was the serpent in America's Garden of Eden. They believed its growing power in the new century had betrayed its workers, supported Jim Crow, demonized immigrants, particularly Jews, and denied women the vote or equal treatment. Those who challenged it were swiftly labeled "Reds" to suppress any rational political debate or new artistic vision.

And yet their lives and dreams flourished, for America still provided a fluid society in which an uneducated miner's son, a young woman with no money, a Jewish intellectual, a Black actor or musician, or an immigrant painter or architect could succeed on grit and merit.

They lived daring lives through two world wars, a depression, and the creation of a new America that they helped to shape.

Ave atque vale!

AUTHOR'S NOTE

Much like Jack and Cammie's spring drive up the hill onto Bound Brook Island in 1937, mine thirty years later to meet my potential father-in-law, Jack Hall, was also fraught with a sense of adventure and new beginnings.

He was then a well-known modernist builder and designer and a gifted painter, as was his daughter Noa, whose hand I was seeking. To my relief, I passed muster with Jack and did marry Noa. Our first Cape house, close to Bound Brook, had been owned by Mary McCarthy and Bowden Broadwater and was where Mary wrote her controversial portrait of the bohemian Cape, *A Charmed Life*. In its studio the *Partisan Review* was edited and Arthur Schlesinger's *Age of Jackson* was written.

Through the Halls, I was introduced to many of the figures who appear in this book. I later acted as a lawyer or literary agent for Edmund Wilson, Serge Chermayeff, Marcel Breuer, György Kepes, Eero Saarinen, Norman Mailer, Gardner Jencks, Joan Colebrook, Shelby Cox, Mary "Bubs" Hackett, Jack Phillips, Ati Gropius, Prince and Princess Chavchavadze, and Daniel Aaron, among others.

As I fell deeper under the spell of the Cape's bohemian magic, it began to occur to me that no one had tried to create a group portrait of their half century. I began to interview them and their children, some of whom had been my contemporaries at Harvard, including Reuel Wilson, Charles Jencks, Michael Macdonald, and Peter Chermayeff.

I became more deeply immersed in the bohemians' work as chair of the Fine Arts Work Center in Provincetown and a trustee of the Institute of Contemporary Art in Boston. But it was more than half a century of living, at least in part, on the shores of bohemia that led me to chronicle these bohemians' remarkable lives.

I am ever mindful of the dangers of such a reconstruction. The late Provincetown poet Mary Oliver once wrote about the lack of a good biography of Edna St. Vincent Millay: "We need to be each other's storytellers—at least we have to try. One wants to know what the beautiful strangers were like—one *needs* to know. Still, it is like painting the sky. What stars have been left out, or their places mistaken, misinterpreted, not noticed at all?"

Admittedly, they led unconventional lives and were neither religious nor respectful of authority. Many drank to excess, were poor spouses and parents, and rarely agreed with America's choice of leaders, but they deeply believed in its potential.

They fought the good fight and had few regrets.

—IKE WILLIAMS

NOTES

I. ARCADIA

1. Robert Motherwell, "Provincetown and Days Lumberyard: A Memoir," in *Days Lumberyard Studios, Provincetown, 1914–1971* (Provincetown, Mass.: Provincetown Art Association and Museum, 1978), 16.

2. GREENWICH VILLAGE AND PROVINCETOWN

1. Allen Churchill, *The Improper Bohemians* (New York: Dutton, 1959), 78.
2. Edmund T. Delaney, *New York's Greenwich Village* (Barre, Mass.: Barre Publishers, 1968), 104.
3. John Dos Passos, *The Fourteenth Chronicle: Letters and Diaries of John Dos Passos*, ed. Townsend Ludington (Boston: Gambit, 1973), 75.
4. Churchill, *Improper Bohemians*, 35.

3. THE 1913 ARMORY SHOW

1. "Reliving the Show That 'Dropped Like a Bomb,'" *New York Times*, Oct. 11, 2013.
2. "Reliving the Show That 'Dropped Like a Bomb.'"
3. Betty Parsons Gallery Papers, Smithsonian Museum.

4. THE PROVINCETOWN PLAYERS

1. Leona Rust Egan, *Provincetown as a Stage* (Orleans, Mass.: Parnassus Imprints, 1994).
2. Mary Heaton Vorse, *Time and the Town: A Provincetown Chronicle* (New York: Dial Press, 1942).

3. Townsend Ludington, *Marsden Hartley: The Biography of an American Artist* (Boston: Little, Brown, 1972).

5. THE MASSES

1. Allen Churchill, *The Improper Bohemians* (New York: E. P. Dutton, 1959), 79.
2. Churchill, *Improper Bohemians*, 91.
3. Churchill, *Improper Bohemians*, 97.
4. Edmund T. Delaney, *New York's Greenwich Village* (Barre, Mass.: Barre Publishers, 1968), 105.
5. Churchill, *Improper Bohemians*, 137.
6. Mary Graham, *Presidents' Secrets: The Use and Abuse of Hidden Power* (New Haven, Conn.: Yale University Press, 2017), 55.
7. Thomas Maik, *The Masses Magazine (1911–1917)* (New York: Garland, 1994).
8. John Dos Passos, *U.S.A.: Nineteen Nineteen* (New York: Modern Library, 1937), 343.

6. THE WAR TO END ALL WARS

1. Daniel Aaron, *Writers on the Left: Episodes in American Literary Communism* (New York: Harcourt, Brace & World, 1961), 346.
2. John Dos Passos, *The Fourteenth Chronicle: Letters and Diaries of John Dos Passos*, ed. Townsend Ludington (Boston: Gambit, 1973), 92.
3. Mary Heaton Vorse, *Time and the Town: A Provincetown Chronicle* (New York: Dial Press, 1942).

8. THE JAZZ AGE

1. Frederick Lewis Allen, *Only Yesterday: An Informal History of the Nineteen-Twenties* (New York: Harper & Brothers, 1931), 109.
2. Louis Sheaffer, *O'Neill: Son and Artist* (Boston: Little, Brown, 1973), 203.
3. Jeffrey Meyers, *Edmund Wilson: A Biography* (Boston: Houghton Mifflin, 1995), 117.
4. Edmund Wilson, *The Twenties*, ed. Leon Edel (New York: Farrar, Straus and Giroux, 1975), 429.

10. THE POPULAR FRONT

1. Geoffrey Wheatcroft, *New York Observer*, March 26, 2006.
2. Nathan Glazer, *The Social Basis of American Communism* (New York: Harcourt, Brace, 1961).
3. Reuel K. Wilson, *To the Life of the Silver Harbor* (Lebanon, N.H.: University Press of New England, 2008), 162.
4. John Dos Passos, *The Fourteenth Chronicle: Letters and Diaries of John Dos Passos*, ed. Townsend Ludington (Boston: Gambit, 1973), 174, 496.
5. Carlos Baker, *Ernest Hemingway: A Life Story* (New York: Charles Scribner's Sons, 1969), 459.
6. Rosalind Baker Wilson, *Near the Magician: A Memoir of My Father, Edmund Wilson* (New York: Grove Weidenfeld, 1960), 127.

7. Elinor Langer, *Josephine Herbst: The Story She Could Never Tell* (Boston: Little, Brown, 1983).
8. Dos Passos, *Fourteenth Chronicle*, 514.

12. COUNTRY LIFE

1. Peter Matson, interview with author, Sept. 1, 2010.
2. Peter McMahon and Christine Cipriani, *Cape Cod Modern: Midcentury Architecture and Community on the Outer Cape* (New York: Metropolis Books, 2014), 117.
3. Frances Kiernan, *Seeing Mary Plain: A Life of Mary McCarthy* (New York: W. W. Norton, 2000).
4. Malcolm Cowley, *A Second Flowering: Works and Days of the Lost Generation* (New York: Viking Press, 1973).

13. WORLD WAR II

1. Peter McMahon and Christine Cipriani, *Cape Cod Modern: Midcentury Architecture and Community on the Outer Cape* (New York: Metropolis Books, 2014), 56–57.
2. Rosalind Baker Wilson, *Near the Magician: A Memoir of My Father, Edmund Wilson* (New York: Grove Weidenfeld, 1960), 128.
3. Edmund Wilson, *The Twenties*, ed. Leon Edel (New York: Farrar, Straus and Giroux, 1975), 120–21.

15. THE ABSTRACTORS

1. Dore Ashton, *The New York School: A Cultural Reckoning* (Berkeley: University of California Press, 1992), 57–58.
2. Ashton, *New York School*, 65.
3. Gail Levin, *Edward Hopper: An Intimate Biography* (New York: Knopf, 1995), 316.
4. Levin, *Edward Hopper*, 376.
5. *Time*, Oct. 8, 1965.
6. Frank Crotty, *Provincetown Profiles and Others on Cape Cod* (Barre, Mass.: Barre Gazette, 1958), 124–25.

17. THE LOST GENERATION'S CHILDREN

1. Dawn Powell, "A Diamond to Cut New York," *New Yorker*, June 26 and July 3, 1995.

18. PROVINCETOWN EITHER WAY

1. Karen Christel Krahulik, *Provincetown: From Pilgrim Landing to Gay Resort* (New York: New York University Press, 2005), 87.
2. Hans Hofmann, *Search for the Real, and Other Essays*, ed. Sara T. Weeks and Bartlett H. Hayes Jr. (Cambridge, Mass.: MIT Press, 1967), 49.
3. *Broad Street Review* interview.
4. Bentley, interview with Julius Novick, *Los Angeles Times*, Jan. 25, 1987.

20. THE NEW, NEW BAUHAUS

1. Peter McMahon and Christine Cipriani, *Cape Cod Modern: Midcentury Architecture and Community on the Outer Cape* (New York: Metropolis Books, 2014), 61.

21. JOAN'S BEACH

1. Frances Kiernan, *Seeing Mary Plain: A Life of Mary McCarthy* (New York: W. W. Norton, 2000), 385.
2. Peter Manso, *Mailer: His Life and Times* (New York: Simon & Schuster, 1985), 262.

22. NEW YORK JEW

1. Sarah Rodman, "Jews amid the Culture of the Broadway Musical," *Boston Globe*, Jan. 1, 2013, review of the PBS *Great Performances* special "Broadway Musicals: A Jewish Legacy."
2. *Time*, Feb. 4, 1935.
3. Lee Seldes, *The Legacy of Mark Rothko* (New York: Da Capo, 1996).
4. Mark Krupnick, *Lionel Trilling and the Fate of Cultural Criticism* (Evanston, Ill.: Northwestern University Press, 1986), 23.
5. Alfred Kazin, *Starting Out in the Thirties* (1965; Ithaca, N.Y.: Cornell University Press, 1989), 16.
6. Alfred Kazin, *New York Jew* (New York: Knopf, 1978), 44-45.
7. Richard Cook, *Alfred Kazin: A Biography* (New Haven, Conn.: Yale University Press, 2008), 216.
8. Kazin, *New York Jew*, 241.
9. Daniel Aaron, *The Americanist* (Ann Arbor: University of Michigan Press, 2007), 140.

BIBLIOGRAPHY

PART I: SPRING

Aaron, Daniel. *Writers on the Left: Episodes in American Literary Communism*. New York: Harcourt, Brace & World, 1961.

Allen, Frederick Lewis. *Only Yesterday: An Informal History of the Nineteen-Twenties*. New York: Harper & Brothers, 1931.

Boylan, James R. *Revolutionary Lives: Anna Strunsky and William English Walling*. Amherst: University of Massachusetts Press, 1998.

Brennan, Susan W. *Truro*. Charleston, S.C.: Arcadia, 2002.

Carr, Virginia Spencer. *Dos Passos: A Life*. Garden City, N.Y.: Doubleday, 1984.

Churchill, Allen. *The Improper Bohemians*. New York: E. P. Dutton, 1959.

Coles, Robert. *Dorothy Day: A Radical Devotion*. Reading, Mass.: Addison-Wesley, 1987.

Cowley, Malcolm. *Exile's Return*. New York: Norton, 1934.

———. *A Second Flowering: Works and Days of the Lost Generation*. New York: Viking Press, 1973.

Delaney, Edmund T. *New York's Greenwich Village*. Barre, Mass.: Barre Publishers, 1968.

Diggins, John Patrick. *Eugene O'Neill's America*. Chicago: University of Chicago Press, 2007.

Dos Passos, John. *The Fourteenth Chronicle: Letters and Diaries of John Dos Passos*. Edited by Townsend Ludington. Boston: Gambit, 1973.

Douglas, Ann. *Terrible Honesty: Mongrel Manhattan in the 1920s*. New York: Farrar, Straus and Giroux, 1995.

Egan, Leona Rust. *Provincetown as a Stage: Provincetown, the Provincetown Players, and the Discovery of Eugene O'Neill*. Orleans, Mass.: Parnassus Imprints, 1994.

Glaspell, Susan. *The Road to the Temple*. New York: Frederick A. Stokes, 1927.

Graham, Mary. *Presidents' Secrets: The Use and Abuse of Hidden Power*. New Haven, Conn.: Yale University Press, 2017.

Heller, Adele, and Lois Rudnick, eds. *1915, the Cultural Moment: The New Politics, the New Woman, the New Psychology, the New Art, and the New Theatre in America.* New Brunswick, N.J.: Rutgers University Press, 1991.

Jensen, Oliver. *The Revolt of American Women.* New York: Harcourt, Brace, 1952.

Lucas, Anthony. *Big Trouble.* New York: Simon & Schuster, 1977.

Ludington, Townsend. *John Dos Passos: A Twentieth Century Odyssey.* New York: E. P. Dutton, 1980.

————. *Marsden Hartley: The Biography of an American Artist.* Boston: Little, Brown, 1972.

Morris, James McGrath. *The Ambulance Drivers: Hemingway, Dos Passos, and a Friendship Made and Lost in War.* Boston: Da Capo Press, 2017.

Noe, Marcia. *Susan Glaspell: Voice from the Heartland.* Macomb: Western Illinois University, 1983.

Nye, Everett L., ed. *History of Wellfleet: From Early Days to Present Time.* Hyannis, Mass.: Ye Olde Town Pump Press, 1920.

O'Toole, Patricia. *The Moralist: Woodrow Wilson and the World He Made.* New York: Simon & Schuster, 2018.

Reed, John. *Ten Days That Shook the World.* New York: Boni & Liveright, 1919.

Russell, Francis. *Tragedy in Dedham: The Story of the Sacco-Vanzetti Case.* New York: McGraw-Hill, 1962.

Schlesinger, Arthur, Jr. *The Age of Roosevelt: The Crisis of the Old Order, 1919–1933.* Boston: Houghton Mifflin, 1957.

Schulman, Robert. *Romany Marie: The Queen of Greenwich Village.* Louisville, Ky.: Butler Books, 2006.

Shay, Edith, and Frank Shay, eds. *Sand in Their Shoes: A Cape Cod Reader.* Boston: Houghton Mifflin, 1951.

Shay, Edith, and Katherine Smith. *Down the Cape: The Complete Guide to Cape Cod.* New York: Dodge, 1936.

Shay, Frank. *The Pious Friends and Drunken Companions.* New York: Macaulay, 1936.

Sheaffer, Louis. *O'Neill: Son and Artist.* Boston: Little, Brown, 1973.

————. *O'Neill: Son and Playwright.* Boston: Little, Brown, 1968.

Steffens, Lincoln. *The Autobiography of Lincoln Steffens.* New York: Harcourt, Brace, 1931.

Strausbaugh, John. *The Village: 400 Years of Beats and Bohemians, Radicals and Rogues: A History of Greenwich Village.* New York: Ecco, 2013.

Vorse, Mary Heaton. *Time and the Town: A Provincetown Chronicle.* New York: Dial Press, 1942.

Wetzsteon, Ross. *Republic of Dreams: Greenwich Village, the American Bohemia, 1910–1960.* New York: Simon & Schuster, 2002.

Wheelwright, Thea, ed. *Thoreau's Cape Cod.* Barre, Mass.: Barre Publishers, 1977.

Willison, George F. *Saints and Strangers.* New York: Reynal & Hitchcock, 1945.

Wilson, Edmund. *The Twenties.* Edited by Leon Edel. New York: Farrar, Straus and Giroux, 1975.

PART II: SUMMER

Aaron, Daniel. *Writers on the Left: Episodes in American Literary Communism.* New York: Harcourt, Brace & World, 1961.

Allen, Frederick Lewis. *The Big Change: America Transforms Itself, 1900–1950.* New York: Harper, 1952.

Bak, Hans. *Malcolm Cowley: The Formative Years*. Athens: University of Georgia Press, 1993.

Carroll, Peter N. *The Odyssey of the Abraham Lincoln Brigade*. Stanford, Calif.: Stanford University Press, 1994.

Carroll, Peter N., and James D. Fernandez, eds. *Facing Fascism: New York and the Spanish Civil War*. New York: New York University Press, 2007.

Cowley, Malcolm. *The Dream of the Golden Mountains: Remembering the 1930s*. New York: Viking Press, 1964.

———. *Think Back on Us: A Contemporary Chronicle of the 1930s*. Carbondale: Southern Illinois University Press, 1967.

Crotty, Frank. *Provincetown Profiles and Others on Cape Cod*. Barre, Mass.: Barre Gazette, 1958.

Elson, John. "No Foolish Consistency: Critic Dwight Macdonald Was a Brilliant, Changeable Gadfly." *Time*, April 4, 1994.

Federal Writers' Project. *New York Panorama: A Comprehensive View of the Metropolis*. New York: Random House, 1938.

Frank, Waldo. *Memoirs of Waldo Frank*. Edited by Alan Trachtenberg. Amherst: University of Massachusetts Press, 1973.

Gay, Peter. *Modernism: The Lure of Heresy*. New York: W. W. Norton, 2008.

Gordon, Alan, and Lois G. Gordon. *American Chronicle: Year by Year Through the Twentieth Century*. New Haven, Conn.: Yale University Press, 1999.

Greenberg, Clement. "The Late Thirties in New York." In *Art and Culture: Critical Essays*. Boston: Beacon Press, 1961.

Hamburger, Philip. *Curious World: A New Yorker at Large*. San Francisco: North Point Press, 1987.

Kazin, Alfred. *Starting Out in the Thirties*. Ithaca, N.Y.: Cornell University Press, 1962.

Langer, Elinor. *Josephine Herbst: The Story She Could Never Tell*. Boston: Little, Brown, 1983.

Laskin, David. *Partisans: Marriage, Politics, and Betrayal Among the New York Intellectuals*. New York: Simon & Schuster, 2000.

Leuchtenburg, William E. *The Perils of Prosperity, 1914–1932*. Chicago: University of Chicago Press, 1958.

Menard, Louis. "Browbeaten." *The New Yorker*, Sept. 5, 2011.

Meyers, Jeffrey. *Edmund Wilson: A Biography*. Boston: Houghton Mifflin, 1995.

Nelson, Cary, and Jefferson Hendricks, eds. *Madrid, 1937: Letters of the Abraham Lincoln Brigade from the Spanish Civil War*. New York: Routledge, 1996.

Olson, Lynne. *Those Angry Days*. New York: Random House, 2014.

Phillips, William. *A Partisan View: Five Decades of Literary Life*. New York: Stein & Day, 1983.

Powell, Dawn. *The Diaries of Dawn Powell, 1931–1965*. Edited by Tim Page. South Royalton, Vt.: Steerforth Press, 1995.

Seldes, George. *Witness to a Century*. New York: Ballantine Books, 1977.

Tanenhaus, Sam. *Whittaker Chambers*. New York: Random House, 1997.

Thomas, Hugh. *The Spanish Civil War*. Harmondsworth: Penguin Books, 1965.

Vevers, Tony. *Lucy and William L'Engle*. Provincetown, Mass.: Provincetown Art Association and Museum, 1999.

Vorse, Mary Heaton. *Labor's New Millions: The Growth of a People's Power*. New York: Modern Age Books, 1938.

Ware, Caroline F. *Greenwich Village, 1920–1930*. New York: Harper & Row, 1965.

Wilson, Edmund. *Axel's Castle: A Study in the Imaginative Literature of 1870–1930*. New York: W. W. Norton, 1984.

———. *A Piece of My Mind: Reflections at Sixty*. New York: Farrar, Straus and Cudahy, 1956.

———. *The Shores of Light*. New York: Farrar, Straus and Young, 1952.

PART III: FALL

Aaron, Daniel. *Writers on the Left: Episodes in American Literary Communism*. New York: Harcourt, Brace & World, 1961.

Agee, James, and Walker Evans. *Let Us Now Praise Famous Men: Three Tenant Families*. Boston: Houghton Mifflin, 1941.

Bultman, Fritz. *Built in USA, 1932–1944*. New York: Museum of Modern Art, 1944.

———. *A Retrospective*. New Orleans Museum of Art, 1993.

Callow, Simon. *Orson Wells: Hello, Americans*. London: Vintage, 2007.

Carroll, James. *Constantine's Sword: The Church and the Jews*. Boston: Houghton Mifflin, 2001.

Crotty, Frank. *Provincetown Profiles and Others on Cape Cod*. Barre, Mass.: Barre Gazette, 1958.

Dreishpoon, Douglas, ed. *Edwin Dickinson: Dreams and Realities*. New York: Hudson Hills Press, 2012.

Duberman, Martin. *Black Mountain: An Exploration in Community*. New York: Anchor Books, 1973.

———. *Paul Robeson: A Life*. New York: New Press, 1996.

Friedman, B. H., ed. *School of New York: Some Younger Artists*. New York: Grove Press, 1959.

Gaddis, Eugene R. *Magician of the Modern: Chick Austin and the Transformation of the Arts in America*. New York: Knopf, 2000.

Grumbach, Doris. *The Company She Kept: A Revealing Portrait of Mary McCarthy*. New York: Coward-McCann, 1967.

Herrera, Hayden. *Arshile Gorky: His Life and Work*. New York: Farrar, Straus and Giroux, 2003.

Kaplan, David. *Tennessee Williams in Provincetown*. East Brunswick, N.J.: Hansen, 2006.

Kiernan, Frances. *Seeing Mary Plain: A Life of Mary McCarthy*. New York: W. W. Norton, 2000.

Laing, Olivia. *The Trip to Echo Spring: On Writers and Drinking*. New York: Picador, 2014.

Levin, Gail. *Edward Hopper: An Intimate Biography*. New York: Knopf, 1995.

Macdonald, Dwight. *Memoirs of a Revolutionist*. New York: Farrar, Straus and Cudahy, 1957.

Nelson, Cary, and Jefferson Hendricks, eds. *Madrid, 1937: Letters of the Abraham Lincoln Brigade from the Spanish Civil War*. New York: Routledge, 1996.

Orlowsky, Lillian, ed. *Hans Hofmann: Four Decades in Provincetown*. Provincetown, Mass.: Provincetown Art Association and Museum, 2000.

Powell, Dawn. *The Diaries of Dawn Powell, 1931–1965*. Edited by Tim Page. South Royalton, Vt.: Steerforth Press, 1995.

Rathbone, Belinda. *Walker Evans: A Biography*. Boston: Houghton Mifflin, 1995.

Schlesinger, Marian Cannon. *I Remember: A Life of Politics, Painting, and People*. Cambridge, Mass.: TidePool Press, 2012.

Secker, Dorothy. *History of the Provincetown Art Colony*. Syracuse, N.Y.: Everson Museum of Art, 1977.

Spender, Matthew. *From a High Place: A Life of Arshile Gorky*. New York: Knopf, 1999.

Weinstein, Allen, and Alexander Vassiliev. *The Haunted Wood: Soviet Espionage in America—the Stalin Era*. New York: Random House, 1999.

Wilson, Edmund. *The Forties*. Edited by Leon Edel. New York: Farrar, Straus and Giroux, 1983.

———. *Letters on Literature and Politics, 1912–1972*. Edited by Elena Wilson. New York: Farrar, Straus and Giroux, 1977.

Wilson, Rosalind Baker. *Near the Magician: A Memoir of My Father, Edmund Wilson*. New York: Grove Weidenfeld, 1969.

PART IV: WINTER

Aaron, Daniel. *The Americanist*. Ann Arbor: University of Michigan Press, 2007.

Bayer, Herbert, ed. *50 Years Bauhaus: German Exhibition*. Stuttgart: Royal Academy of Arts, 1968.

Beam, Alex. *The Feud: Vladimir Nabokov, Edmund Wilson, and the End of a Beautiful Friendship*. New York: Pantheon Books, 2016.

Biddle, Francis. *In Brief Authority*. Garden City, N.Y.: Doubleday, 1962.

Brightman, Carol. *Writing Dangerously: Mary McCarthy and Her World*. New York: Clarkson Potter, 1992.

Gelderman, Carol. *Mary McCarthy: A Life*. New York: St. Martin's Press, 1988.

Howe, Irving. *A Margin of Hope*. San Diego: Harcourt Brace Jovanovich, 1982.

Kazin, Alfred. *New York Jew*. New York: Knopf, 1978.

———. *A Walker in the City*. New York: Harcourt, Brace, 1951.

Krupnick, Mark. *Lionel Trilling and the Fate of Cultural Criticism*. Evanston, Ill.: Northwestern University Press, 1986.

Lennon, J. Michael. *Norman Mailer: A Double Life*. New York: Simon & Schuster, 2013.

"Lochinvar's Return." *Time*. Oct. 8, 1965.

MacCarthy, Fiona. *Walter Gropius: Visionary Founder of the Bauhaus*. London: Faber & Faber, 2019.

Maclean, Caroline. *Circles and Squares: The Lives and Art of the Hampstead Modernists*. New York: Bloomsbury, 2020.

Manso, Peter. *Mailer: His Life and Times*. New York: Simon & Schuster, 1985.

McMahon, Peter, and Christine Cipriani. *Cape Cod Modern: Midcentury Architecture and Community on the Outer Cape*. New York: Metropolis Books, 2014.

Mumford, Lewis. *From the Ground Up: Observations on Contemporary Architecture*. New York: Harcourt, Brace, 1947.

Rudofsky, Bernard. *Architecture Without Architects*. Garden City, N.Y.: Doubleday, 1969.

Washington, Mary Helen. *The Other Blacklist: The African American Literary and Cultural Left of the 1950s*. New York: Columbia University Press, 2014.

Wilson, Edmund. *The Fifties*. Edited by Leon Edel. New York: Farrar, Straus and Giroux, 1986.

———. *A Piece of My Mind*. New York: Farrar, Straus and Cudahy, 1956.

Wilson, Reuel K. *To the Life of the Silver Harbor*. Lebanon, N.H.: University Press of New England, 2008.

ACKNOWLEDGMENTS

First, to those omitted due to my aging memory, my apologies.

Among those I interviewed over the fifty-four years I spent on the Shores, I am particularly grateful to the following:

On Bound Brook Island, Jack, Mardi, Darius, Noa, and Katrina Hall; Ruth Hatch, Sharon Dunn, Charles and Penny Jencks, Sidney Hurwitz, and Harry and Elena Levin.

In Provincetown, Khaki and Dodi Captiva, Johanna Captiva, Tamsin Hapgood, Mary Hackett, Blair and Paul Resika (in addition to the use of his glorious painting on the jacket), Jean and Fritz Bultman, Prudence Grand, Norman and Norris Mailer, and Mike Lennon.

In Truro, Sidney Simon, Joan Colebrook, Daphne Hellman, Peter McMahon, Bud and Joan Stillman, and Hayden Herrera.

In Wellfleet, Peter and Gloria Watts; Elena, Reul and Helen Miranda Wilson; Mike and Nick Macdonald; Seth Rolbein; Rachel Brown; Lloyd Rose; Nina, Paul David, Sasha, and Marusia Chavchavadze; Daniel Aaron; Susanna Deiss; Jack and Flossie Phillips; Anna and Peter Matson; Serge, Ivan, and Peter Chermayeff; Bill and Nancy Webb; and Mary Meigs.

Fortune favored me when this work was acquired by Jonathan Galassi at Farrar, Straus and Giroux (also the publisher of Edmund Wilson's incredible diaries). Jonathan, like no other publisher I have ever worked with, line edited and improved the manuscript beyond my wildest dreams and then introduced me to his equally gifted team at FSG: the incredibly able Katie Liptak, who supervised the book's progress; the copyediting and production editing team extraordinaire of Ingrid Sterner, Laura Starrett, M. P. Klier, Nancy Elgin, and Scott Auerbach; the designer Gretchen Achilles, who further enhanced the book. The photographs were both edited and discovered in many cases by the intrepid Deb Nicholls and her colleague Melissa Flamson.

My beloved friend and the best agent in the business, Jill Kneerim, agented this book as only she can—first finding the essence of the story, organizing it, and then championing it. She also recommended me to David Sobel, who much improved its early draft, drawing on his long, distinguished editorial career.

Never forgetting, those who supported me and its making, led by my longtime publishing assistant, Hope Denekamp, without whose constant support there would be no book, and the many others who typed my ridiculously poor handwritten notes, including Jennifer Grieve, Lucy Cleland, Sarah Khalil, Jennifer Grady, and Eleanor Donahue.

And finally, the family I have been so blessed with: Caroline Courtauld, wife, muse, and deeply gifted author of many books. My three sons, Caleb, Jared, and Nathaniel, each of whom has deep roots in bohemia, were enormously helpful in organizing artwork and photos and recalling stories I had long forgotten.

My deepest thanks to each of you!

INDEX

Page numbers in *italics* refer to illustrations.

ILLUSTRATION CREDITS

236 Courtesy of the Hall family
237 Library of Congress, Prints & Photographs Division, Carl Van Vechten Collection, LC-DIG-ds-05656
240 Courtesy of the Hall family
246 Aufbacksalami (https://commons.wikimedia.org/wiki/File:Bauhaus_Dessau_2018 .jpg); image was converted to black-and-white. https://creativecommons.org/licenses/ by-sa/4.0/legalcode
247 Photograph by T. Lux Feininger
248 © AP / Shutterstock
254 Photograph by Walter Gropius, courtesy of Ati Gropius
255 Courtesy of Cranbrook Archives, Cranbrook Center for Collections and Research
257 Photograph by Richard G. Askew, courtesy of Cranbrook Archives, Cranbrook Center for Collections and Research
259 Photograph by Henry Stone, courtesy of Henry Stone
263 Courtesy of Peter McMahon
264 Photograph by Antoine Lorgnier, courtesy of Antoine Lorgnier
271 Courtesy of Archives and Special Collections, Vassar College Library, Ref. #3.670
272 Library of Congress, Prints & Photographs Division, Carl Van Vechten Collection, LC-USZ62–42506
274 Paul Engle, left, gathered with prominent authors and editors for literary symposium, the University of Iowa, December 4, 1959. Frederick W. Kent Collection of Photographs, Special Collections & Archives, the University of Iowa Libraries.
277 © Jose Mercado / Stanford News Service
284 Portrait of Alfred Kazin, ca. 1954–1955, individual faculty papers, College Archives, SC-MS-01008, Smith College Special Collections, Northampton, Massachusetts
287 Photograph of Daniel Aaron by K. Jaworowska, Daniel Aaron Papers, Smith College Special Collections